Mirrors of Man in Existentialism

ALSO BY NATHAN A. SCOTT, JR.

Rehearsals of Discomposure: Alienation and Reconciliation in Modern Literature (1952)
Modern Literature and the Religious Frontier (1958)
Albert Camus (1962)
Reinhold Niebuhr (1963)
Samuel Beckett (1965)
The Broken Center: Studies in the Theological Horizon of Modern Literature (1966)
Ernest Hemingway (1966)
Craters of the Spirit: Studies in the Modern Novel (1968)
Negative Capability: Studies in the New Literature and the Religious Situation (1969)
The Unquiet Vision: Mirrors of Man in Existentialism (1969)
Nathanael West (1971)
The Wild Prayer of Longing: Poetry and the Sacred (1971)
Three American Moralists—Mailer, Bellow, Trilling (1973)
The Poetry of Civic Virtue—Eliot, Malraux, Auden (1976)

EDITED BY NATHAN A. SCOTT, JR.

The Tragic Vision and the Christian Faith (1957)
The New Orpheus: Essays Toward a Christian Poetic (1964)
The Climate of Faith in Modern Literature (1964)
Man in the Modern Theatre (1965)
Four Ways of Modern Poetry (1965)
Forms of Extremity in the Modern Novel (1965)
The Modern Vision of Death (1967)
Adversity and Grace: Studies in Recent American Literature (1968)
The Legacy of Reinhold Niebuhr (1975)

Mirrors of Man in Existentialism

WITHDRAWN

NATHAN A. SCOTT, JR.

COLLINS

New York Cleveland London

Portions of this book appeared in *The Unquiet Vision* by Nathan
A. Scott, Jr., Cleveland: The World Publishing Company, 1969.

Library of Congress Catalog Card Number 78-69971
ISBN 0-529-05641-0 (cloth)
ISBN 0-529-05487-6 (paper)

Published by William Collins + World Publishing Co., Inc.
2080 West 117th Street, Cleveland, Ohio 44111

First Published in Great Britain 1978
UK ISBN#0-00 215530 3

Printed in the United States of America

To my granddaughter
Priscilla Diana Ashamu

Contents

Foreword

DURING THE latter half of the nineteenth century and the earliest decades of the twentieth, there evolved from a vast ferment of events and ideas an important movement called "Existentialism." In part it is theistic—from Kierkegaard to Buber—but from Nietzsche to Sartre it is nontheistic, often even atheistic. In some circles it has become no more than a fad. But on a larger scale and in many areas of our creative life—the arts, literature, and intellectual thought of the post-World War II era—Existentialism has exerted a widely pervasive influence. Not only is the idea attractive to many people because of its novelty and courage; but its stress on the centrality of individuals and their basic aloneness gives it an extraordinary power. Of parallel significance is its emphasis on a person's reluctant, yet inevitable commitments in life and on man's inescapable freedom in contrast to his limitations and finiteness. Whether pro-theistic or anti-theistic, Existentialism relies on intuition and expects involvement; it emphasizes inwardness and highlights sincerity. Amid social forces generating fierce pressures that can inhibit and destroy, Existentialism—whether with or without God —seeks to protect individuals and their creativity. At the heart of the movement lies a concern with the mood of modern man and the terrible choices thrust upon all who share human existence. Existentialism urges us to retain our sense of individual humanity, to avoid becoming slaves of progress and its spurious goals, and to escape being entranced by objectivity or ensnared by rationalism.

Mirrors of Man in Existentialism presents the major ideas and leading figures of this movement with remarkable clarity and rare insight. The author, Nathan A. Scott, Jr., is a distinguished scholar, an inspiring teacher, a gifted writer and editor. In this fine book Dr. Scott highlights the continuing importance of the existentialist viewpoint as a major shaping force in our contemporary cultural life.

May 1978   CARL HERMANN VOSS

Carl Hermann Voss, Ecumenical Scholar-in-Residence for the National Conference of Christians and Jews, was general editor for a series of books in which parts of this volume previously appeared.

1

Existentialism and the
Tragic Sense of Reality

JUST AFTER the close of World War II, when it began once more to be possible quickly to get current news about European intellectual developments, reports began to filter into the United States of a new philosophical movement that was creating enormous excitement in Paris. Its leaders were not university professors of philosophy, but men whose interests led them to produce novels and plays and political pamphlets as well as philosophical treatises. The chief figures were said to be Jean-Paul Sartre and Albert Camus (though Camus was soon to express some discomfort about being associated in the public mind with Sartre and his friends). And the movement was called Existentialism.

In the late 1940's hardly a week went by when publicity in one form or another was not being given to the existentialists in American magazines and journals of opinion, and in the supplements of the Sunday newspapers. Young suburban matrons displayed the latest book by Simone de Beauvoir or Camus on their coffee tables, and, as they sat under hair dryers in their beauty parlors, looked at

pictures of Sartre in *Vogue*. Students in our colleges
and universities were greatly stirred up by all that they
were learning about these French intellectuals who talked
about the homelessness of the human spirit, about man's
fundamental sensation as being one of nausea, and who
did their writing not in library stacks but in the cafés of
the Parisian Latin Quarter. Their books were bought like
detective stories, in university bookstores all over the
country, and it was considered essential to have at hand a
formulated opinion about "the new men." Everywhere—at
cocktail parties, in fashionable magazines, on the campuses—the chief cultural episode of the time, it seemed,
was the advent of this aggressively revolutionary new philosophy of anguish and crisis, of terror and of what one of
its German representatives called "frontier situations."

The American response to Existentialism in the 1940's
was not, however, wholly enthusiastic. Just as frequently
as it was hailed as a first wave of the future, it was dismissed
as simply another fashion of the day. American philosophy
in our time is predominantly empiricist in its basic attitudes—which is to say that it regards human life as a part
of nature and assumes that man's experience is best illu-
mined by those methods of inquiry most appropriate to the
study of the natural world: namely, the programs and procedures of empirical science. And the indifference of our
dominant philosophic tradition toward those regions of
experience that are not easily encircled by empirical science is but an expression of a great commitment to the
perspectives of "common sense" which is still deeply in-
grained in our culture. We, as a people, have been blessed
in not having had to live through many of the most trou-
bling terrors of modern history; and it is precisely this good
fortune which often makes it difficult for us to respond
with sympathy and understanding to visions of the world
that are rooted in some deep skepticism about the rele-

vance of "common sense" to the great "frontier situations" of human existence.

So, on the occasion of their first encounter with Existentialism, many American thinkers responded with a good deal of impatience and irritation. For here was a movement whose literary expressions all seemed to have the flavor of detective thrillers. Anxiety and homelessness and nostalgia and the death of God were being said to be the central facts of man's condition, and the whole style of mind represented by the existentialists was by many felt to be something too melodramatic: so its sensationalism was dismissed as merely a postwar phenomenon which expressed nothing more than a kind of irrational overreaction on the part of European intellectuals to all the perils that the war years had brought.

But today, at the end of the 1970's, we confront a scene which makes it clear that the existentialist movement, far from having been merely a postwar fad of the 1940's, does in fact mark one of the great central traditions in the thought and literature of our age. And now that it has become, with the passage of time, a part of the established furniture of modern cultural life, we can view its history and scope much more comprehensively than was possible when Sartre and Camus were first bursting into international prominence at the close of World War II. We can see, for example, that, contrary to what was at first widely supposed, Existentialism is by no means chiefly a French phenomenon; that a man like Sartre, for all his brilliant originality and independence of mind, is deeply indebted to the darkly brooding genius of the great German existentialists, Martin Heidegger (1889-1976) and Karl Jaspers (1883-1969). It has also become apparent that existentialist modes of thought need not entail an agnostic or atheistic world view, that they may also be a part of profoundly religious apprehensions of reality, as is

the case with the great Spanish philosopher Miguel de
Unamuno (1864-1936), the Jewish theologian Martin
Buber (1878-1965), or the French Roman Catholic philosopher Gabriel Marcel (1889-1973). And we can also now
see how directly the existentialist vision derives from certain currents of radical thought in the nineteenth century,
most especially from the Danish philosopher and theologian Søren Kierkegaard (1813-1855) and the German
philosopher Friedrich Nietzsche (1844-1900).

Indeed, we cannot hope at all adequately to understand
the basic testimony of Existentialism unless we go back to
the middle years of the nineteenth century. And once this
journey has been made, what we immediately confront
as perhaps the most important hallmark of that period's
mentality is the boundlessness of its faith in the essentially
rational character of reality. This was the outstanding fact
coloring nearly everything that the most truly representative spokesmen of the age had to say about the meaning
of human life—the conviction that there is no real chasm
between the human mind and its world environment.
Man exists in Nature, he is the work of Nature, and the
rationality which he finds in himself is simply a human
expression of that which is universally characteristic of
reality; this was one of the basic tenets of nineteenth-
century thought. And in this the people of the age were
truly descendants of the great men of the eighteenth
century—of Locke and Newton and Voltaire and Diderot—
from whom they inherited their faith that Nature and Reason shall ultimately be found to be one.

In one particular, however, that cluster of ideas which
marks the basic tendency of nineteenth-century thought
represented an important departure from the classic faith
of the great Age of Reason in the preceding century. For,
in the eighteenth century, time and change were not regarded as realities of any very high significance: to a man

like the physicist and natural philosopher Isaac Newton, the vast assemblage of things constituting the universe appeared to be an orderly and harmoniously functioning system; furthermore, to him and to his contemporaries it seemed that it had always been so and would always continue to be so. Indeed, the frequency with which the universe was figuratively conceived to be a sort of vast clock or machine betrayed how little importance was attached to the idea of growth or development in the age of Newton. For machines do not *grow* into what they are: at a certain definite point in time they are created, and thereafter, if well made, they continue with unfailing regularity to perform whatever may be their appointed function. And so it was with the universe itself, in the Newtonian world picture.

But this world picture began to undergo considerable alteration in the early years of the nineteenth century. The revolutionary political developments in Europe and America which brought the preceding century to a close had begun to give men a new sense of human society itself as something not fixed and closed but open, in all sorts of startling new ways, to change and reconstruction. Ways of life that had once been thought eternal now began to seem provisional and transient, particularly under the pressure of all the developments involving the early rise of modern technology and the rearrangements of society consequent upon the growth of great cities. And, increasingly, experimental research—especially in the new field of biology—was suggesting that the world demands to be thought of not as a static and mechanical affair but as something alive, in a state of change and development. So, gradually, the idea of evolution, the idea that reality is an affair of process and growth, began to take hold of the European imagination. And, in an age when the horizons of human life seemed everywhere to be expanding (in politics, in theoretical and applied science, in industry), it was doubtless natural for men after a time to become persuaded, as they did become, that cosmic evolution was itself a guarantee of cosmic progress. A world that had produced so rich a diversity of forms—in nature and in human affairs—must, it was concluded, be moving toward an ever brighter future whose pageantry will present modes of life richer than anything belonging to the past. Thus in the nineteenth century it came to be taken for granted not only that reality is rational but that its most essential law is the law of progress.

This whole way of thinking found its most formidable expression in the writings of the German philosopher Georg Wilhelm Friedrich Hegel (1770-1831), whose career spans the divide between the eighteenth and nineteenth centuries and constitutes one of the great landmarks of modern intellectual history. First of all, the order of experience was, for Hegel, something essentially rational, so thoroughly rational indeed that he considered each finite reality to be but a fragment of one all-inclusive experience forming the content of the Absolute Mind. For to try to understand any particular thing, whether stone or flower or man, is to be driven toward an inquiry into all the manifold relations that constitute the matrix of its existence: the quest for understanding drives us, in other words, from the part to the whole—because the world is rational through and through. And this absolute, all-encompassing framework within which all the fragmentary realities making up experience find their true meaning is itself, Hegel contended, the all-inclusive, infinite experience of the Absolute, of the Infinite Self—which we come to know more and more of as we come to know more of ourselves and of our world. For the Absolute is the inner *life* of the world and achieves self-consciousness in and through the human mind. Or, if we choose to translate the doctrine of the Absolute into conventional religious language, we may say that the Hegelian God is not a God standing outside the world of his creation but a spirit (the spirit of cosmic reason) dwelling wholly within the world, and not only coming to self-consciousness in the human mind but also finding its embodiment in the culture and in the institutions of man. So, therefore, man does not need to turn to any miraculous event for disclosures of divine truth: he has only to turn to his own experience. And if it is in the traditions and institutions of mankind that cosmic reason attains, however imperfectly and fragmentarily, its truest expression, then, as Hegel concluded, the history of civilization must itself be that process whereby the Absolute is ever more fully revealed. In short, the world is, slowly but surely, moving toward what it ought to be. Thus it was that the greatest philosopher of the nineteenth century gave a kind of quasi-official formulation to the myth of Reason and Progress.

But though this was a picture of the world which the broad majority of thinking men in the nineteenth century found deeply satisfying, there slowly began to gather an undercurrent of discontent, a feeling that the world was not quite so tidy as Hegel made it out to be. Amidst the confusions that swept across Europe in the wake of Napoleon's disastrous adventures, there were poets, for example—the Italian, Giacomo Leopardi (1798-1837); the German, Heinrich Heine (1797-1856); the Frenchmen, Leconte de Lisle (1818-1894), Alfred de Vigny (1797-1863), and Charles Baudelaire (1821-1867); and the Englishman, Matthew Arnold (1822-1888)—who began to speak with a new uneasiness about (as Arnold phrased it)

> this strange disease of modern life,
> With its sick hurry, its divided aims,
> Its heads o'ertax'd, its palsied hearts.

Or, again, a student of society like Karl Marx (1818-1883), as he looked out upon the nineteenth-century scene, saw a great tragedy beneath all the glitter and self-satisfaction. For in the economic order of capitalism he found that the worker was outrageously cheated of the fruit of his labor, and was reduced to little more than a commodity in the labor market. In the new factory towns and industrial areas, Marx declared, men were being forced into empty, meaningless patterns of life—performing a dreary task over and over again, day in and day out, on some kind of assembly line, and earning barely enough to keep body and soul together. It was a system, said Marx, that entailed nothing but alienation—the alienation of a man from the fruit of his own labor and thus from his human identity, as well as from his fellow man and his natural community.

And not only were the rumblings of disorder to be overheard in the writings of certain poets and social critics; their echoes were also sounding through the work of novelists like Stendhal (1783-1842), Flaubert (1821-1880), and Dostoevski (1821-1881). Indeed, we can now discern hints of darkening clouds on the European horizon even in the work of a line of visual artists running from Daumier (1808-1879) through Van Gogh (1853-1890) to Edvard Munch (1863-1944).

But among all these dissidents it was perhaps the Danish thinker Søren Kierkegaard who was the most brilliantly prophetic. Just as Marx perceived disorder and alienation in the corporate world of modern society, so Kierkegaard discovered the same realities in the life-world of the human individual; and he could find no peace in the Hegelian dream of unbroken unity between the finite and the Infinite. As he says in the little book called *Repetition* (1843):

> One sticks one's finger into the soil to tell by the smell in what land one is: I stick my finger into existence—it smells of nothing. Where am I? Who am I? How came I here? What is this thing called the world? What does the word mean? Who is it that has lured me into the thing, and now leaves me there? . . . . How did I come into the world? Why was

I not consulted, why not made acquainted with its manners and customs but was thrust into the ranks as though I had been bought of a "soul-seller"? How did I obtain an interest in this big enterprise they call reality? Why should I have an interest in it? Is it not a voluntary concern? And if I am compelled to take part in it, where is the director?

In short, every glimpse, every intuition of himself that he experienced told him, in effect, that he—and not only he but every man—was lost in a strange world with which one could not easily achieve any intimate relationship. The world as pictured in the philosophy of Hegel was, to be sure, a place where everything was fitted nicely together by the coordinating principle of the Absolute. But such a world, in Kierkegaard's analysis of things, appeared to be but the merest phantasm. For wherever he stuck his finger into existence, he could detect only the smell of nothingness: nowhere could he find the world offering up any answer to the great questions—How came I here? Why am I here? What is my human destiny? So he felt forced to conclude that, far from man's being an integral part of such an ordered cosmos as the Hegelian universe, his actual condition is one of homelessness and exile and abandonment.

Hegel could say, "The real is rational, and the rational is real." But, for Kierkegaard, the principal fact of human experience concerns the finality with which the individual, lost as he is amidst the implacable silence of this strange world, is locked up within his own loneliness and solitude. So he contended that any truth which man achieves will be found not to be a part of some objective logic, such as that which swallows up the world in Hegel's system, but will be instead a truth wrested from the vital actualities of a man's own personal existence, something which he has *earned* by experience: it will be *my* truth, a part of the uniqueness of *my* adventure in the world. The world in the large is beyond my reach: so I cannot find anything to steer my life by in any sort of objective truth. No, the truth which is a joy and a gladness to the heart—if it can be found at all—will be a radically *subjective* truth: this is a cardinal principle of Kierkegaard's whole outlook. And thus much of his reflection found its center in the human individual, and in all the concrete realities in which he is immediately and passionately implicated.

Let us imagine, for example, a young man away from home, who for several years, as a university graduate student, has been intensely involved in the mastery of a highly technical discipline—indeed, so involved in his work has he been that he has come to lead a rather solitary and isolated life, moving back and forth among classroom and library and laboratory, and returning at the end of each day to his room. Intermittently he has suffered brief seizures of loneliness, but the pressures of his research have been too constantly felt for him to be very greatly disoriented by these odd moments of unrest. But at last there comes a time when the work for his doctorate is nearly completed: he has brilliantly solved the puzzle with which he has long been struggling in his physics laboratory. And now it is, as the tensions of these years begin to relax, that he suddenly finds, much to his surprise, that the triumphs of his research do not bring the kind of satisfaction that might have been expected. So unpracticed is he in self-reflection that he does not know the trouble to be simply loneliness, the fact that there is no one else to take joy in his triumph—but this is what it is that makes the savor of his success so unsatisfying.

And now imagine that, just at this juncture, he begins to notice an attractive young woman who is also a graduate student in his department, a young woman who (as he at last notices) has occasionally seemed to be trying—hesitantly and reticently—to get to know him. In the past the young man had been too absorbed in his work to be more than momentarily and vaguely aware of these overtures.

But now a kind of crack, a kind of fissure, has occurred in the pattern of his life; so, with some trepidation, he invites her out to dinner one evening. And thus their friendship begins. He is utterly delighted by her gaiety and warmth and sensitivity, and she is charmed by his shy simplicity and honesty. So they see more and more of each other, until finally there comes a day when, without her speaking it, he sees, in the trusting lilt of her face as they walk through a park one afternoon, that she loves him.

But does he observe this fact as coolly as he reads the instruments in his laboratory? Of course not, for here is vital truth. At last the lonely desolateness of his life is utterly dispelled, as he suddenly knows himself truly to be loved by this woman. And till the end of his days the memory of that afternoon, of that park, of how the slanting afternoon sunlight touched her face as she smiled, will be a part of his sense of the world and of who he himself is. He will never cease to be one who was lost until a certain girl on a certain afternoon smiled in a way that said she loved him. This is a permanent truth of his life.

And, in Kierkegaard's view, this is the only kind of truth that deeply matters. For man, as he understood him, is the kind of creature who must find meaning somewhere on the horizons of his life—he must be able, that is, to find that which offers him some assurance that he is accommodated, that he is accepted, that there is some place for *him*; this is his primary passion, to find at the basis of his existence a truth which is *his* as an individual. The latest report of the most advanced social critic—a Herbert Marcuse or a Robert Heilbroner or a Jürgen Habermas—may be fascinating to him; and Fred Hoyle, or whoever else happens to be on the outermost boundaries of scientific cosmology, may offer intellectual stimulation. But the kind of truth which can be said to be genuinely *vital* will in some deep sense be *his,* for the truth on which a man builds his life, as Kierkegaard never tired of saying, is "subjective" and is laid hold of with "passion." In his great book, the *Concluding Unscientific Postscript* (1846), he puts the issue (in the manner of a parable) in this way:

> If one who lives in the midst of Christendom goes up to the house of God, the house of the true God, with the true conception of God in his knowledge, and prays, but prays in a false spirit; and one who lives in an idolatrous community prays with the entire passion of the infinite, although his eyes rest upon the image of an idol: where is there most truth? The one prays in truth to God though he worships an idol; the other prays falsely to the true God, and hence worships in fact an idol.

It was in these terms, then, that this remarkable Danish poet of human existence proceeded to scuttle the Hegelian world picture, which was, in many ways, only a sophisticated formulation of the outlook commonly prevailing in the nineteenth century—a kind of philosophic articulation of the period's faith in the essential rationality of the universe and in the unswervingly progressive direction of history. Hegel, said Kierkegaard in effect to his contemporaries—without for a moment denying Hegel's astonishing brilliance of mind—is the great hoaxster of the age. For, far from the world's being a sort of rationalist system in which man has an assured place, it is in fact a universe without landmarks, without signs, a strange and inexplicable universe which persists in remaining silent before the great question we are forever stammering out—why? why? why? So the human condition is one of homelessness and estrangement and solitude: the primary reality, therefore, is that of the lonely, passionately questing individual who, as he faces the yawning abysses of the world, can save himself from utter despair only by a great leap of faith—by gambling, in fear and trembling, and with his *whole* being (with his reason as well as his emotions), that on the other side of that leap he will find God.

It was such ideas as these that Kierkegaard released into the nineteenth century. The term, said he, which offers the best technical description of the human situation is the term "existence." For the meaning of the verb "to exist" in the original Latin, *existere*, is "to stand out from" or "away from" or "apart from"; and this is what Kierkegaard took the human situation to be—a standing *out* or *apart* from the world, from truth, from God, the chasm being bridgeable only by a leap of faith.

Just a generation later, the second great nineteenth-century progenitor of the existentialist movement, Friedrich Nietzsche, was to conclude that, even if such a leap be taken, it will lead to nothing—since, beyond the leap, nothing is to be found but nothingness itself. The explosively pungent sentence which sets forth his very extreme verdict in his book of 1882, *The Gay Science*, is as brief as can be: "God is dead." And the proof, said this choleric and brilliant German, is to be found in the Church itself, in its faintheartedness, in its cultural mediocrity, in its apathy and inertia: Christendom itself has murdered God, and thus men must now look elsewhere for the ultimate fulfillment of human life.

It is just at this point that we can best see what is involved in the movement from Søren Kierkegaard to Friedrich Nietzsche. For Kierkegaard, too, had voiced a thunderous indictment of Christendom, declaring that the Church was too often bent simply on "making a fool of God" (as he said in *The Attack Upon Christendom*). By which he meant that Christians are too frequently like those tame geese of whom he once spoke, who each week go off to their Sunday service to hear one of the ganders preach about the lofty destiny their Creator reserves for them in the blessed regions of heaven, and who then waddle on home to their Sunday dinners, to become plump and delicate. And when some among them appear to be languishing and growing thin, the others point to them as sad examples of the consequence of taking the preacher too seriously—though these same geese piously go off on the next Sabbath day to hear the gander, before waddling on homeward again for the Sunday feast. Such, Kierkegaard maintained, is the kind of fraudulence represented by conventional Christianity—which is largely, he believed, simply a sort of chaplaincy to the middle classes. Comfortable philistines go off each Sunday to hear the preacher talk about the harrowing sacrifices of Christ, and then waddle on home afterward to stuff themselves at their Sunday tables. And in thus practicing a religion which costs nothing and which has been stripped of any kind of genuine risk, they make a fool of God and fools of themselves. "Christendom," he said in *Training in Christianity*, "has done away with Christianity without being quite aware of it."

For Kierkegaard, the winning of a truly human integrity was predicated upon the achievement of religious authenticity. In his vision of things the primary reality was the single individual, confronting—in his uncompanioned solitariness—the ultimate uncertainty of the world. Like Nietzsche, he, too, believed that there is no possibility of the individual's avoiding the gravest issue that a man can face—whether, beyond all the discords of our mortal music, there is some final Harmony actively at work to resolve the dissonance of this troubled earth. And he further believed that, on those chill and distant boundaries of life where this issue is really met, one must make a leap of faith.

With Nietzsche, however, a generation later, the human situation is being interpreted even more radically. For him the spiritual mediocrity and sham religion of conventional Christianity are simply the last evidence of how absolutely bankrupt and irrecoverable is traditional belief. Like

Kierkegaard, he, too, conceives the ultimate problem for philosophic reflection to be that of how the single individual can achieve a fully human authenticity. And he also takes it for granted that this authenticity will be a matter of *passionately* appropriated subjective truth. But since God is dead and the heavens are therefore empty, it is not a leap of faith that he recommends—for that, in his sense of reality, would be simply a leap into nothingness. What is required now, he declared, is rather that men should summon the courage to rebuild their lives without any of the supports and consolations which Christianity offered to earlier ages; they must somehow manage to face into the bleak emptiness that the world presents, now that God is gone, and try themselves to *confer* meaning upon the meaninglessness of existence. Indeed, the kind of spiritual heroism required by our modern situation calls, he felt, for a "new man," a "higher man," even, as he said, for a "superman." For, as he said in *The Gay Science*, "some sun seems to have set, some old profound confidence seems to have changed into doubt." What is now faced is a terrible new cosmic solitude, and a terrible new kind of liberty in which, having killed God, man must himself become a kind of god—or at least those few men who are capable of bravely launching into the sort of human future that awaits us in the modern world. And between this aristocratic minority and the broad majority of men (who will doubtless for a long time to come cling to all the old fictions) there is such a distance that the minority must be regarded as representing a new kind of man, the superman. As he tells us in *Thus Spake Zarathustra*, "Man is a rope stretched between the animal and the superman—a rope over an abyss." Which is to say that historic European man is but a bridge to a new kind of man—the man who, knowing that we are alone in the world, will have the courage to be an "honest atheist."

In him alone shall we find that style of spiritual life which bears the marks of "authentic" human existence in the time of the death of God.

Here, then, are the large outlines of the testimony offered to the nineteenth century by the two men who deserve to be regarded as amongst the greatest prophets of the modern period. And when the term "prophet" is used in this connection, what is being appealed to is not the idea of "soothsayer," of one who in some mysterious way predicts the future. No, the cultural vocation of the true prophet—whether he be a Jeremiah or a Socrates, an Augustine or a Pascal, a Marx or a Freud—is to be a kind of midwife to his age: in his speaking or in his writing, the prophet brings to birth, through his word, some deep truth of a people's experience which they had not hitherto quite been able to take hold of themselves but which, once his message is listened to, appears to be confirmed by everything else that is known about the human condition. The prophet fishes in deep waters and brings to light some crucial reality that is deeply lodged in the life-world of his contemporaries; then the people whom he is addressing, once they have truly listened to what he has to say, begin to find in his message a new center for their consciousness of themselves and of their common destiny.

But, of course, precisely because the prophet is saying something that is radically new and therefore deeply disturbing, he is likely at first to be met with nothing but derision and scorn. And so it was with Kierkegaard and Nietzsche, who both suffered what Kierkegaard called the "martyrdom of laughter." Neither won what we call "a good press," and, during their lifetimes, they were both dismissed as eccentrics—geniuses perhaps, but unstable, neurotically morbid, and given to hysteria.

The nineteenth century, however, as it is often said, came to an end on the thirty-first of July, 1914. For with the outbreak of World War I it became inescapably clear that the sense of the stability of bourgeois civilization and the inevitability of its progress, which had been accepted for a hundred years, was built upon enormous illusions. And as these illusions began to be shattered by the economic and political upheavals which the war brought, men came to feel that the whole of Western culture, in a new and unprecedented way, was on trial, and that they were without any shelter against the coming storm. Even after the armistice in 1918, the Russian Revolution (launched in the previous year) gave an air of uncertainty to the settlements worked out at Versailles by Orlando and Lloyd George and Clemenceau and Woodrow Wilson. For a brief period, it is true, the founding of the League of Nations aroused fresh hopes of the possibility of subduing the new disorders of the twentieth century. But by the beginning of the 1930's the Western world found its economy in the grip of a great depression, and looming ominously on the horizon were the shadows cast by the rise of Hitler and Nazism in Germany.

It was against this whole background of events that the sense of the human universe as something profoundly alien and immovable began to be an experience not simply of a small minority of sensitive men like Kierkegaard and Nietzsche in the nineteenth century, but, increasingly, of large numbers of thoughtful people. One of the most famous books of the period, *The Decline of the West* by the German historian Oswald Spengler (1918; rev. ed., 1922), gave a kind of advertisement to the widely harbored suspicion that an epoch was coming to an end, and that perhaps even the world itself was hurtling toward doom. With the English poet of the seventeenth century John

Donne, men were more and more prepared to say:

> The sun is lost, and th' earth, and no man's wit
> Can well direct him where to look for it.
> . . . .
> 'Tis all in pieces, all coherence gone.

It is said of a certain self-portrait in the nude by the sixteenth-century German painter Albrecht Dürer that he sent it to his physician with the message: "Right there, the spot colored yellow, where my finger's pointing—that's where it hurts." And in the period following World War I something of the same sort began to be said, with ever increasing urgency, by poets like T. S. Eliot and Ezra Pound and William Butler Yeats; by novelists like Franz Kafka and James Joyce, Ernest Hemingway and William Faulkner; by dramatists like Eugene O'Neill and Bertolt Brecht. Nor was this pervasive sense of crisis being expressed only in imaginative literature: it is also very much to be felt in the great classic painting and sculpture of the twentieth century. Those strange double-faced creatures, for example, which Picasso was producing forty years ago, look out at the world as if they are aghast at what they see; or, again, the figures that were being produced in the same period by a sculptor like Giacometti seem, in their fragile slenderness and delicacy, to express a sense of man as one helpless and naked and utterly vulnerable. And the strange new music that began to be heard in the years after World War I—the music of Arnold Schoenberg and Anton Webern and Edgard Varèse—appeared also, in its eerie dissonance, to be singing out a similar vision. Indeed, even the new science of the period—the physics, say, of Werner Heisenberg and Niels Bohr—was beginning to represent the world as influenced by irrational factors beyond the reach of reason. And the sense of the human situation as something absurd and insecure was, of course, being expressed most emphatically by the new psychology of Freud.

Such was the general climate of feeling and opinion that had already taken form in the 1930's, when the legacy of Kierkegaard and Nietzsche began to be reclaimed and to win a new prestige. Today, forty years later, we have become so habituated to insecurity and panic that they seem almost to be a part of the normal human lot. Man may have seemed a relatively simple and reliably decent creature back in that distant Indian summer of the mid-nineteenth century, but in our own distressed century, when soap has been made of human fat and lampshades of human skin and six million lives snuffed out in Hitler's ovens and gas chambers, we have a sense of the human interior as something infinitely treacherous. And since the explosion of the first atomic bomb at Hiroshima on the sixth of August, 1945, we have settled into an age in which a permanent fact of life is what the dreary language of our time calls "the Cold War," an age in which terror is far-flung and in which affairs among nations are therefore conducted on the basis of what our statesmen call the "calculated risk."

Nor do we in the United States any longer escape these disorders. Here, for a long time, it could be supposed that God in his infinite wisdom and mercy had provided men with a kind of sanctuary, a place of safety apart from all the terrors of modern history. But—as it once used to be said in the Indian summer of our own American past— this is a supposition that can today be thought of only as "square." For even in "the land of the free and the home of the brave" millions are hungry and discriminated against and without hope, and there is often great embarrassment over the clumsiness and ineptitude of the nation's foreign policy. And, as a consequence, many now conceive themselves to be members of the "loyal opposition."

In such a time, it is no wonder that Søren Kierkegaard and Friedrich Nietzsche no longer seem the overwrought alarmists they were once thought to be, that indeed they are today universally accounted two of the most important figures on the whole landscape of modern thought. It seems equally natural that the tradition of thought which has its roots in their philosophies—the tradition that we call Existentialism—should now be regarded as one of the central movements in the intellectual life of this century.

The distinguished French philosopher, the late Gabriel Marcel, who was in many ways himself deeply affiliated with the existentialist tradition, remarked some years ago that "not a day passes without someone (generally a woman of culture, but perhaps a janitor or a street-car conductor) asking me what Existentialism is." But, as he said, "No one will be surprised that I evade the question. I reply that it is too difficult or too long to explain." Yet, in the way of formal definition, perhaps all that need be said is simply that the existentialist tradition embraces that body of twentieth-century thought and literature which finds its center in a certain cluster of ideas descending from Kierkegaard and Nietzsche.

In the order of these ideas, priority is claimed by the conception of the world as a place inaccessible, unintelligible, absurd—and from which, therefore, man is estranged. The hero of Franz Kafka's novel *The Trial* awakes one morning to find himself under sudden arrest for an unspecified crime; or again, the protagonist of his long story "Metamorphosis" finds himself on a certain morning suddenly transformed into a gigantic beetle. And the world which is portrayed in these and others of Kafka's fictions— in its impenetrable mystery, in its absolute ambiguity— figures forth something of that sense of reality which is characteristic of the existentialist imagination. For it is a mode of reflection which takes the fundamental human experience to be one of exclusion, of being shut out, of being unable to find in the world into which one has been "thrown" any place of safety or principle of meaning.

And it is the sense of man as a creature estranged—and as therefore locked up within his own loneliness and solitude—which leads to the second major theme of existentialist thought: namely, the stress upon the subjectivity of truth. Since the world will not yield up its inner secrets and since man is, therefore, unaccommodated, the existentialist thinker concludes that the principal focus of all serious reflection must be man himself, and his passionate search for the true foundations of his life. Given the inaccessibility of the world, it will avail nothing, in other words, to seek after any sort of "objective" truth, to aspire toward knowledge of that which is independent of human existence itself. The important thing, in short, is not the abstract universality of any system of objective ideas, for reality is too slippery to be caught by such a net: no, the important thing is that which I find sustaining of *my* life—and the only sort of truth that really matters is a truth which is "existential," which is "subjective," a truth that *I* have earned and which is therefore *mine*.

It is the emphasis on the essential solitude of man, as he faces an alien universe, which leads to what is a third theme of existentialist thought—namely, the definition of the basic human task as one of achieving an *authentic* life. What is basically at stake here is the notion that, given the uncertainty and insecurity which so largely constitute the human condition, there is little chance of a man's surviving at all unless he can summon the requisite courage. But courage is a virtue painfully and expensively attained; and thus man is constantly tempted to try to escape the arduous solitariness of a truly authentic life by seeking refuge in the social collective, by submerging himself in the routines and customs of what Kierkegaard called "the

public." But, as he never tired of pointing out, such stratagems finally lead only to a deepening of despair; and
thus in his writings, and in existentialist literature
generally, we not only get a definition of the human norm
in terms of "authenticity" but we also get an anatomy of
the various forms of "*in*authenticity" represented by mass
culture.

A fourth existentialist theme, which is a correlate of
these already set forth, concerns the scene or setting of
authentic existence as being what the German existentialist
Karl Jaspers calls the "extreme situation." Kierkegaard and
Nietzsche and the various important existentialists of our
own time are all in agreement in holding this to be the
basic milieu of human life, when it is being experienced
with real seriousness and intensity. Certain significant
differences, it is true, mark the characterizations given
by various writers of what life is like "on the boundary."
But the existentialists do all tend to agree that we do not
begin to discover what it means to be human until we are
brought up short against the great limiting realities of suffering and guilt, or sorrow and disappointment and death.
For it is only when we know what it means to be "shipwrecked," it is only when we have felt the sting of some
radical failure, of blighted hopes and foundered purposes,
of some misfortune that is sheer, unmitigated woe—it is
only then that we begin, in any deep way, to appreciate
our human finitude, how frail and unsheltered and vulnerable we are before the vicissitudes of life. And to be
without any experience of extremity is to lack a certain
necessary equipment (of wisdom and maturity) apart from
which no really authentic life can be achieved.

Then, finally, there is a fifth testimony that existentialists tend to make, which belongs not so much to the
substance of their message as to their sense of what ought
to be characteristic of the *style* of serious discourse, and

here the stress is on "indirect communication." What is being asserted, in effect, is that he who "thinks existentially"—with the passion of personal immediacy—is attempting, at bottom, to make sense of his own life, to find a way of ordering his own experience of the world. But one cannot contain the vital reality of one's own selfhood within the simple syllogisms of logic, and certainly the world itself is too slippery, too elusive, to be captured by any straightforwardly direct and logical proposition. So, therefore, when the existentialist thinker undertakes to communicate with others, he will not undertake to build a system or to employ with any great consistency the methods of direct exposition: instead, his stratagem will be that of indirect communication. Both Kierkegaard and Nietzsche used a great variety of pseudonyms and poetic devices, and contemporary existentialists like Camus and Sartre, in addition to their philosophic essays, have written plays and novels and stories—the purpose of this whole effort being not primarily that of setting forth a body of doctrine but of plunging us into the existentialist *experience*, of nostalgia and anguish, of alienation and extremity.

Now it is undoubtedly the case, as Gabriel Marcel suggests, that the whole phenomenon of Existentialism in modern culture is something too subtle in its make-up and too many-sided in its various literary expressions to permit its being easily defined. But at least we may point to the cluster of ideas descending from Kierkegaard and Nietzsche, and say that those thinkers and artists who have self-consciously adopted the perspectives arising out of this body of thought form that line of testimony which constitutes the existentialist tradition. Its representatives are, of course, too numerous to be considered in their entirety in this book, and the omissions are, therefore, many and various. It is to be particularly regretted, for

example, that room could not be made for any account of
so significant a German figure as the late Karl Jaspers,
who claims a place of large importance in this sector of
contemporary thought. And, among the religious existentialists, it is unfortunate that the Roman Catholic thinker
Marcel and the Protestant theologian Paul Tillich (1886-
1965) cannot be given more detailed treatment than is
allowed for by the pattern of the seventh chapter, in which
they are briefly discussed. Nevertheless, it is hoped that
those readers who are encountering Existentialism for the
first time will find this guidebook to be helpfully charting
a terrain which, though endlessly fascinating, may at first
strike the newcomer as presenting considerable difficulty.

We turn first to the great seminal figures Søren Kierkegaard and Friedrich Nietzsche. Then we move into the
present century to the three men—Martin Heidegger and
Albert Camus and Jean-Paul Sartre—whose careers, more
than any others, have helped to establish Existentialism as
a fact of contemporary cultural life. And from Heidegger
and Camus and Sartre, who brilliantly represent Existentialism in its secular mode, we turn to the distinguished
Jewish philosopher Martin Buber, using him as a central
example of the movement in its religious phase. And, finally, the book terminates in some reflections on those
issues of faith and destiny which have been so powerfully
raised in our time by existentialist thought.

2

Kierkegaard's
Strait Gate

. . . strait is the gate, and narrow is the way,
which leadeth unto life, and few there be that find it.

—*The Gospel According to*
St. Matthew, 7:14

THE INFLUENCE of Søren Kierkegaard has been constantly
felt in philosophic and religious thought for more than a
generation; yet it may be regarded as one of the most
astonishing developments in the intellectual life of our
time. For this tormented and eccentric prodigy of mid-
nineteenth-century Denmark was the product of a little
country that has never formed more than a relatively
insignificant eddy in the backwaters of Continental life,
and he used a tongue that has never been a central language of European culture. Yet by the 1930's—more than
seventy-five years after his death—he had begun to be
universally acknowledged as one of the most creative and
important thinkers of the modern period. We think of him
today as a Christian psychologist who is easily the peer of
Augustine and Luther and Pascal. He has had the same
sort of *general* impact—in his case, on imaginative litera-

25

ture, on secular philosophy, on theoretical and therapeutic psychology, as well as on theology—that we discern in the posthumous career of a Marx or a Nietzsche or a Freud. In the kind of lonely courage with which he challenged much of the "official" wisdom of his time, he manifests a certain tragic nobility, such as we feel to be a part of many of the other great pioneers and prophets of his eventful century. Indeed, when the full import of his legacy begins to be considered, one wants simply to say of this strange, Hamlet-like "poet"—as one does of Freud—that he *added* something to our modern awareness of how twisted and devious are all the paths in the country of the human heart, added something in the way that only genius can.

In the XXIXth Fragment of the *Pensées*, Pascal speaks of the astonishment we sometimes feel when, on picking up a book, we find ourselves to be encountering not an author but a man. It is this sort of response which the entire body of Kierkegaard's work commands, for he was a man whose life was shaped by his thought and whose thought was, in every respect, conditioned by his life. He took it as the major premise of all his reflection that the only kind of thinking which has genuine relevance to human experience is that in which a man puts himself on trial, risking even his sanity in the radicalism with which he probes the foundations of his life. This is what he meant by "existential" thinking: facing the concrete actualities of one's life, undertaking to think through all the questions they raise about the meaning of one's humanity, and doing this in as profoundly serious a way as possible. Existential thinking, in other words, is not the detached cogitation of an uninvolved spectator, but the passionate exploration of one infinitely concerned, and absolutely engaged, by the object of his thought—which is nothing less than the meaning of his own selfhood. The reality which an existential thinker lays hold of is a reality which has cost him something, a reality which he has felt on his own pulses, which he has suffered through and endured: anything less, in the things of the spirit, is of no value at all: this is *the* cardinal principle of Kierkegaard's thought—which means that there is no other route into his ideas except that which leads through the circumstances of his life.

Kierkegaard was born in Copenhagen on the fifth of May, 1813, the seventh and last child of Michael and Ane Kierkegaard. His father, Michael, after gathering a considerable fortune through varied enterprises (haberdashery, wholesale groceries, etc.), withdrew from business affairs at the age of forty and, at the time of Søren's birth, had been living in retirement for sixteen years, devoting himself to theological studies under the guidance of Bishop Mynster, the ranking Danish theologian of the period. Michael Kierkegaard was of West Jutland peasant stock; and in his boyhood, while tending sheep one day, he had stood, shivering and hungry, on the lonely Jutland heath and cursed God to His face, in despair over what was then the apparent hopelessness of his lot. And this moment of the boy's abandonment to anger at the harshness of his life in that primitive heath country was something which he was never to forget, for it left a lifelong burden of immovable guilt. Years later, after he had won security and wealth as a businessman in Copenhagen, he could not help perversely believing his very prosperity to be somehow a sign of his having been forever excluded from the Truth, as a result of that youthful blasphemy which he took to be unforgivable because, as he supposed, it had been a sin against the Holy Ghost itself—the sin than which there can be none greater. So there was a shadow of remorse and melancholy that hung implacably and constantly over his life, and, since he presided over his family and his household as a sternly exacting patriarch, it was inevitable that his morbid severity of conscience should leave its mark on a child so sensitive and susceptible as his youngest son. In his later years Kierkegaard, as he looked back on the nurture he received at his father's hands, was in fact to speak of it as an "insane upbringing," and he declared in his *Journals* that even as a child he was "already an old man," made so by his father's habit of representing life to him as something darkly tragic and perilous. But, he added, "one thing I had: an eminently shrewd wit, given me presumably in order that I might not be [altogether] defenseless."

When he entered the University of Copenhagen in 1831, he dutifully chose to study in the theological faculty, in conformity with his father's desire. Yet that "eminently shrewd wit" with which he was endowed appears to have been the guiding force in his university years: he did not shirk the regimen of formal study and performed brilliantly on his examinations, but all the while he was fast acquiring the reputation of a dandy and man-about-town in the Copenhagen drawing rooms of which he became an *habitué*. He had a great fondness for the theater, and for music and opera, and the whole style and emphasis of his life during this period seems to have been that of a young aesthete and dilettante. Yet he remained his father's son and was at this time confiding to his *Journals* the great need he felt to find "an idea" or "a truth"—"related to the deepest root of my existence"—to which he might wholly devote himself.

This feeling of need to find a truth for which he could both live and die was doubtless intensified by some dread disclosure made to him by his aged father, in Søren's twenty-second year. The references to it in Kierkegaard's *Journals* are all calculatedly ambiguous and oblique, but there is some reason for supposing that the old man, forever nagged by his imperious conscience, felt obliged to confess to his son an act of sexual misconduct. In this connection, it is to be remembered that the first child of Michael and Ane Kierkegaard was born just four months and eleven days after their marriage. Ane had been a servant in Michael's house, working under his first wife who died without children. But she was married to her employer before her former mistress had been dead a year, and the plain fact of the matter would seem to be that this little servant girl—Søren's mother—was seduced and made pregnant by the powerfully domineering master of the house, even before the year of mourning for his first wife was up. It is doubtless to what was for him the shattering experience of his father's recital of this whole event that Kierkegaard was referring (in a brief document on his early years confided by his brother Peter to the friend [H. P. Barfod] who first edited his papers) when he spoke of "the great earthquake," of "the frightful upheaval," which occurred in his twenty-second year. Indeed, it is the knowledge of his father's unbridled sensuality *and* of that early blasphemy on the Jutland heath which, by the time of Søren's twenty-fifth year (the year of his father's death) —when, within a short space, his mother and two of his sisters died—had borne in upon him a sense of his whole house being under the shadow of a curse. It was a foreboding altogether natural, given the kind of melancholia with which his father had endowed him—no doubt exacerbated by a deep shame stemming from some sexual "fall" of Søren's own in this same period, of which there are various hints in his writings.

At least, however, he was left financially secure at the time of his father's death (in August of 1838), as a result of generous bequests.

Then, two years later, when his work for the degree of Master of Arts was very nearly completed at the University, Kierkegaard became engaged to a most eligible young lady of Copenhagen, Regina Olsen. It would appear that in all

outward respects Kierkegaard was not a particularly pre-
possessing young man: the drawings and paintings that
remain all indicate that his figure was that of a scraggy,
rawboned spindling, with a humped back and a high-
crowned head topped with a great thatch of unruly blond
hair: the body was frail and ungainly, seeming always to
be somehow slightly askew. Yet the records also suggest that, in his youth, he possessed a great vivacity and
sprightliness of wit, so that one suspects that, despite his
ill-favored physique, he had considerable charm. It would
otherwise be difficult to account for the apparent ease with
which Kierkegaard swept Regina off her feet. This is his
own recital (in the *Journals*) of the beginning of the affair:

> On September 8 I left my house. . . . We met each other
> in the street outside their [the Olsens'] house. She said there
> was nobody at home. I was foolhardy enough to look upon
> that as an invitation, just the opportunity I wanted. I went in
> with her. We stood alone in the living room. She was a little
> uneasy. I asked her to play me something. . . . She did so;
> but that did not help me. Then suddenly I took the music
> away and closed it, not without a certain violence, threw it
> down on the piano and said, "Oh, what do I care about music
> now! It is you I am searching for, it is you whom I have
> sought after for two years." She was silent. I did nothing
> else to make an impression upon her; I even warned her
> against myself, against my melancholy. When, however, she
> spoke about Schlegel [who had been Regina's teacher, who
> had already courted her, and who later became her hus-
> band] I said, "Let that relationship be a parenthesis; after
> all, the priority is mine." . . .
>
> She remained quite silent. At last I left, for I was anxious
> lest someone should come and find both of us, and she so
> disturbed. I went immediately to Etatsraad Olsen. I know
> that I was terribly concerned that I had made too great an
> impression upon her. I also feared that my visit might lead to
> a misunderstanding and even hurt her reputation.
>
> Her father said neither yes nor no, but he was willing
> enough as I could see. I asked for a meeting: it was granted

to me for the afternoon of the 10th. I did not say a single word to persuade her. She said, Yes.

He had fallen in love with Regina three years earlier, when she was only fourteen; at last, in the late summer of 1840, as she was approaching her eighteenth birthday, the time came for Kierkegaard to press his case, and so he did. It was, most decidedly, a "whirlwind courtship."

The engagement lasted for only eleven months, however, for on the eleventh of August, 1841, Kierkegaard sent back to Regina the ring which she had given him and notified her of his wish to terminate their betrothal. It is indeed a strange story, which cannot here be told in detail: a full chronicling of the tale is given in Walter Lowrie's great biography of 1938 (*Kierkegaard*, published by the Oxford University Press).

The little that does need to be said here about this development in Kierkegaard's life can perhaps best be set forth by an anecdote recounted by a niece of the great French novelist of the nineteenth century, Gustave Flaubert. In a Preface to an edition of her uncle's correspondence, she tells of walking homeward with him along the Seine one afternoon, after they had paid a visit in the countryside beyond Paris to one of her friends whom they had found surrounded by her children, in a charming home. And she says that her uncle, in thinking back over the afternoon and the pleasant hours they had spent in the midst of this attractive family, suddenly exclaimed, "*Ils sont dans le vrai!*"—"They are in the truth!" By which Flaubert meant that the kind of wholesome, normal affirmation of life that this delightful family scene had connoted was, indeed, *le vrai*, containing in itself a quiet sanity and sturdiness quite as valuable as anything belonging to the sophistication and urbanity of his own agnostic world.

One feels that it was a similar "truth" that Kierkegaard,

too, wanted somehow to find himself "in." He had been deeply involved for several years in philosophic and theological studies, and it was already clear that in this area lay his life's work—a work which could possibly exact a supreme effort. Yet one suspects that he hoped to possess also the kind of truth of which Flaubert spoke so wistfully to his niece: the kind of completion which it is the most natural thing in the world for a man to hope for—a good wife, marriage, children, all the joys that are brought by a happy family. And Regina's acceptance of his love promised all this.

Yet, as month after month of the engagement wore on, Kierkegaard's passionate dedication to a contemplative life and an intellectual vocation must have caused him to be assailed with doubts about his capacity to settle into the ordinary, day-by-day routines and demands of a bourgeois household for the rest of his days. And finally, one must conclude, these doubts became so naggingly insistent that he had to beg to be released from a commitment which he could not believe he had the strength to live through. There are those who have contrived ingenious psycho-analytic interpretations which suggest some obscure psychic disability in Kierkegaard that prevented marriage. But the man who is too deeply claimed by an intellectual or religious or artistic vocation to be able to make room in his life for marriage and a family is a familiar human type, too familiar indeed for such farfetched ventures in psychoanalytic conjecture to be required in order to make sense of the story of Kierkegaard and Regina Olsen. Regina "fought like a lioness," says Kierkegaard, and "besought me with tears and adjurations . . . not to for-sake her." But though filled with anguish at the pain he was causing her, he was too convinced of the rightness of his course to yield. As he said in later years, "My sin has never been that I did not love her. . . . My sin was that I did not have real faith, faith to believe that with God all things are possible." Yet this self-judgment, pronounced in retrospect, was excessive, one feels, in its severity, for the real fact of the case was undoubtedly that his was a nature controlled by a most exacting *"either/or"* kind of logic—*either* an ordinary worldly life, with marriage and domesticity and the usual fulfillments in that way; *or* the life of a "solitary" whose one purpose is to disclose to men "what it is to be a Christian"—and it is improbable that either he or Regina would have found their union tolerable for very long.

So, at last, they parted. And fourteen years later Kierkegaard was dead—exhausted utterly by the excruciating labor to which he had submitted himself, of producing in little more than a decade a phenomenally large body of philosophical and theological literature which, as we look at it now, appears to be one of the great adornments of European culture in the modern period.

Kierkegaard's terribly painful ordeal of breaking his engagement to Regina Olsen had a decisive effect on the whole subsequent drift of his thought. For, in giving up this girl he loved, he had cut himself off from a certain area of life, from a whole range of experience and of possible fulfillments. In thus committing himself by his irrevocable choice, he found himself thrust forward upon the naked fact of his personal existence. And, thereafter, the immediate reality of his own mortal selfhood could never be simply a matter of abstract speculation, to be observed and studied in a spirit of aloof detachment and unconcern. For, having deeply experienced the hard drama of Either/Or, he now knew that what is most actual for a man is the burden of his own life. And it was this knowledge that required him, he felt, to hand in a veto against the most influential philosopher of his period—*Georg Wilhelm Friedrich Hegel.*

For Hegel envisaged the universe as one great all-encompassing whole in which every single finite reality has its allotted and logical place. And thus the basic tendency of his metaphysics was to swallow up the human individual in the Absolute, to make the particular self (as Kierkegaard said) merely "a paragraph in a system." But *this* man—Søren Kierkegaard—had lived through the experience of a broken engagement to an adored fiancée, and the experience took on a profoundly religious and philosophical meaning. For in its disclosure of how terrible is the solitude in which a man stands when he dares absolutely to choose one thing rather than another, it had the effect of bearing in upon him the realization that what is radically significant for any human being is not, as Hegel suggested, some cosmic principle of universal reason, but rather the immediate reality in which he is passionately involved: namely, his own existence which cannot be submerged in anything like Hegel's system of Absolute Being.

With that sense of the primacy of the individual person's existence which his own experience had given him, it is not surprising that Kierkegaard should have come to focus his thinking on the various ways in which a man may actually dwell in the world. It is a theme which figures importantly in many of his writings, but the works which take us most directly to the center of this area of his thought are those great books constituting that series of volumes which came from his pen in the period between 1843 and 1845— *Either/Or; Repetition; Fear and Trembling; Philosophical Fragments; The Concept of Dread;* and *Stages on Life's Way.*

In these works Kierkegaard proposes that there are three basic stages, or styles, of human existence—three distinct ways in which a man may face himself and his world. On one level, a person's basic orientation may be toward his external environment, and he may look out upon it as though he were primarily a spectator. Such a man lives forever on the surfaces of things, wholly absorbed by the ever changing outward scene. He is without any great commitments or goals or purposes; he is simply fascinated by the panorama of the world as he encounters it from moment to moment. And this is where he lives—always *in the moment*, and in its fleeting pleasures and satisfactions. He is open to all the adventures, receptive to all the experiences, that life brings his way; but he does not, in the name of any particular experience or value, undertake to judge all other experiences. He finds the human drama enormously interesting, but he is not led by his contemplation of it to make any decisive choices or to embrace any radical imperatives: he refuses to "get out of the poetical and into the existential." And thus Kierkegaard declares life, when it is lived on this level, to be "aesthetic," for when a man proposes to view the world simply as a spectacle in which he is not involved, it is an essentially aesthetic attitude that is being adopted. The aesthete may, of course, appear in various guises: he may, like Don Juan the seducer, be one who spends his days in quest of the grosser sensual pleasures; or, like Ahasuerus, the wandering Jew, he may be one who forever drifts restlessly back and forth across the face of the earth; or, again, he may appear as the detached intellectual who, as it were, takes a stand outside the world, giving himself to nothing but purely theoretical and speculative issues. But, under however many guises the aesthete may be found, what is always to be discovered as his chief distinguishing trait is his neutrality, his unwillingness to submit his life to any kind of binding commitment: it is the distance at which he lives from his own selfhood. And, in the language of Jesus' Parable of the Empty House, his "last state is worse than the first." For his life is most basically controlled not by anything in himself, but rather by the ceaselessly changing panorama of the outer world: this is what he is sustained by, this is what he clings to. But the world is always capricious and untrustworthy and beyond our control; thus, when it becomes the object of a man's primary reliance, his last state is bound to be one of disappointment and despair.

Yet the despair which must eventually overtake the aesthete can be a profoundly fruitful experience, since the discovery of the instability of the aesthetic life is the first step toward that higher stage or level of existence which Kierkegaard calls the "ethical." Here it is, on the ethical plane, that a man, having perceived the impossibility of finding a stable center for his life in any constellation of external circumstance, begins to abandon the detached neutrality of the spectator and to anchor his existence in genuine moral commitments. And what Kierkegaard conceives to be most important in the ethical dimension is not the particular code or standard to which one holds oneself accountable: it is rather, as he says in *The Concept of Dread*, "the energy, the earnestness, the pathos with which one chooses." What primarily distinguishes life in the ethical sphere, in other words, is the seriousness with which a man makes decisions as to how and where he should "apply" himself in the world of which he is a member. And decision, choosing, is the great thing. In the aesthetic sphere, life is an affair of simply being enchanted by the myriad possibilities which existence presents; but in the ethical sphere, a man is no longer sustained merely by the exciting vista of the various alternatives for action that lie before him: he does actually take the risk of choosing one pattern of life rather than another, of unconditionally committing himself to one line of conduct rather than to a dozen other possible courses of action. He consents, in short, to confront the Either/Or—and in so doing he finds himself, for all the aimlessness and inconstancy of purpose belonging to the aesthetic sphere are put behind, and the self now finds its life guided by a new steadiness of effort and objective.

But though there is a dignity belonging to the ethical sphere which can never be a part of aestheticism, not even on this second level of existence is there any final peace for the heart. For when a man undertakes to be obedient to an absolute principle of morality, he will, ever and again, be brought to the point of feeling the need to make a confession something like that which St. Paul utters in his Epistle to the Romans, when he says: " . . . the good that I would I do not: but the evil which I would not, that I do." Life in the "ethical" sphere does, in short, suffer a kind of shipwreck in that crisis in which the individual discovers that merely to know what one ought to do is not necessarily for one's will to be morally empowered to fulfill the ethical imperative. It is, in other words, in the experience of shame, of remorse, of contrition and penitence, that the ethical life is disclosed as insufficient, pointing beyond itself to some larger design.

Thus it is that, in Kierkegaard's analysis of man's search for fulfillment, the human pilgrim is driven on from the aesthetic to the ethical and then on to the third and last stage or level of existence, which he calls the "religious." He did not by any means, of course, want to suggest that the religious sphere is flatly opposed to the ethical; yet he very clearly wanted us to understand that it is something far more than the ethical life simply made more stringent, more exacting, more austere: it is, indeed, an essentially different dimension altogether. When a man, having been brought to the point of despair over the aimlessness of aesthetic existence, is then driven on to undertake an ethical quest, what he tries to do is to link his life with some universal rule or norm; in this way he hopes to become more authentically human. But the trouble with moral absolutes and universal norms is that, however relevant they may be to the general circumstances of life, they tend—precisely because of their universality—to have only a very limited relevance to the concrete and uniquely existing individual. And it is just my search for my own essential reality—for the true ground and ultimate foundation of *my* life—which constitutes the intrinsic nature of life in the religious sphere. In the ethical sphere, it is self-fulfillment which is aimed at; but a man is already on the way toward the religious sphere when he begins to realize that it is precisely his selfhood, in all its fragmentariness and finitude, which needs completion, that it must therefore find its ultimate ground beyond itself, and that "self-fulfillment" is consequently, as an ideal, a meaningless paradox.

Nowhere in the entire body of Kierkegaard's work is the difference between the ethical and the religious more sharply drawn than in his brilliantly written and moving little book of 1843, *Fear and Trembling*, which is a beautifully lyrical sort of meditation on the Old Testament story of Abraham and Isaac. In the biblical account, it will be remembered, Abraham (the legendary patriarch of the Jewish people) is reported to have been so passionately intent on devoting his whole life to God that he did one day become convinced that he must offer to God his adored son, Isaac, as a sacrifice of praise and thanksgiving. Isaac was his most precious possession, and a voice within seemed ever more insistently to be urging that God demanded nothing less, as an expression of Abraham's love toward Him, than the very life of this child. "Take now thy son," said the voice, "thine only son Isaac, whom thou lovest, and get thee into the land of Moriah; and offer him there for a burnt offering upon one of the mountains which I will tell thee of."

So at last Abraham rose up early one morning, with a heavy heart, saddled his ass, and took two of his young men with him, together with Isaac his son. And they proceeded, over three days, to a place far off in a lonely hill country. After they had arrived in this remote and desolate region, Abraham, says the Book of Genesis, turned to his companions and directed them to abide at a certain spot while he and Isaac went farther on to worship. Then he took the child and the implements he had brought for the sacrifice (the wood, and a torch, and a knife), and they went on till they reached a more secluded area. There, finally, they stopped, and Abraham built an altar out of stones which he gathered; then he

> . . . laid the wood in order, and bound Isaac his son, and laid him on the altar upon the wood.
> And Abraham stretched forth his hand, and took the knife to slay his son.

But just in that instant, like an angel from Heaven, the truth burst in upon him, and he found himself addressed by another voice, speaking with greater authority than the first: "Lay not thine hand upon the lad, neither do thou anything unto him." Then—strange miracle that it was!— he suddenly beheld a ram caught in a tangled thicket by its horns: so "Abraham went and took the ram, and offered him up for a burnt offering in the stead of his son." And afterward Abraham and Isaac, who had come up to this place together, went down again, the father filled with a great sense of wonder, and his heart now once more at peace.

So it is that the story is recounted in the Book of Genesis, and from time immemorial it has put the people of Israel in mind of one whose devotion was so great that he was prepared to give up the dearest thing in his life when it appeared that this was what God required of him—and one, therefore, worthy of the promise which came from on high:

> " . . . I will multiply thy seed as the stars of the heaven, and as the sand which is upon the seashore; and thy descendants shall possess the gate of their enemies.
>
> "And in them shall all the nations of the earth be blessed. . . ."

It is not, of course, a story which is "historical" in our modern sense of that term; but it is, nevertheless, one of the great legends in the sacred literature of the world.

It was just here, in this ancient narrative, that Kierkegaard found the difference between the ethical and religious spheres illustrated with crystalline clarity, though one suspects that the story so much appealed to him because he found his own sacrifice of Regina Olsen mirrored in Abraham's readiness to sacrifice his son. In any event, here it is, he said, in the father of Isaac, that we have the religious man *par excellence,* and a fine example of how great is the distance separating the ethical sphere from the religious sphere. For when human existence is considered from the perspective of the ethical sphere, nothing could be more clear than the obligation that a father has to watch over and preserve the life of his son. Yet here was a man who, though filled with a great love for his child, was prepared, nevertheless, to suspend temporarily the requirements of ethics and to slay his offspring, because he believed it to be required of him by his personal relationship to God. By an unsympathetic arbiter, Abraham may be adjudged a potential murderer: yet Kierkegaard would have us remember that, when he approached Isaac with the drawn knife, he was a man filled with anguish, for he had not simply rejected the ethical—he was devoted to his family, he was a man deeply conscious of a father's duty toward his son, and his love for Isaac was the great passion of his life. He was, in short, a man who had truly submitted himself to the universal norms of ethics, and he could suspend those norms only with the profoundest fear and trembling. But what is implied by Kierkegaard's whole analysis of human existence is that, when a man has really submitted himself to the universal norm and found it insufficiently comprehensive of *his* reality, he must then—and *only* then—dare to transcend it, dare to declare himself an exception: namely, one the concreteness of whose individual life is not fully reckoned with by a universal norm. And the name for the courage with which a human being dares to make this declaration is "faith." It is by faith that a man leaps from the ethical to the religious level of existence: which is to say that faith is not a matter of giving one's assent to vaguely obscure propositions about various spooky realities but is, rather, a matter of the courage with which a man, in the most critical situations of his life—when he is faced, like Abraham, with alternatives that appear almost to be equally valid—dares to take a stand *in behalf of his own humanity,* choosing that (however "absurd" it may seem) which promises most deeply to validate what he has found to be the essence of his manhood. This is what living in the religious sphere means: it means living by faith, or with *courage*, and it represents a style of life whose radicalism purely ethical categories can never embrace.

Yet what is perhaps most remarkable about Abraham is that, though he suspends the ethical norm (when he draws the knife) and thus breaks away from "the world," he nevertheless gets it all back again. And this, too, Kierkegaard asserted to be the case with the "knight of faith" who, even though he gives up the world, yet receives it back again—which is why he may often not be easily identifiable, as a man of faith. When he is actually encountered, we may find him to be a solid businessman, and he may appear to be an altogether conventional bourgeois. Yet this manager of the local bank, this pillar of his particular church, knows that his country club membership, the comfortable home over which his attractive wife graciously presides, his modest affluence, his "respectability," do not constitute the real meaning of his existence; none can guarantee his heart's peace or offer any real support in the ultimate emergencies of life. And thus, just because he is not dependent on these things, they are "added unto him," and he can enjoy them with the kind of nonchalance that distinguishes the attitude of the man of faith toward the things of this world.

But though one may speak of a certain kind of nonchalance as distinguishing Kierkegaard's "knight of faith," his meaning would be distorted were "nonchalance" to be taken to imply unruffled serenity, lack of tension, any sort of "positive thinking." On the contrary, for Kierkegaard the inner life of the man of faith is always an intensely dramatic affair of turbulence and struggle, for his strength is something that must ever and again be repossessed and renewed. In Kierkegaard's view of things, faith—genuinely ultimate and radical faith—is not an opinion about something or other or a belief that such-and-such is true. It is, rather, a way of existing—something like "the first flight of a baby eagle, pushed out of the nest by its parents, and then discovering to its amazement that the invisible ocean of light in which it is dropping is capable of bearing it up."[*] Which is to say that faith is a form of radical trust, and its radicalism we do not easily embrace: to press the analogy of the baby eagle, our natural preference is to trust the security of the nest rather than the aerosphere, even though the nest may at any time be blown away. "Letting go" of the material things of this world does not come easily, but nevertheless they must be

---

[*] Karl Heim, *The Transformation of the Scientific World View* (London: S.C.M. Press, 1951), p. 167.

let go if a man is to come into full possession of his humanity. This is what it means to exist religiously: it means taking a great leap, out of the nest. But this leap is not something which, having once been taken, may then be regarded as a feat permanently accomplished. I cannot say to myself, at least with any honesty. "Yes, I made the leap year before last: now things have been set right: now I have faith." For at any moment some great new emergency may develop which requires new resources of wisdom and courage. So the life of faith is one in which a man is continually confronting himself all over again, forever rising to new challenges and venturing new risks—in fear and trembling.

But of course most men do not want to submit themselves to the severe discipline involved in the kind of rigorous self-interrogation which the life of faith constantly entails. As T. S. Eliot remarks at a certain crucial point in his great poem of 1935, "Burnt Norton,"

> . . . . human kind
> Cannot bear very much reality.

There is a great terror which seems inevitably to be a part of self-confrontation. We like to think that we are more charming, more intelligent, more self-contained and independent than in fact we are. "Though he believe it, no man is strong." Yet so incorrigible is our habit of holding flattering opinions of ourselves that no man finds it easy to face his weakness, his frailty, his faults. And—as any practicing psychoanalyst knows full well—in nothing are we so adept as in our various stratagems for evading the concrete reality of ourselves. Which is to say that the strenuousness of the kind of life that is lived in the "religious" sphere is something that we are constantly seeking to avoid.

But the evasion of the true center of our existence can lead only to despair, and much of the Kierkegaardian literature is devoted, therefore, to an anatomy of the various forms of what (in the title of his brilliant book of 1849) he called *The Sickness Unto Death*. In Kierkegaard's analysis of the human situation, despair is the sickness unto death precisely because it is that illness of the spirit which is the consequence of a man's flight from the reality of his own selfhood. And no one, he contended, is altogether untouched by this malady: it is a universal plight of the human creature who never quite musters sufficient courage consistently and constantly to face the real truth of his condition, and who begins to be in despair in each moment in which he chooses to run away from his actual identity. There are, of course, those complacent people who imagine themselves to be utterly safe and sound, but though theirs may be a despair which is unconscious, it is made no less real by its repressions; indeed, when it does finally come to the surface, it may prove to be all the more disruptive for having been so long suppressed. Yet the more conscious forms of despair can on occasion prove to be equally dangerous. For, when a man will not dare to face himself, the likelihood is that he will then imagine the true locus of his reality to be not in himself but in one or another circumstance external to himself: which means that he makes himself captive to the world—over which, in the nature of the case, he can exert no control. Then he will suppose that everything would be all right if only circumstances were different, if only he had this man's looks or that man's wealth. And thus illusion is built upon illusion. Or, instead of some flight into worldliness, conscious despair may prompt a man to try to stabilize his life in the manner, say, of Melville's Ahab—by some arrogant act of defiance, by some act of immoderate self-assertion. Or the individual may instead choose, more passively, to regard his distress as without remedy—in which case he clings to it, because it gives him a grievance, and he finds a perverse satisfaction in the sense of being wronged.

And so the analysis goes in *The Sickness Unto Death*, as Kierkegaard plots the myriad forms and possibilities of man's despair. But, he contends, whatever form the distress may take, despair is, at bottom, a form of sin. And here Kierkegaard flatly contradicts much of what in our time is taken for granted about the various disorders which afflict the human soul. For when a man mistreats his wife, or when he is cruelly betrayed by her in adultery, when parents stifle spontaneity and independence in a child, or when a young person stubbornly refuses advantages generously offered by his mother and father, we are in the habit of casting about for the "cause" of the neurotic behavior: we assume that something has "happened" to the person which, once it is discovered, will "explain" his conduct. And in this post-Freudian age we tend to assume that the psychological disorder is the consequence of some traumatic experience. Nor can we easily dispense with deterministic views of human nature, as long as we look at a man from the outside, as though he were an object. But Kierkegaard's perspective was, of course, always that of a subjective thinker. And he knew that, however much from an external point of view a person's failings may seem attributable to whether he was breastfed or bottle-fed as an infant and to the various sorts of sociological conditions in which he grew up, when he mistreats his wife or violates the trust of his friends, he has done so because he has chosen to be perversely self-indulgent and insensitive. Kierkegaard's speaking of despair as a form of sin was his way, in other words, of declaring the seat of our troubles to be not outside ourselves, but within—deep, deep in the human interior.

This whole doctrine of human nature, in its stress upon the subjective truth as opposed to the objective, and "inwardness" as the locus of what is most humanly real, led Kierkegaard, finally, to move from the issues of individual psychology toward a very radical critique of the Church of his time and of European civilization at large. For everywhere, it seemed to him, the basic structures of nineteenth-century life were calculated to keep a man from saying "I" and from reckoning straightforwardly with his own individual selfhood. It was the crowd, he declared, that was fast becoming the fundamental form of human existence: men, individual men, were coming more and more to be simply units of an impersonal social collective. In a little book called *The Present Age*, which was written in the winter of 1846, he denounced, with a furiously angry eloquence, this whole phenomenon of collectivism, and thus he anticipated that line of existentialist critics in our own time—the German Karl Jaspers, the Spaniard Ortega y Gasset, the Frenchman Gabriel Marcel, the Russian Nicolas Berdyaev—who have produced a similar critique of what we now speak of as "mass society." Men no longer contemplate their existence and accept the risk of facing themselves, he contended in *The Present Age*. Instead, they form a committee—and "in the end the whole age becomes a committee." People have developed so great a passion, indeed, for banding together that the crowd has become the predominant category of life, very nearly displacing altogether the category of the individual.

The result, said Kierkegaard, is the invasion of the world by a new phantom, "the public . . . a kind of gigantic something, an abstract and deserted void which is everything and nothing," and which begins to come into existence when men give up their individuality for the sake of buying the cheap sort of safety that comes when one is engulfed, as an anonymous unit, into a social collective.

"All inwardness is lost. . . ." And the modern period tends more and more to become "an age of leveling" in which the important centers of life are no longer felt to be great individuals—kings and soldiers and poets and sages— but rather the sorts of entities that arise when men are added together: it is the crowd which is taken to be the fundamental form of truth. But since, for Kierkegaard, the locus of distinctively human reality was the individual, he found himself required, by the whole logic of his outlook, to take up an embattled position against what he conceived to be the essential drift of modern society. And it is this attitude of resistance which is being expressed in many of the writings of his last years, most especially in the little book of 1846, *The Present Age.*

But the increasingly collectivist character of social and cultural life was not, Kierkegaard felt, the only factor in the modern situation tending to disable the special sort of seriousness required by "religious" existence; indeed, he found the Church itself to be more a part of the problem than it was a part of any good answer to it. For the Church, too, in its institutionalizing of the Christian faith, was managing to devitalize the great challenge of the Gospel to "Go your own way and be ye separate," and thus it was becoming itself little more than simply another social collective. So, not unnaturally, the last great effort of Kierkegaard's life was devoted to a savage attack upon everything that he conceived to be hollow and evasive and inauthentic in the Danish Church of his time. By 1848 he had declared, in *The Sickness Unto Death,* that " . . . in Christendom the name of God is surely the word which occurs most frequently in daily speech and is absolutely the word to which one attaches the least meaning," that "Christendom is . . . far from being what it calls itself. . . ." And this kind of polemic had consistently figured as a leitmotif in his writings for many years. But in 1854, the

year before his death, he created a great scandal amongst
his fellow countrymen by the unbridled fury with which
he was attacking the established Lutheran Church (the
state church of Denmark) in a series of nine pamphlets
issued at monthly intervals under the title *The Instant.*
In their English translation, these pamphlets are today
available in the form of the book we know as *The Attack
Upon Christendom,* which is undoubtedly one of the most
trenchant indictments of Christian culture produced in the
modern period.

Kierkegaard's explosion was detonated by the eulogy
that the distinguished Danish theologian Professor Hans
Martensen delivered on the occasion of Bishop Jakob
Mynster's funeral, in which he declared that Mynster had
been "a link in the sacred chain of witnesses to Apostolic
Truth." And it was most especially the word "witnesses"
by which Kierkegaard was aroused. For the term in the
original Greek means "martyr," and he felt that nothing
could be more excessive than the claim that Mynster and
his kind (namely, the Danish clergy who were, in effect,
well-paid civil servants) were people from whom the
proclamation of the Christian Gospel exacted any great
cost, that they were in any true sense of the term at all
"martyrs." So it was Martensen's sermon which prompted
Kierkegaard, with all the scorn he could muster, to trumpet
forth the "mediocrity of Christendom."

It was not, of course, that he held any personal dislike
for either Martensen or Mynster. He was quite prepared
to acknowledge that they both represented considerable
urbanity of scholarship and devotion to the Church, as
they understood it. Indeed, Bishop Mynster, who had been
his father's confessor and closest friend, was a man for
whom Kierkegaard had borne considerable affection since
childhood. And it was this affection which had long kept
alive in him the hope that he might find it possible to avoid

any public criticism of Mynster's career. The bishop was an eloquent preacher, and Kierkegaard had nothing but admiration for "his incomparable sermons." "But . . . alas, the week, as is well known, has seven days. . . . And in the remaining six days," he said of Mynster, "worldly shrewdness is his element." He had hoped over a long period that there might come a time when the bishop would admit in some way that his was a style of Christianity lacking any prophetic power, and deeply flawed. But this admission had never come—and now, here was Professor Martensen, on the occasion of Mynster's funeral, declaring him to have been a "witness"—that is, a "martyr" —in behalf of Christian truth. So Kierkegaard confided to his *Journals* on the first of March, 1854, "What I have to do now, I do with sorrow; yet it must be done, about that I am perfectly clear; I can find no peace until it is done."

No, said Kierkegaard to Denmark, Bishop Mynster was no more a "witness" than the mother of a large family is a "virgin": he was, rather, an urbane administrator who was adept in making the machinery of the established Church run smoothly and efficiently. And thus he had been one of the great enemies in the land of the real Gospel of Jesus Christ, for his chief work had largely consisted in building up the illusion that Christianity did exist in Denmark. He was, in short, nothing but the chief representative of a Church which had lost all resemblance to the Church of the New Testament. And Kierkegaard insisted that no verdict less harsh could be rendered of a Church whose bishops and clergy and laity were principally concerned only to maintain in their handsomely appointed buildings a schedule of stately services, with beautiful music and invigorating sermons and comforting prayers. The Church, he said, had in fact become simply another bulwark of bourgeois respectability. One of its great functions in cultural life ought to be that of summoning men out of the blind mediocrity of conformity and into an acceptance of their true human vocation to be responsible individuals who know what it means to be the Single One before God. But now, Kierkegaard declared, the life of the Church itself is very largely a life *en masse*, governed by rule, by convention, by conformity: and thus it is a travesty of the Church of Christ.

Indeed, he was convinced that a pagan culture would be found to be more permeable by the Gospel than Christendom itself. For, he contended, any effort at "reintroducing Christianity into Christendom" will encounter a most formidable hindrance in the conviction that is held by those who live in Christendom—that they are in truth Christians because they have been baptized and regularly attend services, and faithfully pay whatever they are taxed for the support of the ecclesiastical machinery. In Christendom, in other words, the illusion still persists that Christianity is a decisive force in human affairs. But it is only an illusion, for Christians have lost all understanding of what it means to live Christianly, and, as he says in *Training in Christianity* (1850), "Christendom has done away with Christianity without being quite aware of it." Parsons are simply well paid, comfortably situated professional men who, in their preaching, poeticize the stern mandates of Christ into a sort of saccharine religiosity which is without any power at all to arraign a man's conscience; and Kierkegaard would have approved of the sharp edge of truth in the satirical *New Yorker* cartoon of a few years ago which showed a rotund little clergyman saying from his high pulpit to the congregation out in the nave of the church, " . . . present company excepted, of course." And the laity? Well, said he, they are what might be expected, in a Church whose clergy have forgotten the meaning of Christian nurture and education: they sit in their fashionable churches, listening to the preacher expound such a text as "God hath elected the base things of the world, and the things that are despised"—and then, after shaking hands with the minister after the service is over, they get into their carriages—or now, into their expensive cars and station wagons—and off they go for a martini and Sunday dinner, having no slight understanding even of what it has meant to partake of the body and blood of Christ in the service of Holy Communion from which they have just departed.

So it is that Kierkegaard's indictment proceeds. Nowhere could he discern any evidence that Christians still remembered what the Church was meant to be—that is, an embattled and militant people prepared, indeed, to be witnesses, to be martyrs, for the Truth; and everywhere he beheld compromise and mediocrity and a deadening drift towards bourgeois conformity and respectability. So he declared Christendom to be of a piece with the "total bankruptcy toward which the whole of Europe seems to be heading."

Here, then, is the kind of challenge which Kierkegaard threw down to the nineteenth century and to the modern generations that were to come after him. It did not at first win any respectful hearing. For a brief time, to be sure, it achieved a certain notoriety for him on the Danish scene: cartoonists poked fun at him—as a loony little hunchback who gazed witlessly at the stars, or as a rooster wearing a top hat in a noisy pen of cackling chickens. He was cruelly satirized in the smart papers of the day. Little gamins on the streets of Copenhagen ran after him shouting, "Either-Or," the title of his first major book, and, when they were disobedient, their mothers, it is said, had only to mention his name by way of quieting an unruly child. But though the ill-usage which he received in drawing-room gossip and in the local press suggests that he did to some extent manage to trouble the conscience of Copenhagen, the masterpieces that came from his pen in the period between 1843 and 1854—*Either/Or, Fear and Trembling, Philosophical Fragments, The Concept of Dread, Stages on Life's Way,* the *Concluding Unscientific Postscript, The Sickness Unto Death,* and various others—gained no immediate entry into the main stream of European culture, and this is not altogether surprising, given the fact that they were written in the Danish language. Toward the end of the century, however, there was one Dane who achieved international prominence in intellectual life—the literary critic and cultural historian Georg Brandes. Though Brandes' sympathy for Kierkegaard's thought was very limited, he did nevertheless write about his work with a brilliance that began to attract considerable attention, so that long before World War I a German edition of Kierkegaard's "literature" was already well under way. By the mid-1930's his presence was everywhere felt in European philosophic and religious and literary circles. Nor was he to be long without a sizable Anglo-American audience, for it was just at this time that the distinguished Kierkegaardian scholar Walter Lowrie, through the generous cooperation of the Oxford and Princeton university presses, began to release his long series of brilliantly rendered English translations—which were supplemented, with equal brilliance, by the translation work of another American, David Swenson, who was one of the first Kierkegaardians in the United States and who for many years was an eminent figure in the philosophy department of the University of Minnesota.

So by the close of World War II this melancholy Dane had become an important presence on the modern intellectual scene, and, for all the parochialism of his inherited language, it was clear that he had in truth used a common tongue and was a major source of that whole tradition which we have now learned to speak of as Existentialism.

Though we have been primarily reviewing here his analysis of "the human condition" rather than his exposition of the Christian faith, Kierkegaard's thought was guided at every point by consistently theological perspectives; and much of his prodigious literary activity was devoted to an exploration of what is involved in a man's embracing the Christian Gospel. Yet, though many of his heirs—such as Heidegger, Jaspers, Sartre, Camus—are equally radical in their commitment to a secularist outlook (whether it be of an agnostic or atheistic sort), his paternity with respect to modern existentialist tradition is, nevertheless, not to be gainsaid. For it is from him, as well as from Nietzsche (to whom we turn in the following chapter), that all those standing in the existentialist line inherit that method of inquiry and that general pitch and temper of mind which constitute their characteristic tendency.

A man can be related to what is most ultimately real, says the *Concluding Unscientific Postscript*, only "by virtue of the infinite passion of inwardness," for "Truth is subjectivity"—or, as it was phrased in *Training in Christianity*, "Truth consists precisely in inwardness." And in this emphasis, which is so much at the basis of his entire thought, Kierkegaard struck a note which is consistently echoed throughout the whole of existentialist literature. One of his interpreters, in an interesting book of a few years ago devoted not only to Kierkegaard but also to Nietzsche and Camus, spoke of the three together as "lyrical existentialists," because the idea of lyricism, with its notion of the singing voice, "draws us inward to become absorbed in the only existence we shall ever directly encounter: ourselves"*—which is, as the author was rightly proposing, precisely where these three men would have us

* Thomas Hanna, *The Lyrical Existentialists* (New York: Atheneum, 1962), p. 178.

turn for the essential human reality, not toward the outer
world but toward the world within, where all is immediate
and without any intervening medium. But in this respect a
man like Camus is in no way different from an Unamuno or
a Heidegger or a Marcel, and the notion of "lyrical" Existentialism marks off no particular party of existentialists,
for the idea of lyricism (with its suggestion of non-objec-
tive, rhapsodic modes of statement) points to the kind of
emphatically subjectivistic outlook which is generally characteristic of existentialist thinkers. In this commonly shared
bias, they are all descendants of Kierkegaard, for it was pre-
eminently he who gave a new dignity and importance in
modern tradition to the intellectual quest for the nature of
the existing individual—by way of "passionate" exploration
of one's own selfhood.

Furthermore, in his analysis of the "stages" of existence, he proposed that a great "leap of faith" is the most
daring act that any man can perform—the act whereby
(like the baby eagle leaving its nest for the first time)
he launches out, as it were, onto a sea "70,000 fathoms"
deep; and he insisted that, without such a leap, no really
authentic life is possible. Even when existentialist thought
(as in a man like Sartre) is more nearly in the Nietzschean
than in the Kierkegaardian line, and when therefore it is
atheistic or agnostic rather than theological, it nevertheless retains a Kierkegaardian stamp. Jean-Paul Sartre,
for example, may consider Kierkegaard's leap to be only
a leap into nothingness: yet he, too, in one whole phase
of his thought, is, in effect, defining the authentic life as
a sort of adventure, as a sort of launching out onto 70,000
fathoms: and, like Kierkegaard, he conceives it to be a
main task of any thinker dealing with the concrete realities of human experience to identify and dissect the various forms of *in*authentic life, as they are to be encountered
in the hypocrisy and conformity and timorousness that

are forever threatening to entrap men in utter mediocrity. Which is to say that Sartre is an essentially iconoclastic thinker, and his iconoclasm—like Heidegger's and Camus' and that of the existentialists generally—is indelibly stamped by Kierkegaard's influence.

Nor can we also fail to discern the influence of Kierkegaard in the common tendency of existentialist thinkers to conceive human life as essentially an affair of restlessness and struggle, of tension and combat, of risk and suffering. They do all, as it were, invite us to consider our lives —to use one of Sartre's favorite terms—as a *project*, to be undertaken with seriousness and passion and courage; the human reality is imagined in ways that imply it to be something finite, unfinished, incomplete. And the world which is the scene and setting of man's existence is not to be taken for granted—it is too mysterious, too full of surprises, too infinitely astonishing. One's posture must therefore be one of vigilance and resolute tenaciousness, if what is fragmentary and unfulfilled in a man's life is, finally, to stand any chance of completion. This emphasis is deeply a part of the testimony of thinkers so diverse as Berdyaev and Heidegger and Sartre and Buber—who do all in this way express what is a part of Kierkegaard's bequest to the existentialist movement.

Then, finally, there is a certain consistency of emphasis characterizing the way in which existentialist thinkers have tended to experience their own personal vocations, and this also is something that we may find already prefigured in Kierkegaard. There is, for example, a charming passage in the *Concluding Unscientific Postscript* in which Kierkegaard, under the pseudonym of Johannes Climacus (the feigned author of the *Postscript*), reflects on how he came to be a writer. He says that one Sunday afternoon, as he sat smoking a cigar in one of the parks of Copenhagen, he began to ponder his life and to submit

himself to candid reappraisal. And as he sat there that day
in the Frederiksberg Garden, he was not a little troubled
by his stock taking, for it told him that he had as yet
realized no large accomplishment. Over a good many
years he had been in residence as a student at the University, and though he had been intensely involved in
intellectual labors, he had yet to turn his hand to a major
piece of work and to undertake a career. As he looked
out that afternoon on the bustling scene of the nineteenth
century, it seemed that all around him men were making
great reputations by way of the ingeniousness with which
they were either designing material improvements of life
(such as steamboats and railroads and new forms of technology) or devising various sorts of intellectual nostrums
calculated to offer some quick and easy access to a comprehensive view of the world. He alone, he momentarily
felt, had yet to make his mark. And since, as it seemed
to him, very nearly everybody was bent on making the
world an easier place to live in, perhaps, he felt, someone
ought to take it upon himself to make things hard, and to
speak of some of the baffling, worrisome perplexities which
men normally avoid. Perhaps what was needed was a
great troubler of the common peace—and here, it occurred
to him, might be his life's vocation.

Now the splendid irony with which this little tale is
recounted in the *Concluding Unscientific Postscript*
makes for a marvelously exact rendering of the kind of role
to which Kierkegaard felt himself elected in the nineteenth
century. And it also puts us in mind of many of his heirs
in the more immediate world of our own time, for the men
who have established Existentialism as a major line of
twentieth-century thought are people who, all of them, have
in one way or another been troublers of our peace. In
their more purely theoretical work, they have called into
question the predominantly rationalist character of

Western philosophic tradition which, as they make us feel, appears indeed to them to be something like what Alfred North Whitehead conceived it to be—namely, "a series of footnotes to Plato." Plato, it will be remembered, at the very outset of the tradition, regarded all the finite realities of our space-time world as simply reflections or replicas of the transcendent realities making up that eternal world of what he called "Ideas." And he conceived the Idea of man, the Idea of the state, to be more real than any existing man or historical community, because the particular man, the particular state, exists only for a time and then perishes and passes away. But the Idea of man is outside time, is eternal: so it is the Idea which is "really real." It is the business of human intelligence, therefore, to deal with universals, since it is the *essence* of a thing that constitutes the locus of its reality. Now this "essentialist" drift of Platonism has been consistently characteristic of the basic tendency of the entire Western philosophic tradition, even when it has on occasion supposed itself to be anti-Platonic—for it has almost always assumed that the universal is more real than the particular, that reason (which is the human faculty whereby universals are apprehended) is therefore the seat of man's humanity, and that theory is a more humanly important activity than practice. But the existentialists have undertaken to trouble our peace by calling all these certitudes into question, declaring in one way or another that *existence* precedes *essence*, and that no "essentialist" philosophy can do justice to the concrete experience of a flesh-and-blood man. Man, says Jean-Paul Sartre, for example, is not an essence, not a universal, but a *project*: for what makes the individual a radically unique creature is his freedom: he is what he *makes* himself to be, in his historical circumstances. The essential being of a man is formed by his way of existing. This has been a crucial emphasis of the existentialist movement, and its chief representatives—like the Kierkegaard who so fiercely attacked the rationalism of Hegel—have tended very sharply to arraign a philosophic tradition whose essentialist bias robs it of relevance to "existential" reality.

But—again, like Kierkegaard—existentialists have maintained a polemical stance not only in their theoretical work but also in their more practical critique of society and politics. For whether one turns to Ortega (*The Revolt of the Masses*) or to Jaspers (*Man in the Modern Age*) or to Berdyaev (*The End of Our Time; The Bourgeois Mind; The Fate of Man in the Modern World*) or to Marcel (*Man Against Mass Society*), one is struck by how consistently existentialist social criticism entails a great protest against the increasing standardization of life in contemporary civilization. Long before William Whyte began to look at the lives of junior executives in Park Forest, Illinois (in *The Organization Man*[*]), and David Reisman began to talk about "other-directedness" (in *The Lonely Crowd*[**]), existentialist thinkers were calling our attention to how steadily the world of the modern West is moving toward a kind of mass society in which the fundamental form of human existence becomes that of the faceless herd, or what Kierkegaard called "the public." And they have consistently conceived it to be a part of their mission to say to the people of our time that a truly authentic human life is not to be achieved by a man's slipping off into the featureless anonymity of the social collective. As it is put by one of the characters in Jean-Paul Sartre's play *No Exit:* "Hell is—others." And most of the principal strategists of the existentialist movement have wanted, like their Danish progenitor, to expose what

[*] See William H. Whyte, Jr., *The Organization Man* (New York: Simon and Schuster, Inc., 1956).

[**] See David Riesman, *The Lonely Crowd* (New Haven: Yale University Press, 1950).

they have found to be baleful and threatening in the special forms of "otherness" by which the men and women of our period tend to be so greatly seduced.

But it is not Kierkegaard alone who has taught existentialist thinkers how to ruffle our peace, for theirs is a patrimony which also derives from another great troubler of the modern conscience belonging to the nineteenth century—namely, that fascinating German who declared (in the Preface of *The Will to Power*) that his work did, at bottom, entail "a summary judgment . . . on the entire modern age. . . ." And thus it is to the testimony of Friedrich Nietzsche that we must now turn.

3

Friedrich Nietzsche— Evangelist of the Death of God

AT A CERTAIN POINT in his book of 1843, *Either/Or*, Kierkegaard says, "My sorrow is my knight's castle. It rests like an eagle's nest upon the summit of a mountain and towers high above the clouds. None can storm it." And in the tone of bravado which marks this declaration one hears an accent which is being sounded again and again by many of the most creative writers and thinkers and artists of the nineteenth century. For amidst all the social and intellectual dislocations that were a part of that tumultuous time, many of the century's most sensitive men, suffering the loss of traditional faiths and being assailed by new doubts, began to think of human life as a thing of extreme insecurity and danger. Man seemed somehow to be abandoned and alone, in a world deprived of familiar landmarks and in which therefore he could no longer firmly grasp anything at all. So the desert and the sea were images to which the poet and the artist were increasingly drawn, for the universe did indeed begin to seem to many like a kind of wasteland, or like the uncharted waters of the trackless deeps. And the situation of the man of courage and vision was very often felt to be something like that of a towering and lonely cliff, a great seagirt rock, or (as in Kierkegaard's figure) like one perched on an isolate mountain peak thrusting out into the empty spaces of the world. The hazardous element in which man dwells came more and more to be conceived an immeasurable domain, like the sea; and his encounter with the ultimate meaning of his existence was frequently imagined in the terms of a brave and solitary residence atop some austerely mountainous crag or summit. These are themes that one meets in the work of such diverse figures as Byron and Melville and Baudelaire and Ibsen and Wagner, and they are in fact pervasively present in the poetry and drama and fiction (and even philosophy) of the nineteenth century.

The man who knows himself to be alone in the world and without anything to hold on to is also to be found in much of the century's visual art—in the late canvases of Goya, in many of Daumier's drawings, in the paintings of Van Gogh, in much of the work of the sculptor Rodin. But it is undoubtedly the distinguished German painter Caspar David Friedrich (1774-1840) who, above all others, gave expression in graphic form to that sense of reality expressed in the frequently invoked imagery of the mountain and the sea. Many of his pictures may be recalled in this connection—the *Chalk Cliffs at Rügen*, the *Monk of the Seashore, The Wreck of the "Hope"*—but there is one in which the whole spirit not only of Friedrich's genius but also of German Romanticism itself is most especially to be felt: it is that remarkable painting called *The Wanderer Above the Mists* (which is sensitively discussed in Erich Heller's book of 1965, *The Artist's Journey Into the Interior**).

* See Erich Heller, *The Artist's Journey Into the Interior* (New York: Random House, 1965), pp. 75-86.

What we see in Friedrich's picture is the solitary figure
of a man, with an air of great authority in his bearing
and with his back turned toward the spectator, standing
at the summit of a great broken cliff. Just beneath him
there is a vast expanse of mist, and Erich Heller reminds
us that "Wherever he came from, he must have wandered
through the night or toward the night; for only now, when
he has reached this mountaintop, the sun is rising or setting." Through the mist, he gazes out upon the peaks of
other mountains in his neighborhood, but they are
shrouded in vapor; and the sharpness with which the picture sets his own vividly rendered rock against the haze
that rises from below makes one feel that the place where-
on this lone pilgrim stands is the very edge of the world.
What is perhaps most impressive, though, in Friedrich's
composition is its curiously *auditory* power; for, at this extreme limit of the earth to which the wanderer has come,
one *hears* a most profound silence, an eerie stillness that
gives a heavy and foreboding sort of solemnity to the
whole scene. Here, indeed, is a man who, as he stands at
the edge of the abyss that yawns below and as he faces
the cracks and chasms that scar the landscape stretching
out before him, is absolutely homeless and alone—without
any attachments, without any abiding place. Yet as he surveys this bleak and chilling prospect he stands erect, calm,
apparently unperturbed—and there is even a touch of arro-
gance in the regal composure of this nonchalant, unim-
passioned aristocrat. It is in fact the best portrait of
Nietzsche that we have (though painted a few years before his birth), for the solitariness of spirit, the elevation
above the lowlands of our common humanity, the standing atop a lonely crag (which "none can storm") in a
desolate mountain district, the staking of a post at the
outermost boundary of the world, the vision of a distant
grandeur—all this belongs most essentially to the extra-

ordinary spiritual adventure which Friedrich Nietzsche undertook in the closing years of the nineteenth century.

"A man of spiritual depth," he once wrote, "needs friends, unless he still has God as a friend. But I have neither God nor friends." And it was in such utter nakedness that this most audacious heretic of his age proceeded to wrestle with all the fearsome riddles that he believed to be looming before man at the end of the modern period —in a time when some old sun that had once lit up the world seemed now to be extinguished and when, as he declared, a great collapse had occurred in the very courts of heaven, even in the city of God Himself.

In many respects, to be sure, the basic style and emphasis of Nietzsche's thought bring him very close to Kierkegaard, who, together with him, stands at the source of modern Existentialism. Like Kierkegaard, Nietzsche was a subjective thinker who was prepared to honor as true only those conceptions whose validity he had himself felt on his own pulses. And he was also like his Danish progenitor in the fierceness with which he trumpeted forth an indictment of what was hollow and bankrupt in the bourgeois society of modern Europe. Nor was his mistrust of systematic philosophy any less profound than Kierkegaard's: he, too, was convinced that no system— such as Hegel's metaphysic of the Absolute—could render any sort of adequate justice to the concrete actualities of human experience. But, in what was perhaps the most important particular, the author of *Thus Spake Zarathustra* stood poles apart from the author of *Training in Christianity*. For whereas Kierkegaard's whole critique of Christendom was calculated to puncture all the sham and dishonesty of institutional Christianity and to make the primitive simplicities of the New Testament effective once again in the lives of men, Nietzsche's arraignment of the historic Christian culture of the West was launched for

the sake of unmasking what he took to be the essential
falseness of the story about human existence which is told
by the Christian Gospel. He knew the loss of confidence
in the Christian faith to entail a terrible kind of agony of
spirit for any man who has been reared under the classical heritage of Western culture. But it was an agony the
willing sufferance of which he was prepared to praise,
as representing a new sort of maturity in spiritual history;
and it is indeed such praise that is being sounded by many
of the most brilliant testaments that came from his pen.
"The greatest of recent events," said he, "is that 'God
is dead.'" And it was the promulgation of this momentous occurrence that constituted the central element of his
entire message.

Friedrich Nietzsche was born on the fifteenth of October, 1844, in the little village of Röcken in the Prussian
province of Saxony. His father was a Lutheran pastor, as
both his grandfathers had been. But Pastor Nietzsche was
dead of a brain hemorrhage before Friedrich's fifth birthday, and, following his death, the family moved to Naumburg, where Friedrich grew up in a wholly feminine household presided over by his mother and grandmother and
including his sister Elisabeth and two maiden aunts. In
school his exceptional precociousness was early recognized, for soon after he was entered at the *Gymnasium*
(a secondary school devoted to pre-university studies) in
Naumburg his mother was advised that he belonged in a
school specializing in the training of outstandingly gifted
youngsters. So, at the age of fourteen, he was transferred
to such an institution, the famous boarding school of
Pforta located just outside Naumburg. Here he was submitted to the kind of intensity and exactitude of intellectual discipline that had long made Pforta one of the great
centers of German secondary education, and he excelled
in his studies in classics, in German literature, and in religion.

In 1864, at the age of twenty, the young Nietzsche entered the University of Bonn, where he fast cultivated an interest in philosophy.' But it was the classics of Greek and Roman antiquity which constituted the central focus of his university work, and thus his principal professor at Bonn was the renowned classical philologist Friedrich Ritschl. When Ritschl left Bonn to accept a professorship at the University of Leipzig, Nietzsche felt it to be the natural thing to do for him to follow his revered teacher on to Leipzig, and so he did. But—and here is the measure of the high distinction which the young scholar had already attained, while still a student—before Nietzsche had even completed his doctorate at Leipzig under Ritschl, he was offered (on Ritschl's recommendation) the chair in classical philology at the great old University of Basel in Switzerland. So, at the unheard of age of twenty-four, he found himself the incumbent of a distinguished university professorship; and, in recognition of this extraordinary accomplishment, Leipzig exempted him from the final examinations for his degree and forthwith conferred it.

Nietzsche remained a member of the faculty at Basel for ten years, from 1869 till 1879. But his physical constitution had never been strong, and the strenuousness of his service in the German ambulance corps during the brief period of the Franco-Prussian War (1870-1871) seems to have permanently depleted his none too abundant energies. And not only was he physically frail but (in the increasingly severe attacks of migraine and the many troublesome illnesses which would appear to have been psychosomatic in character) there were also recurrent signs of a deep psychological instability that may now be seen as having augured the total collapse of his last years. So, while still quite a young man, after having had to take more than one leave of absence because of various disabilities, Nietzsche finally retired from the Basel faculty in 1879, at the age of thirty-five, when it seemed that his health was very nearly broken altogether. The leisure brought by his retirement enabled him, however, in the months that followed, to achieve a sufficiently substantial recovery to resume his researches and writing. By this time he had already completed *The Birth of Tragedy* (1872), his *Untimely Meditations* (1873-1876), and *Human, All-too-Human* (1878-1880); and it was in the period between 1880 and 1889, following his retirement from Basel, that, with a great burst of creativity, he produced many of his most important books: *The Dawn* (1881), *The Gay Science* (1882), *Thus Spake Zarathustra* (1882-1885), *Beyond Good and Evil* (1886), *Genealogy of Morals* (1887), *The Twilight of the Idols* (1889), and various other works.

Perhaps the most important relationship in Nietzsche's life during the years of his Basel period was that which he had with the eminent composer Richard Wagner. They had first met in Leipzig in 1868, and each had been pleased to find that the other shared his enthusiasm for the philosopher Arthur Schopenhauer (1788-1860) and for his magnum opus, *The World as Will and Idea*. After Nietzsche settled at Basel, they began to see each other frequently, for Wagner had a villa not far from there at Tribschen, on the shores of the Lucerne. There he had lived for some years with his mistress, Cosima (the illegitimate daughter of Franz Liszt and the wife of the famous pianist and conductor Hans von Bülow), whom he finally married in 1870, after their union had resulted in a family of several children. The Wagners were brought especially close to the young Basel professor after Wagner's generous praise of his first book, *The Birth of Tragedy*, led him to begin to travel out to Tribschen for visits. Nietzsche had an immense admiration for Wagner, believing him to be the towering figure in German cultural life, and he doubtless felt enormously flattered by the warmth with which he was received by the composer of *Tannhäuser* and *Lohengrin* and *Tristan*. But he was also quickly smitten by Cosima, who was the most interesting woman he had ever met; and, unattainable as she was, he soon fell in love with her, secretly but everlastingly, for it was a passion which he was to keep for the remainder of his life. Indeed, in the madness of his last years he was on occasion to speak of her insanely as "my wife Cosima Wagner." And it is thought by some that Nietzsche's eventual break with Wagner was prompted by an impotent hatred of him who possessed his own heart's darling.

It would be, however, very greatly to misconceive Nietzsche's relationship to Wagner, were its final rupture to be accounted for simply in terms of a sexual jealousy in Nietzsche (of which in fact it appears that he was himself barely conscious). Initially, of course, he had been drawn to Wagner not because of the attractiveness of the great composer's mistress but because he felt a profound ideological sympathy for the kind of cultural program he found being expressed in Wagner's music. Like Kierkegaard before him, this young German scholar supposed one of the besetting afflictions of the nineteenth century to be its pervasive mediocrity: everywhere, in his estimate of things, the fabric of the age seemed to be distinguished, in its social and intellectual and artistic expressions, by nothing but drabness and triviality and stagnation. Only in the soaring majesty of Wagner's revolutionary music-dramas did he find the promise of greatness, the eruption of true passion and authentic genius. Not only was he deeply moved by Wagner's music, but he also shared Wagner's aversion to the Christian faith and was more than a little aroused by the kind of German paganism which this audacious composer was attempting to revive in his work for the operatic theater.

The young Nietzsche had already been intoxicated by

Schopenhauer's atheism, by the sort of doctrine that he encountered in *The World as Will and Idea:* that what is required for the redemption of human life is not a savior (as Christian teaching asserts) but, rather, man's achieving a resolute confidence in his own capacity to shape the destiny of the world toward some happy end. There is, Schopenhauer had argued, an energizing power at work everywhere in the universe—in the instinct of the animal, in the biological processes of vegetation, even in the sort of stability represented by inorganic matter. He had called this power "Will," and since, as he claimed, it is in man that this essential reality—of Will—comes to reflective self-consciousness, it is man himself, he reasoned, who deserves to be thought of as the true custodian of the world. And its redemption awaits only his winning the courage to assume his high mission.

These were ideas that had already begun to fascinate Nietzsche during his student years at Leipzig, and it was the kind of echo that they found in Wagner which led him to be even more greatly fascinated by the composer of *The Ring of the Nibelung.* For Wagner's antipathy toward the Christian tradition was based not only on his belief that its Jewish roots made it something essentially alien to the Germanic spirit, but also on his conviction that its ethic of love and humility made for a kind of strangulation of the will to power, the result of which must finally be a weakening of man's capacity for a robust and virile life. He therefore wanted to replace the Christian myth with ancient Teutonic legend, electing its gods and demigods (Wotan and Erda, the Valkyries, Siegmund and Sieglinde) to the place of pre-eminence. The whole project struck Nietzsche at first as marvelously bold and enterprising.

Increasingly, though, after the establishment of Wagner's great festival theater in Bayreuth in 1876, Nietzsche grew more and more discomfited by what was coarse and vulgar in the maestro's racial doctrine. And with the staging at Bayreuth in the summer of 1882 of *Parsifal*, Nietzsche did at last feel utterly betrayed by his old friend; for, in basing this massive opera on the legend of the Holy Grail, Wagner was in effect returning, as Nietzsche concluded, to the otherworldly hocus-pocus of the Christian myth. So he felt that there was no other tack for him to take except that of outright denunciation, and the statement of his case is to be found in two furious pamphlets—*The Wagner Case* of 1888, and the work entitled *Nietzsche contra Wagner* (published by his sister in 1895, after Nietzsche had collapsed into total insanity).

But though the relationship with Wagner fizzled out into bad feeling and bitterness, and Nietzsche therefore never saw Cosima again after his breach with her husband, she was by no means the only woman who figured in his life. There was a young French matron, a certain Mme. Louise Ott, whom he met at Bayreuth in 1876 and of whom for a few months he was intensely enamored—though nothing really ever came of the infatuation. Or, again, in that same year he was briefly in love with a young woman from the Baltic provinces, Mathilde Trampedach, who refused his proposal of marriage.

Then, in 1882, while visiting in Rome, he was introduced to Lou Salomé, the intelligent and charming, though not particularly beautiful, daughter of a Russian general. As she was later to write, "Loneliness . . . was the first strong impression which Nietzsche's appearance conveyed. . . . He had a soft laugh, a way of talking almost inaudibly. . . . He showed great politeness and an almost womanly tenderness, a steady, benevolent equanimity."

These two spent the summer of 1882 together at Tautenburg in Thuringia; and, given the warm sympathy with which Lou responded to all of Nietzsche's ideas and enthusiasms, by the autumn he had become so deeply attached to her that he begged his close friend Paul Rée to plead his case. The three were together in Leipzig when Nietzsche laid this commission on Rée, and, in his agitation, the ardent suitor fled to Basel to await Lou's answer. One suspects that Lou Salomé had not only a great admiration for Nietzsche's intellectual distinction but also a genuine affection for the man himself. Yet she doubtless also had misgivings about entering into marriage with a man the instability of whose temperament she could hardly have failed to discern. And she was perhaps even more greatly put off by his sister, Elisabeth, who regarded her brother with intense possessiveness, was furiously jealous of anyone—most especially a woman—who threatened to displace her in Nietzsche's affections, and who had predictably conceived a great hostility toward Lou. So Lou's answer, finally, to Nietzsche's proposal was a gentle but firm refusal. Elisabeth was later to declare that "Lou Salomé was never sincere"; but this is a charge no doubt prompted more by sisterly jealousy than by anything else.

In his last years, however, this domineering woman was finally able to attain exclusive and unchallenged control of her brother's life. In 1888 Nietzsche was living in Italy, in the city of Turin, where he had been at work on *The Anti-Christ* and *Ecce Homo*. But his mind, always most delicately organized, was steadily weakening—perhaps in part as a result of a syphilitic infection he had contracted some years earlier. Finally, on the third of January, 1889, after witnessing the brutal flogging of a horse by a coachman, he collapsed sobbingly on the street, with his arms thrown round the horse's neck, screaming invective at whoever attempted to approach him. He had to be carried back to his residence where, when he regained consciousness, he imagined himself to be at once Christ and the Greek god Dionysus.

It was clear now that this unhappy genius had descended into utter darkness. So his friend Franz Overbeck (a distinguished theologian on the faculty of Basel University), came to Turin and, with the help of the German consul, completed the arrangements for his removal back to Switzerland, where he was immediately entered in a Basel clinic —from whence he was taken on back to Germany and placed in the asylum for the insane in Jena. By the end of March, though his madness was now absolute, he had grown sufficiently quiet to be released from the asylum. So his mother, having now moved from Naumburg to Jena, received him into her home and cared for him until her death in 1897.

Then it was that Elisabeth at last could take complete charge. Her husband, Bernhard Förster, was now dead. And, with the immense royalties which Nietzsche's writings were beginning to earn, she purchased an estate at Weimar, near the famous Goethe house, where Nietzsche died on the twenty-fifth of August, 1900, being then buried in the churchyard at Röcken, beside his father's grave.

Frau Förster-Nietzsche (as she called herself) was not only, however, frequently the bane of Nietzsche's life, but even after his death she remained a nagging nuisance who managed over a long period to obscure and distort the true meaning of his legacy. Once it became clear that her brother was destined for a place of immense and permanent fame in the history of modern intellectual life, she gathered together all his books and manuscripts and, after legally obtaining exclusive rights to his literary remains, established at the estate in Weimar, as a center of research for students and scholars, the Nietzsche Archive. And this she controlled as tightly and shrewishly as, given her grasping nature, she might have been expected to do. But far less forgivable even than her monopolizing of manuscript material and her unconscionably profiteering

schemes of publication was the tenaciousness with which
she propagandized in behalf of her own misinterpretations
of Nietzsche's thought. Her husband had been a vulgar
little rabble rouser who was prominent in the anti-Semitic
movements of the Germany of Bismarck, and she was
more than a little touched by his fanatical racism. Her
great purpose came finally to be that of convincing the
world that Nietzsche had been an apostle of precisely
those things which he had in fact most greatly despised—a
chauvinistic folk mysticism and a Teutonic faith, an idolatry
of racial purity and of the German *Reich*. And by skillfully
lifting out of their context in his writings such notions as
the superman, master morality, and the will to power, and
by artfully drawing on the conversations she had had with
her brother (which were not, of course, in the nature of
the case verifiable), and by disingenuous editing of his
books, she was able to promote her own version of
Nietzsche so successfully that it is only recently that even
specialist scholars have been able to penetrate the legend
she manufactured and recover Nietzsche's actual legacy.
Indeed, it was Frau Förster-Nietzsche who persuaded Hitler to visit the Nietzsche Archive at Weimar, who persuaded
the Nazis to adopt her brother as their quasi-official
philosopher, and who was responsible for the intellectual
community's generally supposing over a long period that
the Nazi acceptance of Nietzsche was something perfectly
consistent with the basic emphasis of his own testimony.
It was a remarkable performance, and one whose way-
wardness has begun to be properly corrected only in the
last quarter-century, largely as a result of Walter Kaufmann's brilliant book of 1950 (*Nietzsche*, published by
the Princeton University Press).

Even now that Frau Förster-Nietzsche's distortions have
at last been corrected, Nietzsche's fundamental concepts

remain very extreme ideas, marked by a kind of melodramatic sensationalism whose violence is perhaps without any real equivalent elsewhere in modern philosophy.
Some have supposed that this extremist quality of his
thought is simply attributable to that strain of instability
which finally erupted into utter madness, but this is surely
too facile a disposition of the matter. What needs above
all else to be remembered in this connection is that the
utterances of a psychotic never have as their consequence
any profound alteration in the way we shape the material
of our own experience. Indeed, they do not even objectify
and make imaginatively available his own suffering: to be
sure, what he says may convey an impression of suffering, but of a suffering which is all chaotic and confused,
tongue-tied and indistinct. True, the man of real genius
may be one deeply wounded by psychological illness, and
his special perspective on human experience may have
been significantly conditioned by that illness; but not only
is he endowed with a great power to express his vision
with cogency and persuasiveness: he also speaks to us in
ways that lead us beyond himself to the public world of
which we are all members, and what he says has some
effect on the way we subsequently perceive and understand that world. This is the whole difference between
sanity and insanity. When we consider the immense influence that Nietzsche has exerted on much of the most
important art and literature and philosophy of this century,
it must then seem inconceivable that the psychological disorders which finally overwhelmed him could have been
the fundamental *root* of his thought. He was, admittedly,
a man often desperately distressed, but it makes very little
sense—in his case, or in any other—to regard the illness as
the *source* of the genius. For the literary and intellectual
power sprang from that in him which was strong. And
though he was a man who often knew what it is to suffer,

his power to shape his pain—and ours—into a compelling vision of the world cannot itself be derived from illness and suffering but only from the residual health that remained in him till his final collapse.

We shall, then, be better advised to think of what is extremist and radical in Nietzsche not simply as an expression of his personal ordeal, but as an expression of the great crisis that an extraordinarily sensitive and far-seeing genius beheld at the very center of the modern world. In his definition of it, that crisis was nothing less than the death of God. The whole of Nietzsche's thought rests on this most decisive conception—that a change of enormous consequence has occurred in the reality of Western man; that the fundamental problem underlying all the immediate issues which are faced by the men and women of the modern age is a problem of faith, or of the loss of that in which for centuries man's faith has ultimately been reposed.

It is in a passage of his book of 1882, *The Gay Science*, that we get Nietzsche's most pungent statement of this theme, and despite its length it deserves to be fully quoted. The passage (which is entitled "The Madman") has the form of a parable:

> Have you not heard of that madman who lit a lantern in the bright morning hours, ran to the market place, and cried incessantly, "I seek God! I seek God!" As many of those who do not believe in God were standing around just then, he provoked much laughter. Why, did he get lost? said one. Did he lose his way like a child? said another. Or is he hiding? Is he afraid of us? Has he gone on a voyage? or emigrated? Thus they yelled and laughed. The madman jumped into their midst and pierced them with his glances.
>
> "Where is God?" he cried. "I shall tell you. *We have killed him*—you and I. All of us are his murderers. But how have we done this? How were we able to drink up the sea? Who gave us the sponge to wipe away the entire horizon? What did we do when we unchained this earth from its sun?

Whither is it moving now? Whither are we moving now? Away from all suns? Are we not plunging continually? Backward, sideward, forward, in all directions? Is there any up or down left? Are we not straying as through an infinite nothing? Do we not feel the breath of empty space? Has it not become colder? Is not night and more night coming on all the while? Must not lanterns be lit in the morning? Do we not hear anything yet of the noise of the gravediggers who are burying God? Do we not smell anything yet of God's decomposition? Gods too decompose. God is dead. . . . And we have killed him. . . . What was holiest and most powerful of all that the world has yet owned has bled to death under our knives. Who will wipe this blood off us? . . . Is not the greatness of this deed too great for us? Must not we ourselves become gods simply to seem worthy of it? There has never been a greater deed; and whoever will be born after us—for the sake of this deed he will be part of a higher history than all history hitherto."

Here the madman fell silent and looked again at his listeners; and they too were silent and stared at him in astonishment. At last he threw his lantern on the ground, and it broke and went out. "I come too early," he said then; "my time has not come yet. This tremendous event is still on its way, still wandering—it has not yet reached the ears of man. Lightning and thunder require time, the light of the stars requires time, deeds require time even after they are done, before they can be seen and heard. This deed is still more distant from them than the most distant stars—*and yet they have done it themselves.*"

It has been related further that on that same day the madman entered divers churches and there sang his *requiem aeternam deo*. Led out and called to account, he is said to have replied each time, "What are these churches now if they are not the tombs and sepulchers of God?"

Here we have, in the story of the madman, what is in fact the real marrow of Nietzsche's whole vision. For what his entire message comes down to is the proclamation of the death of God. He is himself, in other words, the madman who comes charging into the marketplaces of the modern world with news that no one quite wants to face

—that God is in eclipse and perhaps even dead, that man himself is therefore on trial, more gravely so than ever before, and that we must reckon anew with the question as to where it is that the true meaning of our lives is to be found.

In one of his most searching meditations the American poet Conrad Aiken says:

> We need a theme? then let that be our theme:
> that we, poor grovellers between faith and doubt,
> the sun and north star lost, and compass out,
> the heart's weak engine all but stopped, the time
> timeless in this chaos of our wills—
> that we must ask a theme, something to think,
> something to say, between dawn and dark,
> something to hold to, something to love.°

Aiken's poem, in concise and beautifully framed language, offers what is in effect a striking summary of Nietzsche's central argument—that the theme of modern man is that he no longer has any theme. With "the sun and north star lost, and compass out," it is our not having anything to hold to now which constitutes the great new fact of our human condition; this is the pith and substance of everything that Nietzsche wanted to say.

It is significant, however, that Nietzsche is never to be found engaging in any debate with the historic rational arguments for the existence of God, in the customary manner of the conventional academic philosopher who espouses an atheistic or agnostic position. His characteristic method, in other words, is not that of a metaphysician —and thus, when he declares that God has died, he is not putting forward a proposition about an event that has occurred in some realm of reality beyond that which is accessible to our human senses. Instead, his chosen role is that of cultural critic; when he speaks of the death of

---

° Conrad Aiken, *Time in the Rock* (New York: Charles Scribner's Sons, 1936), p. 2.

God, he is speaking not primarily as metaphysician, but in his capacity as observer and diagnostician of modern civilization—and what he really wants to announce is a "great refusal" which modern man has made.

Throughout his career Nietzsche kept up, it is true, a continual quarrel with the Christian faith. "What differentiates *us*," as he said in *The Anti-Christ*," "is not that we find no God—neither in history, nor in nature, nor behind nature—but that we do not feel that what has been revered as God is 'godlike.' " And he never tired of reiterating his contempt for Christianity, which was partly aroused because (as he said in *The Will to Power*) "Christians have never practiced the actions which Jesus prescribed to them." But his more fundamental reason for rejecting the Christian faith was that its understanding of the relation between man and God had, he felt, the effect of promoting an outrageous underestimation and belittlement of the world and of man himself. Yet, for all his aversion to Christian doctrine, he was never at pains to present any carefully reasoned metaphysical arguments for atheism. And thus the late Albert Camus was altogether right in saying (in *The Rebel*) that "Nietzsche did not form a project to kill God" but that he simply "found Him dead in the soul of his contemporaries" and then undertook to discover what the shape of human life consequently had to be. What he took for granted, in other words, as a fundamental fact of our culture, was its commitment to a radically secular outlook; and the vocation he accepted was that of laying bare what it means for man to live in a world in which he is, as it were, utterly alone, and in a world which is therefore without any meaning or purpose except that which man himself manages to confer upon it.

The new reality with which we must now reckon, said Nietzsche, is the very absolute kind of freedom which befalls man in a world that has survived the death of God.

We are, indeed, now on our own. And though this independence of any master may bring exhilaration, it also brings a most profound disquietude, since absolute freedom also entails absolute responsibility—responsibility in fact, said he, "for everything alive, for everything that, born of suffering, is condemned to suffer from life." In short, the emancipation that has come to man at the end of the modern age carries with it a terrible burden. Since God is dead, nothing is any longer authorized or certain— nothing, that is, except man's own sovereignty. Man is therefore answerable not only for the management of his own destiny, but also for the introduction of such law and order into the world as will make its primal lawlessness tolerable. He is thus plunged into an "immense void." "We have left the land," says *The Gay Science*, "and have gone aboard ship! We have broken down the bridges behind us—nay, more, the land behind us! Well, little ship! Look out! Beside thee is the ocean. . . . Times will come when thou wilt feel that it is infinite and that there is nothing more frightful than infinity." But though we must send our ships into uncharted seas, we cannot permit them to become lost. We must somehow mark out lanes and chart these seas—which is to say that the modern nihilist, though he is above all law, must somehow himself bring some order into the lawlessness of the world, if the human enterprise is to retain any dignity and meaning. And if we fail to invent values of our own, then God's death will be followed by man's suicide, for, though man's freedom is absolute, he cannot live in absolute anarchy. So we are brought finally to a great paradox, that the only way in which the creature who is above law can defy the universal chaos is by inventing new law and new systems of value.

Here, then, are the general lines along which Nietzsche's analysis of the modern situation proceeded. He was convinced that the traditional faith of Christendom was an irreparable debris, that all attempts at buttressing it up against the new skepticism were worse than futile. To have any traffic at all with what he called "the will to believe in what comforts us" was, he thought, the way of cowardice and evasion. And finally, he insisted, there is no evading the terrible new kind of solitude which awaits us; it is simply our fate, the fate of men who, having killed God, inherit a terrible new kind of liberty in which they must themselves become gods. That is to say, the great human task is now that of imposing on the world a purely human meaning and a purely human value. For the universe into which we have been thrown is one where (as it was once phrased by Bertrand Russell) man is "the product of causes which had no prevision of the end they were achieving"; and if he is to live by any hope at all, amidst the world's immense indifference, it must be by a hope which he himself invents. Humanity must somehow, in other words, learn a way of giving to itself a great validating purpose: in all its dealings with the world, it must learn how to confer order upon disorder, and rationality upon fundamental irrationality. What is needed, as Nietzsche termed it, is a radical "revaluation" of existence.

It is in the eccentric and quasi-autobiographical work *Ecce Homo*, written in 1888 just before his final collapse, that Nietzsche gives us perhaps his clearest hint as to what he means by "revaluation," when he speaks of it as his "formula for an act of ultimate self-examination by mankind." Here we may find a suggestion of the line that needs to be taken in correcting a certain overinterpretation of this phase of Nietzsche's thought, for some have supposed that his project of "revaluation" did in effect involve a turning, as it were, of the whole Western tradition on its head. It has sometimes been thought that

his call for "revaluation" was a call for an absolute re-
placement of the inherited values of European Christendom by completely new values, but the virtues which
Nietzsche did in fact seem most greatly to admire were
traditional virtues, the virtues of courage and honesty and
benevolence and gallantry. When he tells us that "revaluation" is his "formula for an act of ultimate self-examination," it would seem that he was not really advocating
the legislation of an absolutely new code of morality, but
was most probably wanting to suggest that, whatever
values a man chooses to live by, if he is a truly modern
man, these will be values, even when they are tradition-
alist in character, which he will have embraced only after
the most careful self-confrontation. Since they will have
been freshly appropriated, they will in a certain sense
have been reinvented, and will therefore be new. In his
view of the modern crisis, no other estimate of things is
possible; for man, no longer inheriting effective cultural
or religious imperatives, must now steer his own course,
freely improvising at every point the direction he takes,
since the world itself is unpropelled in any direction at
all.

"Revaluation" may, then, be regarded as Nietzsche's
name for what he conceived to be the one spiritually authentic mode of life for modern man—for the man who
knows that God is gone and that he must, therefore, now
produce out of himself that which will fill the Void and
give the world a new meaning and significance.

But, of course, revaluation presupposes a very stern
kind of moral courage of which Nietzsche never expected
the majority of men to prove capable. He took it for
granted that the majority of men will doubtless continue
for a long time to come to sleep in the old myths and to
cling to the old fictions. He was certain that there are
not many who will be found able to face, straightfor-

wardly and relentlessly, all that is implied by the fact that God is now dead. But he was equally certain that at least a few can be counted on to launch bravely into the kind of human future that awaits us in the modern world. And between the aristocratic minority and the broad majority there is such a distance that the minority, said Nietzsche, must be regarded as examples of a new kind of man. His most important discussions of this theme are to be found in that brilliant book of the early 1880's which is the great masterpiece of his life, *Thus Spake Zarathustra*, and in the large body of notes which have been collected under the title *The Will to Power*. Here, the term which he uses for this new type of man is *Übermensch*; and the English equivalent preferred by some of his interpreters is "overman," which is the literal rendering of the German. But the more customary and the more felicitous rendering is "superman."

Now it is a vulgar misinterpretation of this whole phase of Nietzsche's thought to conceive his doctrine of the superman as the keystone of a kind of proto-Nazi Caesarism. This, to be sure, was the tack taken by Hitler's official philosophers who were, of course, guided by that tradition of Nietzsche interpretation which Frau Förster-Nietzsche had helped to promulgate. It is an erroneous reading of his work, which has yet not altogether been laid to rest. Nor can it be absolutely denied that Nietzsche's writings offer any pretext for this kind of interpretation. For the superman is "beyond good and evil"; and, believing that God has been dethroned, he *does* "create" his own values, deliberately and unflinchingly. But Nietzsche despised anti-Semitism, as many of his writings amply indicate, especially *The Anti-Christ*. Indeed, he most warmly advocated racial mixture, believing that each racial group had certain valuable traits and that the offspring of interracial unions might, therefore, be expected

to be superior human types. He did, to be sure, occasionally use the term "master race," but his context generally indicates that this for him was never an affair of
"blood" but rather of intellectual and philosophic creativity. And the whole notion of the superman is misunder-
stood if it is taken to designate a "blond beast" who is
cynically committed to some sort of amoral self-aggran-
dizement.

The popular image of the Nietzschean superman is an
image of a blustering bully with a raised fist and a threatening grimace on his face—a distortion so absurd as not
even to be a caricature. For the Übermensch—as presented, say, in Zarathustra—far from being an amoral
gangster, is the mortal enemy of unscrupulousness and
violence, of lawlessness and terrorism. And he is "beyond
good and evil" chiefly in the sense of being one who is
prepared to undertake the task of "revaluation." He is, in
Nietzsche's account, a rare aristocrat of the spirit. For,
unlike the broad majority of men who constitute an un-
thinking herd, he is one whose maturity of consciousness
and culture is signalized by his clear awareness that man
is alone in the world, and that if the world is to be re-
deemed it is man himself who must do it, by arduously
struggling toward unattained heights. Which is to say
that the superman is not afraid to live dangerously and does
not shrink before the awesome challenges presented by
the death of God.

Indeed, it is, in Nietzsche's reckoning, the superman
alone who, after facing all the hazards of human existence in this late and difficult time, can nevertheless muster
sufficient poise and equanimity to say "Yes" to the world.
His early studies in Greek tragic drama—which culmi-
nated in his first book, The Birth of Tragedy—had convinced
him that the test of maturity was to be found in a man's
being able (like the tragic hero) to say "Yes" to the "sad

and suffering" world. In *The Gay Science* and *Thus Spake Zarathustra* and wherever else he sets forth his idea of world affirmation, he uses the Latin term *amor fati* ("love of [one's] fate") to speak of the kind of profound acceptance of reality which he took to be an essential mark of man's having truly come of age. *Amor fati*, he liked to say, was his "formula for the greatness of a human being." And it was a formula that he never tired of reiterating, that he who has achieved his full stature as a man is one who is able (as he said in *Ecce Homo*) "not only to bear the necessary, even less to conceal it . . . but to *love* it."

But there is still another formula which is an essential part of Nietzsche's vision and which has the effect of dramatizing how remarkable is the achievement represented by the superman's embrace of *amor fati*: it is the doctrine of Eternal Recurrence, which is his formula for the world's absurdity. Perhaps no other single theme gripped his imagination as did this idea, which so fascinated him that he spoke of the moment of its conception as "the Great Noon" of his life. He returns to it again and again in his writings, in *The Gay Science* and *Beyond Good and Evil* and *Ecce Homo* and *The Will to Power* and various other works; but it finds its most elaborate exposition in *Thus Spake Zarathustra*, where it constitutes the great leitmotif in this book which, more than any other, presents the richest orchestration of Nietzsche's thought.

While he himself (in *The Will to Power*) spoke of the doctrine of Eternal Recurrence as "the *most scientific* of all possible hypotheses," it would be a mistake to regard it as having been for Nietzsche simply a kind of abstract hypothesis. Indeed, far from being merely a speculative hypothesis, it was for him a powerfully poetic symbol of the utter meaninglessness of the world. For a world in which all things are dominated by the iron necessity of repeating themselves in an endless cycle is a world which is radically absurd. It is a world in which everything is a consequence of the interplay of blind forces which operate only to bring to pass that which once was. Thus there is no longer the prospect of any kind of hope or fulfillment; for the universe, having been utterly emptied of God, moves in a circle, and its sovereign law is the eternal return of the same.

Yet, even to such a world, the superman—great stoic that he is—says "Yes," for he (as Nietzsche said in *Beyond Good and Evil*) "has not only learned to accept and come to terms with what was and is, but wishes to have it again as *it was and is*, for all eternity. . . ."

It is this dual theme of the Eternal Recurrence and *amor fati* which brings us, finally, to Nietzsche's doctrine of the Will to Power. For if it be asked what it is that enables the superman (that is, the fully mature man who has come of age) not only to endure a world dominated by Eternal Recurrence but even to affirm it, Nietzsche's answer is that the source of his strength is to be found in the Will to Power. The term which best conveys what he means by the Will to Power is that which is first used in *Thus Spake Zarathustra*—"self-overcoming": for this is that at which the Will to Power aims in man, at overcoming oneself. But it is conceived to be present not only in man but in all living things: as he says in the chapter of *Zarathustra* entitled "On Self-Overcoming," ". . . where there is life, there is also will: not 'will to life' but . . . 'will to power.' "

Zarathustra does not, however, present any systematic development of this theme, for this was a task which Nietzsche in the late 1880's was projecting as the next great project of his life: his ambition was to produce a vast book which would be the magnum opus of his career —*The Will to Power: An Attempted Transvaluation of All*

Values. But after the completion of *Zarathustra*, other projects intervened, such as *Beyond Good and Evil* and *The Genealogy of Morals* and *The Anti-Christ;* and, unhappily, all that we have of the promised work is an immense array of notes which were jotted down in the period between 1884 and 1888.

Yet, despite Nietzsche's never having got round to a systematic exposition of the doctrine of the Will to Power, it is possible to discern in his last writings the broad outlines of the conception toward which he was heading. What is clear is that he conceived reality to have a fundamentally dynamic character: nothing is static, everywhere reality is in a state of becoming, all living things are infused with an energy that lures them away from what they are toward some higher and hitherto unattained condition. This principle of dynamism—the sovereign principle of reality—Nietzsche denominated as the Will to Power, which was his metaphoric way of designating that urge towards self-transcendence which he believed to be everywhere present in the world. He also believed that it is the fullness with which this dynamic principle finds expression in the superman that empowers him to "overcome" what is harrowing and oppressive in a world that has survived the death of God. This it is (the Will to Power) that enables the superman, the fully mature man, to triumph over all the dragons he encounters in his earthly journey, so that, alone though he be in the dark, he is yet borne on—elsewhere, toward other stars.

Nietzsche has sometimes—perhaps more often than not—been unfortunate in the quality of his disciples. And the doctrine of the Will to Power has occasionally been converted by some of his heirs into a crudely fanatical apology for a kind of Machiavellian *Realpolitik*. Thus it needs to be remarked that it is, indeed, just in this phase of his thought that the great moral subtlety and refinement of the man ought to be most keenly felt. For Nietzsche did not exempt the intellectual life itself from the dynamic principle of the Will to Power, and he took it for granted that any and every philosophy—his own included—demands to be transcended. As he said in *Beyond Good and Evil*, "As soon as ever a philosophy begins to believe in itself, it always creates the world in its own image; it cannot do otherwise; philosophy is this tyrannical impulse itself, the most spiritual Will to Power, the will to 'creation of the world.' " And not only is philosophic creativity a highly spiritualized expression of the Will to Power: it is also in effect, in the degree to which it has genuine profundity, a kind of invitation to man to attempt some *further* penetration of reality. Consequently, no honest philosophy will be found believing very deeply in itself; and it will even go on to invite skepticism about itself in the interests of giving full play to the Will to Power. There is, in short, a finely grained modesty that is deeply a part of the basic texture of Nietzsche's vision. So, in whatever kingdom of the spirit it may be from which he now surveys the human scene, one imagines that, at those who have responded in a fanatical way to any phase of his thought, he (like George Meredith's Comic Spirit) looks "humanely malign" and aims "volleys of silvery laughter."

His final importance consists perhaps not so much in the particular body of doctrine to be derived from his writings as in the total attitude toward existence to which he was among the first to give effective and candid publicity in the modern period. It was the genius of the man to create a beautifully simple formula for the expression of the crisis of faith that forms the background of much of the most representative art and literature and philosophy of our time. If one wants to know what that crisis entails, one may turn to the literature created by those modern sociologists who have specialized in the problems arising out of what is called "mass society." Or one may turn to the writings of the psychologists who specialize in what is called "the identity crisis." And the literature of twentieth-century philosophy may also be found occasionally illuminating, when it is not exclusively focused on the issues of logic and theory of science. But in these areas one gets relatively subdued accounts of the modern situation, and if one wants a quick and pungent summary, then one must go back to this German radical of the late nineteenth century who told us simply that "God is dead."

The distinguished German existentialist Karl Jaspers (1883-1969), in his book *Reason and Existence,* pinned the issue down very nicely when he said that Nietzsche "cannot be classed under any earlier type"; not "poet, philosopher, prophet, [nor] savior," he represents, rather, "a new form of human reality . . . in history." Like Kierkegaard and like Dostoevski, he is a kind of saint and a kind of martyr who, in totally staking his whole nature in a critical effort, administered a shock to the modern consciousness which has had the effect of casting a great searchlight on the soulscape of our time. And thus, with Kierkegaard, he helped to initiate a tradition of inquiry—which we call Existentialism—into what it means to be human now, at the end of the modern period.

4

Heidegger's Path—Towards the Recovery of Being

MARTIN HEIDEGGER'S DEATH, on May 26, 1976, just four months before his eighty-seventh birthday, brought to a close one of the supreme careers in the intellectual life of this century, for, after Husserl and Whitehead and Wittgenstein and Dewey, he was the last great innovating genius of modern philosophy. But though his work in its own sphere is as seminal as that of Picasso and Stravinsky and Joyce in theirs, he is himself—unlike these other modern masters—wholly concealed behind it, to so great an extent indeed that very little is known about the details of his personal history.

Heidegger was born on September 26, 1889 in the little town of Messkirch in the German province of Baden, as the first son of Friedrich and Johanna Heidegger. The Heideggers' was a devout Roman Catholic household, and, after Martin's early years in the public school of his home town, it was no doubt natural, as he began in 1903 his preparatory studies for the university in the Gymnasium of Konstanz, that he should then have been aiming at the priesthood. But by 1909, when he had completed his secondary studies in the Bertholds-Gymnasium in Freiburg-im-Breisgau, he had already been wholly claimed by what was to be the great commanding passion of his life, and thus, though he was by no means neglectful of opportunities for the study of theology at the University of Freiburg, his chief work there was done under the philosophical faculty. He took his doctorate in 1913. Then, with the publication in 1916 of his first major post-doctoral monograph—a study of a medieval text on the nature of metaphysical language, the so-called *Grammatica speculativa* (once attributed to Duns Scotus but actually the work of Thomas of Erfurt)—he became eligible for appointment to the Freiburg faculty as *Privatdozent* (comparable, in the German system, to an instructorship in an American university). This post he held until 1920, when he was appointed to a professorship at Marburg, where he was to remain for the next eight years; and, from the perspective of a much later time, Heidegger did himself declare the Marburg period to have been "the most stimulating, composed and eventful" phase of his life.

Indeed, it was during the Marburg years that, by dint of the extraordinary power and originality of his teaching and by way of a kind of student underground, Heidegger's name began to travel across the German university scene "like the rumor"—as the late Hannah Arendt recalled—of a "hidden king." It was a time, very much like our own, when, as Hannah Arendt said, "Philosophy was no bread-winner's study, but rather the study of resolute starvelings who were, for that very reason, all the harder to please." Amidst the disenchantments and hardships of German life after World War I, university students working in humanistic faculties were quick to be impatient with the conventional lecture being droned out from the professorial platform, and, though they were uncertain as to precisely what they wanted, they knew at least that they required something more vital, something more pertinent to their condition, than the old systems and the old academic rigmarole. And, as the word soon began to get about in the early 1920's, here at Marburg was a man who—to use Heidegger's own words—knew how to distinguish "between an object of scholarship and a matter of thought" and who was proposing that it is the latter with which genuine philosophical enterprise is concerned. So he began to win a following—but not at first because he was himself advancing a new doctrine that could be summarized and bruited about: on the contrary, his seminars, semester after semester, were devoted to the analysis of a single text, to Aristotle's *Rhetoric* or Descartes' *Meditations* or Kant's *Critique of Pure Reason* or Hegel's *Logic* or Husserl's *Logical Investigations*—and the method was simply that of week after week worrying the text at hand into some fresh disclosure of its essential meaning and of the urgency with which that meaning bore upon the contemporary intellectual situation. But, amongst German professors of the period, so revolutionary was Heidegger's pedagogy that it carried an enormous impact, and by the mid-'twenties notes taken at his lectures and in his seminars were being circulated among students everywhere. "The rumor about Heidegger," says Hannah Arendt, "put it quite simply: Thinking has come to life again; the cultural treasures of the past, believed to be dead, are being made to speak, in the course of which it turns out that they propose things altogether different from the familiar, worn-out trivialities they had been presumed to say. There exists a teacher; one can perhaps learn to think."[*]

The intense creativity of Heidegger's early Marburg years, however, bore little fruit in the way of published work, so that one day in the winter term of 1925-26 the

[*] Hannah Arendt, "Martin Heidegger at Eighty," in *The New York Review of Books*, Vol. XVII, No. 6 (October 21, 1971), pp. 50-54.

dean of the philosophical faculty came into his study to say, "Professor Heidegger—you have got to publish something now." And the reason for this enjoinder was that the faculty had unanimously decided that it was he who should succeed their distinguished colleague Nicolai Hartmann in the University's chief philosophical chair: indeed, the appointment had already been proposed to the Ministry of Education in Berlin and been rejected on the ground that the candidate's record of publication was insufficiently impressive. But now, given the eagerness of his Marburg associates to offer him the finest honor they could bestow, he at last undertook to put into systematic form his reflections of the previous years, and the result was his epoch-making book of 1927, *Being and Time* (*Sein und Zeit*), which, indeed, left the Ministry in Berlin no recourse other than that of reversing its earlier negative judgment and offering him the chair from which Hartmann had retired.

Heidegger's growing prominence now made it natural that the Freiburg faculty should undertake to woo him back, as they did, and in 1928 he returned as *professor ordinarius*—destined the following year for induction, at the time of Edmund Husserl's retirement, into the chair that Husserl's immense distinction had made the most prestigious philosophical berth in the German academic world.

The period was, of course, one in which German life was becoming increasingly troubled by internal disorders. In the early 1920's the country was struck by a wave of inflation so catastrophic that by the end of 1923 the American dollar was worth two hundred billion marks—which meant that money had simply ceased to have any value at all. Though the leading industrial magnates and feudal landowners profited from the crisis (which they had helped to engineer), the middle classes, given their old habits of saving and investing, were utterly pauperized by it and finally convinced themselves that their woes were a result of nothing other than the anarchy entailed by the "democratic system" of the Weimar Republic. True, a considerable economic recovery was managed in the period between 1924 and 1930, but, once Germany was overtaken, like every other nation of the West, by the world depression of the early 'thirties, the deep cynicism about parliamentary democracy that had taken hold in the post-war years cooperated, as it were, with the weakness of the Republic being administered by the aged Paul von Hindenburg—toward the end of inducing a great ground swell of sentiment in behalf of the kind of "order" promised by the new National Socialism. President von Hindenburg's naming of Adolf Hitler as chancellor of Germany at the end of January in 1933 signalized the death of the Republic, and, within a matter of months, the last vestiges of government under constitutional law disappeared, as all the principal agencies of political and cultural life—banks and trade unions, the courts and the police, the arts and the press, schools and universities—were "coordinated" in the interests of "nazifying" the Third Reich.

It was in this context that Heidegger in 1933 was appointed Rector of the University of Freiburg, and his inaugural address—*The Self-Preservation of the German University* (*Die Selbstbehauptung der deutschen Universität*) —expressed a warm affirmation of the Hitlerian movement. This indiscretion frequently makes now an occasion of astonishment, that one so deeply steeped in the Western humanistic tradition could have been prepared to make common cause with the thugs and rabble of Hitler's confederacy and could have failed to discern all that was ominous in the barbarism that was so aggressively insurgent. This astonishment, however, will surely be felt only by those who expect creative genius in literature and philosophy and the arts to be endowed with what in fact it rarely is—namely, the talent for a shrewd perspicacity with respect to the concrete actualities of politics. In the case of Heidegger, so exacting a critic of totalitarian mentality as Hannah Arendt, though she could feel no impulse to grant her former teacher any easy indemnity, had simply to conclude that, living at the remove he did from the swirling currents of German politics in the early 'thirties, he made the mistake of not reading *Mein Kampf* and was thus unable initially to see how much the new fascist mystique of the *Herrenvolk* was a product of the gutter. But the harsh reality soon impressed itself upon him, and, though he never publicly committed himself to any brusque disavowal of the dispensation of Hitler and Goebbels, his distaste for it was so easily discernible that, by the early 1940's, an order had been issued forbidding the publication of his writing.

At the time of the occupation of western Germany by the Allied forces, Heidegger had not for many years had any sort of role in public life, but the Freiburg address of 1933 was not forgotten; and those who were charting a new course for the German people felt that it would be inappropriate for him to be allowed to resume his professorship. So thereafter, though he continued till the early 1960's occasionally to conduct seminars and deliver lectures in university settings, the remainder of his life was spent in retirement, at his cottage amidst the isolateness of the little mountain village of Todtnauberg in the Black Forest, not far from Freiburg. And there (as Stefan Schimanski has described it) "on top of a mountain, with the valley deep down below, with nothing but space and wilderness all around, in . . . [his] small skiing hut," "his only relationship to the world . . . a stack of writing

paper,"* he continued a lifetime's meditations and produced the profoundly exciting essays and books of his last
years—the most notable being the *Brief über den Human-
ismus* of 1947 (*Letter on Humanism*), the *Holzwege* of
1950 (*Paths in the Forest*), *Einführung in die Metaphysik*
of 1953 (*An Introduction to Metaphysics*), *Was heisst
Denken?* of 1954 (*What Is Called Thinking?*), *Der Satz
vom Grund* (*The Principle of Ground*) and *Identität und
Differenz* (*Identity and Difference*) of 1957, and *Gelassenheit* (*Releasement*) and *Unterwegs zur Sprache* (*On the
Way to Language*) of 1959.

Heidegger is generally associated with that family of
thought called Existentialism, and one of its most prominent representatives, Jean-Paul Sartre, has insistently
claimed him as one of his principal mentors (notwith-
standing their many sharp divergences). He himself, however, was somewhat embarrassed by Sartre's homage, and
—despite his having been more than a little influenced by
both Kierkegaard and Nietzsche—he was steadfast in
disowning any affiliation with this whole line of thought.
"For me," as he said, "the haunting question is and has
been, not man's existence, but 'being-in-totality' and 'being
as such.'" And such a definition of his interest would,
indeed, seem to be in accord with the stresses that belong
to the major statements of his career. Yet it is undeniable
that the Heidegger of *Being and Time* conceived the meaning of "Being" to be accessible only by way of a very strict
analysis of the *human* modes of being, for the fundamental
assumption underlying the great book of 1927 is that the
philosophic imagination, when it seeks to approach not a
particular entity or substance or attribute or class but

* Stefan Schimanski, "Foreword," in Martin Heidegger's *Existence
and Being*, trans. by Douglas Scott *et al* (Chicago: Henry Regnery Co.,
1949), p. 10.

rather that which is constantly present in all the things of this world, will find its most direct *entrée* in and through the particular being whose nature requires that the question of Being be raised—namely, man. Since that which "assembles" and most essentially constitutes everything that exists is not itself any sort of "object" standing over against the human "subject," since it does not at all belong to the category of "things" and is "above" the ordinary categories of reflection, it cannot be advanced upon—as Heidegger was assuming in the 1920's—by some process of inference that moves, with the help of the principle of causality, from the realm of finite, contingent realities toward something like the Absolute of Idealist philosophy. On the contrary, given (as traditional philosophy would say) the "transcendental" character of Being, if it is to be approached at all, it must be approached not theoretically but existentially, by way of the one creature who stands not out from or over against it but within it as a conscious participant. Which, in Heidegger's sense of things, was to say that, at the level of truly fundamental philosophy, what is at stake is not some theoretical process of deduction but rather a descent into the depths of one's own humanity, not a "transcendental analytic" but an "existential analytic," and it is to this that his book of 1927 was dedicated.

So it is not surprising that *Being and Time* should have found its decisive theme in *Dasein* (which means *being-there* and which it is customary not to translate in non-German discussions of Heidegger). Since man, by the inner dynamism of his own nature, is irresistibly driven to search out the ultimate ground of his existence, Heidegger reserves *Dasein* as his chief technical term for the distinctively human mode of being. "*Dasein*," as he says, "is an entity for which, in its Being, that Being is an issue." And thus, as he appears to have felt at the time this book was being written, our best path into Being-itself is one that leads through those structures of existence that belong to the particular being whose unique vocation it is to be obsessed with the question concerning what it means to *be*. In short, *Dasein*, as he was proposing, is the primary datum with which any "fundamental ontology" must reckon; and it is the brilliant originality with which it probes the essential modes of *human* being—anxiety (*Angst*), care (*Sorge*), temporality (*Zeitlichkeit*), the "resoluteness" (*Entschlossenheit*) with which death is faced, transcendence (*Transzendenz*)—that makes *Being and Time* one of the classic texts in the literature of modern Existentialism.

In Heidegger's analysis, the fundamental truth about *Dasein* is that it finds itself to be simply "thrown" into the world, and he considers the sure sign of the *in*authentic life to be that of passive resignation to one's "thrownness" (*Geworfenheit*). He who exists in the world as "one-like-many," who shirks any responsibility for discovering the meaning of his own existence and who finds his norms in the routinized responses of those who live *en masse*, who dwells wholly within the featureless anonymity of what Kierkegaard called "the public," and whose one great concern is merely a matter of "what one does" or "what one does not do"—such a person (whom Heidegger speaks of pejoratively as *das Man*) is the very type and example of inauthenticity. His life is an affair of utter banality, because he is alienated from the great purposes and possibilities that give significance and dignity to the human venture: he is one who, finding himself to have been thrown into the world, spiritlessly accedes to his thrownness as a kind of ineluctable fate, and thus in effect he chooses to be simply one *thing* among others.

But when *Dasein* wins through to a truly authentic stance, it is marked above all else by concern ("care"— *Sorge*) about its possibilities: no longer is it lost in externalized anonymity, in a servile acquiescence to the way things happen to happen: on the contrary, now, it sees itself as, in its very essence, something to be striven for, something to be achieved—and the acceptance of the challenge brought by this sense of itself as possibility is precisely that which certifies its authenticity. Moreover, amongst all the myriad possibilities which the self confronts, it finds its "capital" possibility, its "extreme possibility," to be nothing other than that of death itself, so much so indeed that Heidegger is prepared to say that *Dasein is* "dying" or "being-toward-death." That is to say, a part of the special burden that man bears by virtue of being human entails his living under the shadow of this ultimate and inescapable threat: it is at once his unique privilege and his peculiar affliction to be able to anticipate his eventual annulment, to *know* that he shall die: so the existential structure of our being-in-the-world is a being-toward-the-end, toward-death, toward that point beyond which we shall be no more. And it is just as we measure and evaluate the more proximate possibilities of our lives in relation to this ultimate possibility that we are able fully to appreciate their essential finitude and urgency.

Das Man will, of course, seek to alleviate the sting of the ultimate and inescapable *annihilatio* that awaits us by regarding it merely as something that "one" reads about over one's breakfast coffee on the obituary page of *The New York Times*, or he will suppose that it is simply a matter of some such very general proposition as that which says "all men are mortal." But over and again *Dasein* will be summoned back into the region of fundamental truth by the "call of conscience" and will be reminded that the ultimate emergency of death is no merely abstract postulate but is the final potentiality of *my* life—and it is only when the individual consents candidly to face this capital possibility of his existence that he begins to be entrained towards a truly authentic lucidity, the kind of lucidity that will enable him to discern the relative triviality of the concerns to which the daily round is normally devoted and that will prompt him to undertake such projects as may give some really high significance to his human career.

The call of conscience, then, evokes in us a sense of "guilt," a sense of deficiency, a sense of having failed in allegiance to the high possibilities that ought to have claimed us and of therefore being less fully human than we might otherwise be. But, again, the achievement of a genuinely authentic selfhood begins to be possible only as *Dasein* deeply realizes its actual guilt, its indigence, its incompleteness. The tidings brought by conscience will, of course, incite a very disturbing kind of "anxiety": none of us wants to be sharply touched by a sense of really fundamental failure, and our first impulse is likely to be that of dodging or repressing in some way the disquietude that conscience brings forth. Yet, as Heidegger insists, apart from a readiness to accept the embarrassments entailed by this kind of moral distress there can be no real growth in the self's capacity creatively to "project" its own finest possibilities. For it is out of this open receptivity toward "conscience" and "guilt" and "anxiety" that there develops what he speaks of as "resoluteness" or "resolve" (*Entschlossenheit*)—the resolve, that is, to enter into one's full human stature and to come of age.

Now that fulfillment of life at which resolve aims is, for Heidegger, most especially marked by a certain orientation to "temporality" (*Zeitlichkeit*), for, in his analysis, authentic *Dasein* is, above all else, distinguished by its capacity to make a certain kind of order prevail amidst the relations between the past, the present, and the future. Since man is constituted of possibility and proves his maturity in the degree to which he wins adeptness in the

"projection of possibilities," he is in the nature of the
case (in Gabriel Marcel's phrase) *homo viator*—man voya-
ging towards the future, towards that which is ahead.
towards that which is not yet realized. But not only is
he entrained towards the future: he is also in every moment
of his existence that which he has *become*—and since he
has *become* "guilty," *Dasein* takes on its past by taking
on its guilt, by candidly facing into its incompleteness and
unfulfillment. Indeed, on Heidegger's reckoning, we move
forward—towards authentic selfhood—only by moving backward in such a way as fully to incorporate into our own
identities a clear awareness of the guilt into which we have
been "thrown." And when resolve—which is, of course,
aiming at the future—so appropriates the past, then it is
prepared to deal creatively with the present, with all the
challenge and opportunity presented by the concrete now.
Since the determinate nature of *Dasein* is defined by
possibility, it is, therefore, a being "in-advance-of-itself"
and grounded in the future; but, given its "thrownness,"
it is also grounded in the past; and, furthermore, embedded
as it is in the world of its "cares," it is likewise grounded
in the present. And the consequent necessity under which
man stands, of inwardly coordinating and holding together these three dimensions, inevitably thrusts him ir-
removably into the realm of temporality.

Indeed, as Heidegger suggests, it is precisely because
Dasein is ineradicably temporal that it is also essentially
"historical" (*geschichtlich*). For the being of a man, unlike
the being of a thing (*Vorhandenheit*), exists not merely
within time (*Innerzeitigkeit*): it is, rather, itself inwardly
constituted by its past, present, and future, and we find
the meaning of our existence only in the degree to which
we manage a sensitive coordination of our lives in these
three dimensions. A tree, though it undergoes change
and subsists through a process of succession, may not, in

Heidegger's sense of the term, be said to have a "history." And, of course, that which is lacking in the life of a tree and which is the critical factor making for "history" is nothing other than decision, for it is by way of certain decisions that a man determines what is valuable and what is no longer serviceable in the funded bequests he inherits from his family and his religious community and his country, just as it is decision that enables him to relate his heritage to his present and his future. Moreover, the whole endeavor of seeking a proper attunement of past, present, and future is occasioned by man's most fundamental engagement—which is the "projection of possibilities." In short, *Dasein* is "historical," because its nature requires it to seek authentic existence—which is to say that its "historicity" is grounded in its inherent tendency to "run forward" towards the future and towards the fulfillment of vital possibilities.

So, in the final analysis, it is the human individual who actuates and energizes history, both the historical reality itself (*Geschichte*) and the scientific study of it (*Historie*). In the ordinary significations of the vulgate, as Heidegger reminds us, "history" refers (a) simply to the past, as when we speak of something or other "belonging to history"; or it refers to (b) a past which lingers on into the present, as when we speak of the impossibility of "escaping history"; or it refers to (c) "the transformations and vicissitudes of . . . human groupings and their 'cultures,' as distinguished from Nature";° or it refers to (d) the traditional, to whatever has been handed down to us by the institutions of our culture. But, as he insists, all these various implications of the term "history" presuppose that it is man who is the real source and "subject" of events. Which means, he then concludes, that history must be

° Martin Heidegger, *Being and Time*, trans. by John Macquarrie and Edward Robinson (New York: Harper and Row, 1962), p. 430.

understood not in terms of the categories applicable to things (substance, causality, etc.) but in terms of those categories (the "existentials") that are alone applicable to human existence, that describe the fundamental possibilities open to *Dasein*. The real stuff of history, in short, is not the happenings that are recorded by the chroniclers of "facts" but the great possibilities that form the human horizon, since the circumstances and events and vicissitudes that constitute the scientific historian's subject-matter are "ontologically possible *only because Dasein is historical in its* [*essential*] *Being.*"* History, in other words, in the most radical sense, *belongs* to *Dasein*.

It is in such terms that the "existential analytic" of *Being and Time* proceeds. Unfortunately, however, the entire project was never finished. The book that we now have was originally projected as but the first part of a larger work the second part of which was to be devoted to a phenomenological "destruction" of the history of metaphysics. But this second phase of Heidegger's enterprise never materialized: indeed, massive as it is, even the book of 1927 as it stands is incomplete, for, though we are told at the end of its second chapter that it will be comprised of three major sections, in point of fact it breaks off with the analysis of *Dasein* and temporality, and the promised third section (which was to have taken us back from Time to Being) is simply missing. So the book, as we have it, is, for all its monumentality, but a fragment, and this doubtless accounts for the tenuousness of its deliverances on what it declares to be its basic theme. It is, of course, to be recalled that the whole program of inquiry into the nature and situation of *Dasein* was undertaken for an ontological purpose, for the sake of making some determination about the nature of Being in its unity and totality. And, as we have remarked, this procedure—of starting with

* *Being and Time*, p. 431.

Dasein—was chosen because it was supposed that, since man is the particular being distinguished over all others by his needing to search for the nature of Being, his own inner constitution may provide the best clues regarding the fundamental character of what (by adapting a phrase of Teilhard de Chardin) might be called the *milieu ontologique*. Yet, once Heidegger's "existential analytic" of *Dasein* is fully laid out and we are at the point where some new disclosure about the nature of Being-itself is expected, the great thing, the promised thing—as Basil Willey remarks of the doctrine of Imagination in Coleridge's *Biographia Literaria*—"slips lizard-like into a thicket of learned . . . [circuities], leaving in our hands . . . [its] tail only."°

Yet that tail itself is sufficiently substantial for us to be able with some measure of confidence to divine what Heidegger in the 1920's intended the main direction of his testimony to be. For, in taking man as the point of departure for his "fundamental ontology," he clearly reveals his inclination to think of *Dasein* as the measure and ground of whatever may be considered to have the status of reality: *everything*, in other words, is by way of being conceived to be relative to *human* existence. True, the aim of his inquiry was nothing less than Being-itself, but the crucial decision on which his whole method rested was that of making the immediate object of his investigation the particular being whose nature it is to raise the question of Being—and thus the inevitable consequence was the conversion of ontology into philosophical anthropology. Indeed, the circularity of the reasoning that underlies *Being and Time* can hardly go unheeded. Heidegger says in effect that *Dasein* is the real center of Being and that it must, therefore, be your point of beginning, if

° Basil Willey, *Nineteenth Century Studies: Coleridge to Matthew Arnold* (London: Chatto and Windus, 1949), p. 13.

you want to define the nature of Being-itself. *Dasein*, of course, finds its *raison d'être* in the "projection of possibilities"—and, since it is only by way of this projection of possible modes of Being that Being is disclosed, the world itself, at least by implication, is finally at the point of being represented as nothing other than the totality of the concerns to which *Dasein* dedicates itself. Being "happens" (*weltet*), as it were, in the self-disclosure of *Dasein*, in the world of the human understanding: this, it would seem, is the kind of radical subjectivism ultimately implied by the book of 1927—which no doubt constitutes as radical a "humanism" as is to be found anywhere amongst the major proposals of recent philosophy.

Very shortly after *Being and Time* had appeared Heidegger seems, however, to have undertaken quite a drastic reassessment of his whole program, and his reflections of the 1930's yielded at last in the 1940's and 50's a series of remarkable books and essays that represent so radical a revision of the doctrine being advanced in the book of 1927 that this reversal or "turning" (*Kehre*) has made it customary now sharply to distinguish between the earlier Heidegger (of *Being and Time*) and, as we say, "the later Heidegger" who came to the fore in the years following the close of World War II. Indeed, with what may be felt to be an astounding *volte-face*, this later Heidegger wants chiefly to register a great protest against "the humanization of truth," against the doctrine that truth resides in some human category or perspective or activity rather than in Being itself. In *Being and Time*, to be sure, he had himself been inclined to regard the "world" as everywhere so besmudged by human intentionality as to be in effect virtually an achievement of *Dasein*, the result of all those unitive analogies and principles wherewith man organizes the welter of existence into a coherent universe. But, apparently by the end of the 1930's, he had come to feel that such a humanization of reality is, as a matter of doctrine, radically mistaken and is in fact precisely the great blighting error involved in the whole Western intellectual tradition. Far from truth being resident in this or that *human* perspective, he was now convinced that we manage to make contact with What-Is not by dint of the sheer creativity of the human spirit and its capacity to impose some sort of order upon experience but, rather, in consequence of nothing other than the "unhiddenness" of Being itself which forms the great milieu encompassing all encounters between man and the things of earth. So his foremost project came to be that of mounting a strenuous polemic against the whole heresy of "humanism."

Already in his essay of 1942, *Plato's Doctrine of Truth* (*Platons Lehre von der Wahrheit*), he was taxing the Greeks with the responsibility for having first launched the program of "humanizing" the world, and, there, his chief exhibit is Plato, whose theory of Ideas he takes to be, at bottom, simply an attempt at reifying into ultimacy the schemata of human reason. Indeed, as he charges, it was Plato who first introduced into Western mentality the superstition that it is human principles and human postulates that hold the sovereign place in the kingdom of the world. And this superstition, in its power of persistence, causes Heidegger to marvel: he finds it at work in medieval Scholasticism, with its doctrine of truth as consisting (by Aquinas's account) in the "adequation" of the intellect to the created things of nature; or, again, the view of truth as something *achieved* by human intelligence he discerns, at the dawn of the modern period, in all that was implied by Descartes' *Cogito*; and, of course, the whole tradition of Idealist metaphysics, as it descends from Kant, represents for the later Heidegger, in the primacy it accords the synthetic categories with which the self orders experience, an inordinate exaltation of the *human* principle, as the final and absolute measure of all things. So, as he suggests, with Kant (at the end of the eighteenth century) we are already in close range of Nietzsche (at the end of the nineteenth), who, in a way, brings down the curtain on the whole drama enacted by the *philosophia perennis*, of seeking to convert the world into a merely human "project." That is to say, in Heidegger's reading of our intellectual history, the man who in 1882 announced the death of God bears the special distinction of having revealed a major premise of the precedent tradition, for, in declaring "the will to power" to be the world's sovereign reality, Nietzsche was simply making (albeit in a highly melodramatic way) a testimony toward which the whole of Western philosophy, given its incorrigible "humanism," implicitly moves. Such is the verdict that this very exacting arbiter renders.

Nor should it be supposed that the polemic against "humanization" implies nothing more than a querulous academician's impatience with certain aspects of the inheritance he has received from his predecessors. For, in Heidegger's sense of things, it is precisely the "forgetfulness" of Being sponsored by the humanization of reality in the West that accounts for our present captivity to the *in*human positivism of a rampantly technocratic civilization: which is to say that his critique of the philosophic tradition forms the basis of a very radical critique of the whole drift of our culture, as we approach what seems now to be the end of the modern age.

When, as he contends, reality in every dimension is conceived to be an essentially human project and when man himself is taken to be the absolute measure of all things—when the sheer ontological weight and depth of our received universe are forgotten, and when Being has been "lost"—then, inevitably, we shall deal with the world

aggressively and predatorily, as something to be brought
to heel and regulated and manipulated and turned to practical account: the great penchant of the age comes to be
one for what he calls in his little book of 1959, *Gelassenheit* (entitled in its English translation *Discourse on
Thinking*), "calculative thinking." And, says Heidegger,
at this present late stage in the whole Western experiment in "humanization" so committed are we to the calculative approach to reality that, as we hurry on to master
and manipulate all of nature and of human life itself, we
begin to be enveloped by that impoverishing "second
nature" comprised of the wholly artificial environment
with which a technological culture surrounds and overwhelms us. The cunning of history is strange indeed, for,
despite our prodigious successes in making all the
things of earth obedient to our science and engineering,
our last state is worse than the first, since we are now by
way of becoming merely automatons of "the will to
will." So mesmerized are we by our own purposes and
so committed are we to an essentially predatory attitude
towards the world that it ought not be a cause for wonder
that our times and places and circumstances seem dull
and dreary, seem merely to be *there*, uncharged with any
kind of grandeur. For when the body and the substance of
the world are approached simply with an intention to
control and to convert to use, then things are bound to
droop and wither, to descend into the banality of the pro-
fane, into what Heidegger calls "godlessness": when we
have lost any capacity for marveling at the miraculous
way in which they are inwardly steadied and supported by
the power and presence of Being, then they become "silent"—and this silence is but the measure of how greatly
we need to recover a range of sympathy and conscience
that will permit us, as Heidegger would say, to journey
homeward, back into "proximity to the Source," there

where we may once again rejoice in and be renewed by (as Hopkins phrases it) "the dearest freshness deep down things."*

But how may we overcome our "forgetfulness" of Being —or, when the "voice" of Being has fallen silent, how may it be newly quickened into speech? This is for Heidegger, one feels, the central question needing to be reckoned with by the people of our age. And clearly, of course, in the terms of his analysis, if we are once again to become adepts in the art of "paying heed" to the radically immanent presence of Being in all the things and creatures of earth, what is required is that we stop "attacking" the world, as though it were nothing more than material for a scientific experiment or a technological project. We must somehow manage for a time to repress our grasping manipulativeness, to throttle "the will to will," and to shut down all the well-driven machines of the calculative reason: what must be taken to heart is Blake's brusque imperative—"Damn braces, bless relaxes."

Yet it remains to be said just how, in our dealings with the world, we may learn to stop attacking it and begin to learn the great discipline, as Heidegger puts it, of "letting-be." And on this vital point he makes a surprising testimony. For, as one whose professional career of more than sixty years was wholly devoted to an enterprise of philosophic reconstruction, it was surely to be expected that he would be wanting to propose some new philosophic scheme as that whose acceptance would make possible the necessary reorientation. But, here, he takes quite a different tack: for one so passionately committed to philosophic enterprise as Heidegger was, it is a very surprising tack indeed, for in his book of 1944, *Erlaüterungen zu*

* Gerard Manley Hopkins, "God's Grandeur," in *Poems of Gerard Manley Hopkins*, ed. Robert Bridges (London and New York: Oxford University Press, 1938), p. 26.

Hölderlins Dichtung (*Interpretations of Hölderlin's Poetry*), and in his brilliant book of 1950, *Holzwege* (*Paths in the Forest*), he is proposing that, for the kind of renovation of sensibility which is now required, we must turn not to philosophy but to poetry. For, in the view of "the later Heidegger," the poet (*der Dichter*) is far more adept than the thinker (*der Denker*) in leading us back into the neighborhood of Being, in offering us the right sort of tutelage in the discipline of paying heed to that marvelous power or energy that so assembles things into themselves that they are simply enabled, in their stark specificity, to be what they are.

And, of course, had the question as to *what* "Being" is been directly put to Heidegger, he would have said that the very question itself expresses a profound misconception, since Being is not something to which one may point as one points to a chair or a swan but rather that which enables all objects to have their objectivity: he would have said something like what one of his interpreters says, that Being "is beyond all 'whats' and 'whiches,' "* that it is that which enables things to be *present*, which keeps them assembled so that they can be beheld in their radical actuality. Whereas *a* being is simply that-which-is-present, that-which-is-in-the-open, Being-itself *is* that Openness (*Offenheit*) which lights up and shows forth the things of earth—that luminous Presence, that primal Power of "letting-be," which allows things to stand out before the gaze of the mind. This is the fundamental affirmation underlying the *Letter on Humanism*, the *Introduction to Metaphysics*, the book of 1954, *Was heisst Denken?* ("*What Evokes Thought?*"—entitled in its English translation *What Is Called Thinking?*), and the two books of 1957, *The Principle of Ground* (*Der Satz vom Grund*) and *Identity and Difference* (*Identität und Differenz*).

* Majorie Grene, *Martin Heidegger* (London: Bowes & Bowes, 1957), p. 111.

Now since he conceives the craft of poetic art to be largely dedicated to the disclosure of the things and creatures of this world "in the starkness and strangeness of their being what they are,"* Heidegger suggests that it is to the poet that we must turn for tutelage in how Being is to be "hailed." In this connection, one might wish for a larger and more diversified body of citation, given the appositeness to his purpose that he might have found in Wordsworth and Keats, in Hopkins and Yeats and Wallace Stevens, or in Eugenio Montale or St.-John Perse. His recourse, however, not surprisingly, is to poets in the German tradition—most especially to Friedrich Hölderlin, but also to Rilke and Stefan George, and to Georg Trakl and Gottfried Benn. And it was his deep immersion in this literature that quickened his sense of the poet's distinctive office being that of awakening in us an attitude of enthrallment before the sheer specificity of the various particulars and quiddities with which the world is furnished. St. Teresa of Avila says: "I require of you only to look"—and this, indeed, is what Heidegger takes to be the principal requirement of the poet.

In his great essay in the *Holzwege* on "Der Ursprung des Kunstwerkes" ("The Origin of the Work of Art"**) he invites us to recall a Van Gogh painting of a pair of farm shoes and to think of the pictorial image in relation to its original subject. The old peasant woman who actually used these shoes, as she trudged day by day through the damp furrows of her fields, knew them, he suggests, only as a piece of "equipment," and for her their "equipmental being" consisted in nothing other than their "serviceability." But we, as we stand before Van Gogh's painting, be-

* H. D. Lewis, "Revelation and Art," *Morals and Revelation* (London: Allen and Unwin, 1951), p. 212.

** A splendid English version of this essay is now available in the collection of Heidegger's essays translated by Albert Hofstadter—*Poetry, Language, Thought* (New York: Harper and Row, Inc., 1971).

come increasingly aware of how these old clodhoppers, in their weather-beaten raggedness, vibrate with "the silent call of the earth," of how they allude to "the loneliness of the field-path as evening declines," and of how, frayed as they are, they irradiate "the wordless joy" of "ripening corn." Which is to say that the painting releases the old woman's shoes from their captivity unto themselves and into what they most essentially are. And so it is, Heidegger maintains, with poetic art: it brings things into "the Open" and enables us to behold them in the dimension of "presence"—and thus it brings us into the region of Being, which is itself nothing other than Presence.

Indeed, it is a line of Hölderlin's that says what Heidegger himself most wants to say—namely, that "poetically,/ Man dwells upon the earth." Or, as Heidegger might have put it, we dwell upon the earth in a truly human way only in so far as we win some heightened alertness to what things appear to be as they come into the Open. But normally, of course, we are so bent on realizing our practical intentions that we take notice of our surroundings only in the degree requisite for the fulfillment of our workaday purposes. We hasten from one occasion to another, mindful only of that merest minimum of things having to do with the urgencies of our common affairs: so our experience is full of dead spots: we are like the shipwrecked men in a story of Stephen Crane's who, adrift in their small boat, do not see the color of the sky, so intent are they on reaching a port. Moreover, we are even more deeply inured in these habits of somnambulating our way through the world by the whole ethos of such a culture as our own which, with its vast panoply of technological matériel, imprisons us in a universe of artifact that—except for the occasional emergency of flood or storm—effectively shuts us off from the primitive realities of the earth. So, as a consequence, we are frequently by way of losing altogether any appetite for what Wordsworth in Book II of *The Prelude* calls "the sentiment of Being," for marveling, that is, at the extraordinary munificence with which Being bestows itself upon each bird, each tree, each blade of grass, each flowing stream—and our loss of any reverential awe before the dignity and the sheer amplitude of Creation, before the unplumbable Mystery of Being, is itself the result of our simply not paying heed to that-which-is-in-the-open.

In Heidegger's view, however, it is precisely the vocation of the poet to be a "watchman" (*Wächter*) or "shepherd" (*Hirt*) of Being, in its immanence within the things and creatures of earth. But his exercise of this pastoral office does not entail his playing such a role as Shelley attributed to the poet when he declared him to be "the unacknowledged legislator of the world." Nor is Heidegger's poet a votary of Orpheus: he does not undertake to build worlds alternative to that of our present habitation; on the contrary, it is not the "light that never was on land or sea" that he aims at but rather the concrete actualities of the world already at hand, and he wants so to "deconceal" them that they may be seen as tabernacling grace and glory and as charged with "a kind of total grandeur at the end."* The poet, says Heidegger, "names all things in that which they are . . . so that things for the first time shine out . . ." He is, in other words, the great proficient in the art of "paying heed," in (as it is put in "The Origin of the Work of Art") "the letting happen of the advent of the truth of what is." The poet, of course, specializes most immediately in the supervision of simile and metaphor and analogy, and he is likely to work with an elaborately measured language—and these are all de-

* Wallace Stevens, "To an Old Philosopher in Rome," in *The Collected Poems of Wallace Stevens* (New York: Alfred A. Knopf, 1955), p. 510.

vices that he uses for the sake of creating images that will interrupt our normally routinized procedures of thought and feeling and lure us into some fresh engagement with the salient, palpable immediacies of our well-trodden, familiar world. Poetry offers no cues or signals or techniques for mastering and exploiting things: it wants only to release them from their "self-seclusion," to light up their essentiality, and to solicit a rapt attentiveness toward that by which they are gathered into themselves (which is nothing other than Being itself)—and in this way, in the spirit of "letting-be," it invites us to offer a kind of *Amen* to the outgoings of the morning and evening, to the north and the south, to the wind and the rain and the children of men, to all the round world and they that dwell therein.

So, by reason of the courteous artfulness with which it disarms us of our penchant for "calculative thinking," Heidegger is persuaded that "truth is at work" in poetry. Truth is at work, because the poet is by way of inviting us to approach the world in the spirit of *Gelassenheit*, in the spirit of surrender and acquiescence. And it is only when the things of earth are approached in this way that we can be laid hold of by that wherewith they are enabled to be what they are: which is to say that, in the measure to which the poet persuades us to submit to the discipline of *Gelassenheit*, he does to that extent bring us back into the neighborhood of Being, into the one region where selfhood can be securely constituted since this is the original and proper domain of the human spirit. The poet, in short, brings us back into "proximity to the Source," and thus it is alone through his ministries that we may begin to escape the manifold confusions in our time that are consequent upon the "humanization" of the world.

So it is that the meditations of this great German

teacher proceeded in his last years—from the search for an analytic of *Dasein* to an attempt at a recovery of Being itself; and the knottily convoluted books to which they gave rise constitute one of the richest and most deeply stirring bodies of philosophic reflection in modern literature. True, even in the context of the German tradition where the idioms of systematic philosophy have generally been intimidating in their snarled and periphrastic abstruseness, Heidegger's highly eccentric vocabulary, drenched as it is in neologism, and his curiously lumbering rhetoric represent in their inelegance something very notable indeed. Yet, as they gradually move from book to book through his vast *oeuvre*, his most sensitive readers find themselves increasingly surprised by the degree to which the rough, clumsy, faltering stiltedness of his speech becomes at last a strange kind of poetry, a profoundly moving *enactment* of his unexampled quest for a new way of grounding the reality of *Dasein*.

Anglo-American philosophy, with its strong commitment to a common-sense empiricism, has not, of course, permitted itself to be much influenced by Heidegger's thought, and its tendency is to dismiss him as an obscurantist whose heavy, ponderous Teutonicisms are simply a huge irrelevance. But he has had an immense influence on the European scene, and not only there but in Japan and Latin America as well, and not only in philosophical circles but also in the adjacent fields of theology and philosophical psychology.

Yet, whether his legacy is to be assessed in a positive or in a negative way, many will doubtless feel that the question as to the appropriateness of our regarding "the later Heidegger" as an existentialist is an issue that remains very much open, despite the regularity with which the general parlance of intellectual life affiliates him with the existentialist tradition. Though he himself disavowed any such affiliation, we will not, certainly, find it difficult to see the author of *Being and Time* as standing in the line of Kierkegaard and Nietzsche and Unamuno and as associable with Jaspers and Sartre and Merleau-Ponty. In this stage of his career, to be sure, Heidegger's principal interest, as he insisted, was already finding its primary focus in the problem of Being and in the systematic definition of the fundamental structures of human existence, and this highly speculative bent did no doubt make for a certain difference of style as between himself and those whom we think of as most typically representative of existentialist method. For it is not ontology that constitutes the main direction of a Kierkegaard or a Nietzsche or an Unamuno but, rather, anthropology*—and their thought is chiefly concerned with the question as to how the individual may win a really authentic humanity. Yet, however much Heidegger's early ontological preoccupations may in certain ways have distanced him from the more normative forms of Existentialism, the basic stress and tenor of *Being and Time* did, nevertheless, carry much of the flavor belonging to this whole ambience. The book of 1927 is, after all, in large part devoted to the analysis of such themes as "dread" and "care" and "temporality" and "transcendence," and it is more than a little touched by the existentialist *frisson*.

But, as the question will be pressed, given the large priority he accords to "Being" over "existence," how may the author of the *Letter on Humanism* and the *Introduction to Metaphysics,* of *Identity and Difference* and the *Holzwege,* be considered to be an existentialist? For surely, it will be contended, in the dialectic between *Being* or *essence* on the one hand and *existence* on the other, the true existentialist is one who finds his primary

* The term "anthropology" is one which in its classical sense speaks, of course, not (as it customarily does today) of the study of primitive society but of fundamental inquiry into the nature of man.

datum in *existence*. And since this is not the case with the "late" Heidegger, is it not simply obfuscating to ally him in any way at all with existentialist tradition?

Now the answering of this question begins to be possible only as it is recalled that, for Heidegger, "The 'essence' of *Dasein* lies in its existence."[*] This is one of the major propositions underlying the book of 1927, but the doctrine it enunciates was fundamental not only for the Heidegger of *Being and Time* but also for "the later Heidegger" as well: which is to say that, early and late, he took it for granted that it is, indeed, *existence* that defines the human condition. Certainly he never espoused any sort of "essentialism," any view of the human reality as merely a replica of some eternal and immutable hypostasis: on the contrary, despite the various shifts of emphasis that the development of his thought reflects at other points, he remained always constant in his view that it is the term "existence" which is alone appropriate for the definition of the nature of *Dasein*—and thus it is surely not amiss to regard him as in point of fact, and (for all his own disclaimers) in the most radical sense, an existentialist thinker.

But, early and late, Heidegger was, of course, an existentialist with a difference, for with him the concept of *Existenz* was not merely a watchword for summoning the individual (in the manner of a Kierkegaard) to authentic selfhood, but it was, far more, an ontological category. To say, in other words, that *Dasein* "exists" is not merely to say, in Heidegger's sense of things, that man is extant, that he is a creature who is, as it were, "at hand" (*vorhanden*). A non-instrumental being, such as a pebble on a beach, is simply extant, a "mere entity" (*Vorhandenes*); and an instrument or tool, such as a pot or a knife, is merely a thing "ready-at-hand" (*Zuhandenes*). But to say that *Dasein* "exists"—and "existence" may be predi-

[*] *Being and Time*, p. 42.

cated only of man, of *Dasein*—is to affirm something more than its mere "facticity" (*Faktizität*). For Heidegger, with his great fondness for etymology, wanted always to insist that the concept of *Existenz* be defined in terms of its root meaning in the original Latin, where "to exist," *existere,* means "to stand out." And thus, in his lexicon, to say that man "exists" is not merely to say that he "is," that he is extant, but it is rather to say that he is a creature whose condition is one of "standing out." A tree or a stone does not "stand out": it simply "stands in itself." But *Dasein* "stands out"—stands out into the infinite realm of Being itself which, by way of its "unhiddenness" (*Unverborgenheit*), imparts to *Dasein* not only its own self-understanding but also its understanding of the world within which it dwells.

It is in this way, then, and on these grounds, that in Heidegger an existentialist vision is united with a profound ontological interest, and neither cancels the other out, so that he may indeed, therefore, for all his commitment to a "fundamental ontology," be considered to be one of the great masters in modern philosophy of the existentialist project.

Moreover, when we consider the immense influence of Heidegger on, as Hannah Arendt speaks of it, "the spiritual physiognomy of this century" (in not only philosophy but also psychology and theology and theory of literature and art), we need to say of him—as of such other avatars of modern Existentialism as Kierkegaard and Nietzsche and Marcel and Buber—that it is not so much in his *philosophy* as in his *thinking* that the intellectual community of our time has found a great inspiring example. This thinking, says Hannah Arendt,

> has a digging quality peculiar to itself, which, should we wish to put it in linguistic form, lies in the transitive use of the verb "to think." Heidegger never thinks "about" some-

thing; he thinks something. In this entirely uncontemplative activity, he penetrates to the depths, but not to discover, let alone bring to light, some ultimate, secure foundations which one could say had been undiscovered earlier in this manner. Rather, he persistently remains there, underground, in order to lay down pathways and fix "trail marks". . . .

This thinking may set tasks for itself; it may deal with "problems"; it naturally, indeed always, has something specific with which it is particularly occupied or, more precisely, by which it is specifically aroused; but one cannot say that it has a goal. It is unceasingly active, and even the laying down of paths itself is conducive to opening up a new dimension of thought, rather than to reaching a goal sighted beforehand and guided thereto.[*]

So the term which depicts the whole body of Heidegger's published work, perhaps more comprehensively and concisely than any other, is that which he bestowed as a title on the remarkable collection of essays issued in 1950—*Holzwege*, or "Paths in the Forest." For this is indeed what the Heideggerian texts offer, not such a system as we get from an Aquinas or a Hegel but *pathways*, pathways through the vast forest of human experience which, even if they do not lead out into the open precincts beyond, do nevertheless describe a course whereby we may pick our way through the thickets of the world. And thus he deserves to be thought of as one of the great *directeurs de conscience* of our time.

[*] Hannah Arendt, *op. cit.*, p. 51.

5

Albert Camus—
Resistance, Rebellion . . . .

A GREAT SORROW was felt throughout the Western world on the fourth day of January, 1960, when it was learned that, early that morning, the distinguished novelist and playwright Albert Camus had been killed in an automobile crash, about seventy-five miles southeast of Paris. Though only forty-six years of age at the time of his death, he had already become one of the great thinkers and artists of modern France. Not only was he honored by his fellow countrymen as one who had brought a new glory to their literature; he was also a man in whose writings the whole civilized world had found a nobility of spirit which seemed to offer to men everywhere fresh encouragement amidst the perplexities of twentieth-century life. Just two years earlier, in December of 1957, he had been awarded the Nobel Prize in Stockholm, because, as the Swedish Academy declared, he had illuminated "the problems of the human conscience in our time." The testimony of his Swedish friends expressed, with a remarkable exactness, the general consensus about the meaning of the career of this extraordinarily eloquent and farsighted Frenchman whose novels and plays and essays have been read by the people of our time with an intensity of interest such as few writers of this century have been able to claim.

It may at first seem strange that our age should find something so inspiriting and even ennobling in Camus' legacy, for in one area of his thought he represents a very dark and severe kind of pessimism. It is the pessimism of a man who conceives ours to be a world without God, a world adrift and without any guiding purpose at all. Indeed, this was perhaps his most fundamental conviction, that the universe in which man dwells lacks any ultimate significance of the sort it might have, were its government in the hands of a righteous God who guaranteed some clear and absolute meaning to human life. In Camus' understanding of our basic condition, man faces a world which is simply *there* and which he knows no more about than what modern science reveals. It is a world simply hurrying through space and offering no objective justification for the moral values which man calls into existence in his effort to give some slender dignity to his life on earth. Thus it is a world which is "absurd," a world into which man feels himself to have been hurled by a blind and senseless fate. Our deepest yearnings—for the evidence of some ultimate principle of justice and reason at work in the affairs of men and of nations—remain unanswered. And the final outrage is what Camus called "the cruel mathematics that command our condition"—namely, the certainty that the life of every man must finally be snuffed out in death, that all his striving and hoping and loving will at last be as if they had never been, and that he will be swallowed up into the silence of the earth—ashes to ashes, dust to dust. Such, Camus affirmed, is the bitter and tragic destiny appointed for man in the absurd world to which he is condemned.

It might be concluded, then, that, finally, *nothing* matters and that a man need therefore be obedient only to impulse and appetite: if the shadow of the Absurd falls over human life at every point, then, it might be reasoned, there is no avoiding the decision reached by Ivan in Dostoevski's great novel *The Brothers Karamazov*, that "everything is permitted."

It is just here, however, that the greatness of Camus' moral vision finds its clearest expression. For it was precisely in the absurdity of the human situation that he found a kind of challenge and discipline. "If God does not exist, then everything is permitted," declared Ivan Karamazov. And if *everything* is permitted, then even murder, then even genocide, become legitimate. Yet to reach so desperate a conclusion, and then to proceed to act upon the basis of it, is to reduce the world to an even more intolerable desert than it already is: it is, in effect, to "take sides" *with* the Absurd and *against* man. One must not allow oneself, in other words, to become so intoxicated with despair that one ends up betraying the only value that remains sacred in an absurd world—namely, man himself. For, as Camus maintained, the great challenge which is leveled at man by the absurdity of his universe is that of finding a way of honoring the sacredness of the human community and of being faithful to one's brother—*in spite of* "the cruel mathematics that command our condition." And it is the steadiness with which he himself carried on a search for that style of life which would give dignity to the human pilgrimage *even* in an absurd world ultimately hostile to man —it is just this which has made Camus such a great source of encouragement to the people of our age. So one felt a certain rightness in the phrase which one of his interpreters used as the title of an essay on his work some years ago in *The Atlantic Monthly*—"Albert Camus: A Good Man."

Albert Camus was born on the seventh day of November,

1913, in the little Algerian village of Mondovi, near Constantine—"on the shores of a happy sea," as he later said. His mother was Spanish, and his father was a Frenchman of Alsatian background who was killed in the Battle of the Marne in World War I only a few months after Albert's birth. Throughout Camus' childhood the family was desperately poor, for his mother, as a cleaning woman, was able to earn only the most meager living for Albert and his brother in Algiers, to which she and her sons moved following her husband's death. She lived with her two boys in the working-class district of Belcourt, and it was here that Camus received his early education in the public schools.

In 1923 one of his teachers, Louis Germain, helped him to win a scholarship to the *lycée* in Algiers, and here he pursued the studies that prepared him to enter the University of Algiers in 1932. As a university student he specialized in philosophy, but in the early 1930's he was also reading very widely in modern French literature, and it was probably the impact upon him of such writers as Marcel Proust, André Gide, Antoine de Saint-Exupéry, and André Malraux that gave birth to his desire for a literary career. Yet it was never a part of his nature to shut himself up amongst books alone; and, throughout this period, in addition to his literary and intellectual interests, he kept alive his enormous enthusiasm for sport (particularly swimming), despite occasional flareups of the tuberculosis he first contracted in early adolescence.

Like so many other young men of his generation, Camus found the attitude of neutrality impossible with respect to the important issues of domestic and international politics in the 1930's, and, in 1934, he joined the Communist Party: it was a gesture of identification with the worker and the underdog which many other young people throughout the Western world found it natural to perform at the time. But he remained a Communist only for a few months, soon leaving the party in disgust with the lack of good faith evident in its policy toward the Moslem population in Algeria. Yet, despite his quick disillusionment with the Communist movement, in one respect he was deeply affected by the cultural atmosphere of which it was a part; this concerned the new connection being striven for between the arts and the life of the working classes. It was largely as a result of his being influenced by this aspect of Communist thought that he devoted himself to the establishment in 1935 of a workers' theater in Algiers, which came finally to be known as *Le Théâtre de l'équipe* (or, as it might be translated, the Theater of the Workers' Guild). Camus himself was the central figure in the company, and this was a project—involving numerous adaptations for the Algerian stage of novels and plays from both classical and modern literatures—which claimed much of his time and energy for a period of two or three years.

But Camus was not only deeply involved in theatrical work as the 1930's drew to a close: he was also a busy reporter and editorial writer on the staff of the leftist newspaper *Alger-Républicain*, though not interrupting meanwhile his philosophic and literary studies. And his creative work had already begun, a first volume of essays (*L'Envers et l'endroit*—or, *The Wrong Side and the Right Side*) appearing in 1937 and still another (*Noces*—or, *Nuptials*) in 1938. With the outbreak of World War II in the fateful month of September 1939, both writing and creative labor in the theater were, however, brought to a halt, and Camus immediately volunteered for military duty. The frailty of his physical constitution made his rejection inevitable, and after spending several months in a futile effort to secure some sort of government post in which he could be useful in the crisis, he went to Paris in March of 1940, there to join the staff of the evening paper *Paris-Soir*. But then came the German invasion in May, and the subsequent Occupation meant, of course, the end of a free press in France. So, after a few months amidst the dreariness of Lyons where he completed his first major book, *Le Mythe de Sisyphe* (*The Myth of Sisyphus*), he returned to Algeria in January of 1941, and there he began to plan the novel which was to be published six years later as *La Peste* (*The Plague*).

By 1942 the Resistance movement was well under way, and Camus joined the network whose headquarters were in Lyons and which called itself *Combat*. After a time his chief assignment with this group was an editorial job on the staff of the network's paper which bore the organization's name; and it was through his work for *Combat* that he was brought into close association with the distinguished novelist André Malraux, whom for so many years he had admired, and the poet René Leynaud, who was executed by the Germans in the spring of 1944. *Combat* quickly became one of the leading newspapers in France after the liberation of Paris in August of 1944, and for the next three years its influential editor was Albert Camus, the brilliant young writer whom the French public was coming to know as the author of the remarkable first novel *L'Étranger* (*The Stranger*), published by the Paris firm of Gallimard in 1942. His reputation was also being enhanced by his two exciting plays—*Le Malentendu* (*The Misunderstanding*), first presented at the Théâtre des Mathurins in 1944; and *Caligula*, which caused a great sensation at its initial performance in the Théâtre-Hébertot of Paris in 1945.

By 1947 the author of *The Myth of Sisyphus* and *The Plague* was a famous and celebrated figure in French literary and intellectual life. It was in the year 1947, after numerous policy disagreements with his *Combat* colleagues, that Camus resigned his editorial post, having

brilliantly demonstrated to postwar France the possibility
of a working newspaperman's being firmly committed to
a radical position on social and political questions without at the same time being a tool of the Communist party.

After his resignation from *Combat*, Camus withdrew
from public life. There followed a period of feverish
involvement in various writing projects, a period which
saw the brilliant first productions of *L'État de siège* (*State
of Siege*) at the Théâtre Marigny in Paris in October of
1948 and of *Les Justes* (*The Just*) at the Hébertot in
December of 1949. In 1950 his first collection of political
essays, *Actuelles* (*Realities of the Present Time*), appeared;
and then, in 1951, *L'Homme révolté* (*The Rebel*) was
published, a book which brilliantly traces the history of
the idea of rebellion in modern thought. Indeed, the 1950's
constituted perhaps the most important period of Camus'
life, years of the most sustained and varied labor and of
the largest accomplishment. In this last decade of his life
he produced a half-dozen adaptations for theatrical performance of the work of such diverse writers as the Italian
Dino Buzzati, the American William Faulkner, and the
Russian Dostoevski. In the second and third volumes of his
Actuelles he continued, through his social and political
essays, to establish himself as one of the most thoughtful
interpreters in contemporary France of modern society.
In his volume of 1954, the book called *L'Été* (*Summer*),
he brought together a number of essays which make up a
body of deeply felt and lyrically eloquent testimony about
the image of the sea, the experience of travel, the meaning
of exile, and various other themes. His novel *La Chute* (*The
Fall*) appeared in 1956, and the collection of stories *L'Exil
et le royaume* (*Exile and the Kingdom*) in 1957. In addition to all these literary projects, he worked throughout
these years as an editor for the publishing house of Gallimard.

His election by the Swedish Academy in 1957, at the age of forty-four, to the high eminence of the Nobel Prize came as a great shock to him—on being notified of the Academy's action, he exclaimed, "Had I been on the Swedish jury, I would have voted for [André] Malraux." In his acceptance speech in Stockholm he chose to speak of the idea by which he had been comforted and sustained throughout his life, even in the most difficult and trying circumstances: the idea of his art and of the writer's vocation. "To me," he said, "art is not a solitary delight. It is a means of stirring the greatest number of men by providing them with a privileged image of our common joys and woes." Thus he declared his conviction that the artist "by definition . . . cannot serve today those who make history; he must serve those who are subject to it. Otherwise he is alone and deprived of his art. All the armies of tyranny with their millions of men cannot people his solitude—even, and especially, if he is willing to fall into step with them. But the silence of an unknown prisoner subjected to humiliations at the other end of the world is enough to tear the writer from exile, at least whenever he manages, amid the privileges of freedom, not to forget that silence but to give it voice by means of art."

To give voice to the burdens and perplexities of the human creature: this was, indeed, the guiding purpose of Camus' career. As one looks back now at his entire work, one feels that he had found his own voice early in his life, in those first youthful books of the 1930's—*The Wrong Side and the Right Side* (1937) and *Nuptials* (1938). For here he was making the two affirmations that were to be at the center of all his writing over the next twenty years: that human life is governed by a most cruel mathematic, and that it is yet a thing of glory. These are, of course, books that remind us that Camus was by birth a North

African, for, whether he is exploring some phase of Algerian working-class life or simply dwelling on the heavy
fragrances of an Algerian summer evening, it is the
splendor of the Mediterranean countryside that forms the
background for his meditations. Amidst its "intolerable
grandeur" he cannot, to be sure, escape reckoning with the
fact that man is ultimately "alone, helpless, naked" in the
world. For the very warmth and opulence of the North
African landscape most poignantly awaken a sense of the
terrible cheat involved in the tragic brevity of man's life.
Yet the loveliness of quiet Mediterranean dusks, the melo-
dious sighings of the Algerian countryside, the sultry
beaches, the magnificence of the sea and of "that sky
gorged with heat"—all this does have the effect of commanding an act of "lucid attention" before the great
enchantments of the earth; and it had, too, the effect of
helping the young Camus discover that there was, indeed, in himself "an invincible summer" which saved
him, finally, from despair.

It was not, however, until he produced his novel of 1942,
The Stranger, that Camus achieved the first major statement of his sense of the world and of the human plight.
The protagonist of the story is Meursault, a clerk in an
Algerian shipping firm, who receives one day a telegram
notifying him of the death of his mother in the home for
the aged where she has for some time lived. He requests
a brief leave from his firm and then proceeds to the remote country district in which the home is located for the
funeral. But, there, he gives no evidence of any grief; his
only feeling is that of drowsiness prompted by the summer
heat. After the funeral he returns to Algiers and goes to
the beach the next morning where he meets Marie, a girl
who used to work in his office. They swim together, then
go to a movie, and return to Meursault's apartment; and
the afternoon they spend together marks the beginning of
their affair.

In the course of the ensuing summer, an acquaintance of Meursault's, Raymond, beats up his girl friend, and Meursault obligingly consents to offer testimony on his behalf to the police. Then, one weekend, he and Raymond encounter the girl's Arab relatives on the beach; there is a fight in which Raymond is knifed by one of the Arabs. Later on that same day, Meursault, on returning to the beach, finds one of the Arabs sprawling in the shade. He sees the man draw a knife, and then, says Meursault, "I felt as if a long, thin blade transfixed my forehead. . . . I was conscious only of the cymbals of the sun clashing on my skull. . . . Then everything began to reel before my eyes. . . ." At this moment he reaches for the revolver he had taken from Raymond earlier in the day. "Every nerve in my body was a steel spring, and my grip closed on the revolver. . . . I fired four more shots into the inert body. . . . And each successive shot was another loud, fateful rap on the door of my undoing."

Now the second part of the novel is largely devoted to an exploration of the meaning of this strange occurrence. There is, of course, an official interrogation which is followed by the trial. And throughout these proceedings Meursault remains as impassive and indifferent as he was on the occasion of his mother's funeral: indeed, it is this aspect of his behavior which seems most to outrage the courtroom. The magistrate and prosecutor and jurymen are as much affronted by his not having wept at his mother's funeral as they are by his having murdered the Arab. It is his unshakable nonchalance, one feels, which does in truth make him a "stranger," an "outsider." He is a man who has long felt blowing in upon him the "slow, persistent breeze" from "the dark horizon of [his] future"—which is the novel's way of asserting Meursault's central obsession with the inevitability of his eventual death, a fact which for him has kept any one action or experience or value from being more important, finally, than any

other. This is why, when he is offered a promotion in his
business firm or when Marie offers him her love or when
Raymond offers him his friendship or when he is faced
with his own mother's death, his response is little more
than a shrug of the shoulder. For how can a man have any
genuine commitments or loyalties when he finds himself
in a world where everything is finally canceled out by
death? Given the ultimate indifference of the universe itself toward man, how can *any*thing really *matter*? Oughtn't
one, therefore, confront the indifference of the world with
an equal indifference of one's own? It is in such a way,
it appears, that Meursault has reasoned: he is a man who
will not permit himself to be comforted by the illusions
and emotions which ordinarily screen men from the cold,
bitter stone of their actual condition. And *this* is why,
the novel suggests, he goes to the guillotine. Yes, to be
sure, he did not weep at his mother's funeral, and he has
taken the life of another man (though with as much indifference as he displays in relation to every other event
in the story). Yet what most scandalizes the courtroom is
the evident coolness with which this little clerk has turned
aside from the myths in which men normally sleep.

But perhaps the most crucial scene of all comes at the
end, in Meursault's jail cell. The trial is over, and the
sentence has been passed—that " 'in the name of the French
people' [he is] to be decapitated in some public place."
Now comes the priest, who serves as prison chaplain, to
offer the condemned man the consolations of supernatural
religion. He wants to say to the prisoner that this earthly
life is not very important after all, that there is another life,
another world, more real and more gladdening than this
one, and that admission into it depends only upon the
human sinner's true repentance. As he drones on, Meursault begins to be filled with a great rage:

> I started yelling at the top of my voice. I hurled insults at
> him, I told him not to waste his rotten prayers on me. . . .

> He seemed so cocksure, you see. And yet none of his cer-
> tainties was worth one strand of a woman's hair. Living as
> he did, like a corpse, he couldn't even be sure of being alive.
> . . . Actually, I was sure of myself, sure about everything,
> far surer than he; sure of my present life and of the death
> that was coming. That, no doubt, was all I had; but at least
> that certainty was something I could get my teeth into—just
> as it had got its teeth into me.

The stale, monotonous platitudes of the priest about what
may be hoped for in an afterlife are simply not convincing:
yet their very absurdity, irritating though at first it is, has
finally the effect of reminding Meursault that (as Camus
once remarked in his *Notebooks*) our "kingdom is of this
earth [alone]" and that in fact he has not altogether been
cheated of the joys of this earthly life. He remembers
the "sun-gold" of Marie's face and all the wonderful sights
and smells of the eternal Algerian summer, and he knows
that, though every human life is finally canceled out by
death, the world is nevertheless a glorious thing. "It was
as if," he says, "that great rush of anger had washed me
clean. . . ." And he faces his last hour with the quiet
serenity of one who, being sustained by "the wine of the
absurd and the bread of indifference," can lay his heart
open to "the benign indifference of the universe."

Two years after the publication of *The Stranger* in 1942,
Camus' first major works for the theater appeared—
Caligula and *The Misunderstanding*. Of the two, it is perhaps the former which more impressively extends the kind
of account of human experience begun in the book of 1942.

Caligula became Emperor of Rome at the age of twenty-
five, and the brief, stormy period of his reign is narrated
in the *Lives of the Caesars* by the Roman historian Sue-
tonius. Though the monstrous savagery of this young tyrant
was that which doubtless first attracted Camus' attention,
his play does, of course, transform the historic personage
into an imaginary figure. In the opening act Caligula

appears as one grief-stricken by the recent death of his sister Drusilla, for whom he had borne an incestuous love. Most importantly, her death, as he explains to his friend Helicon, has come to stand for him as a kind of symbol of the fact that "Men die and . . . are not happy." What troubles him most deeply, in other words, is that he finds himself, along with all other men, in an absurd world, in a world without meaning or purpose in which the human spirit is ultimately destroyed. He has also found that what is really bitter and tragic in human life is fully understood by only the smallest minority of men. So he has decided that the service he shall perform for Rome will be that of shocking its citizens into an awareness of how irrational the universe in fact is. This he proceeds to do by launching a reign of terror, a program of systematic famine and confiscation of property, of torture and murder.

Indeed, this young madman plunges Rome so deeply into chaos it does at last appear that no one at all is any longer safe. Thus, finally, he provokes a wave of revolt, even amongst that handful of his friends who share his conviction that the world is without order or meaning. A plot formed to remove him from the throne is led by Cherea, his closest friend, who acknowledges that, yes, the Emperor's philosophy is "logical from start to finish," but, as he says, if pushed to its final conclusion, Caligula's program for Rome would simply make it impossible for anyone at all to live there. Cherea is a man who is as deeply convinced as is Caligula of the world's ultimate absurdity; as he says, "The same flame consumes our hearts." Yet he does not want to commit himself to any campaign against the Absurd which is, in effect, a campaign against man himself. So, in the decisive scene of his confrontation with the Emperor, he resolutely says, " . . . you've got to go." And shortly afterward he and his fellow assassins fling themselves upon Caligula and stab him to death. The only consequence of this madman's attempt at impersonating Fate has been corpses, and Cherea and Scipio and the others have had at last to face the intolerableness of permitting a rebellion against the human condition to become itself a betrayal of man. Indeed, Caligula himself is compelled to acknowledge at the very end that he had "chosen a wrong path, a path that leads to nothing."

A similar path is being explored in the second major play of Camus' early period, *The Misunderstanding*. This is a work which has the same tightness of plot and swiftness of movement we associate with classical Greek tragedy. The action occurs in some remote central European village, at an inn operated by two women, a mother and daughter. The climate of the region is dark and damp and dreary: so the two women dream of sunlight and of open spaces by the sea. As they have cherished this dream over the years, they have regularly murdered the guests who have occasionally patronized their little inn, slaughtering them for the sake of whatever money could be pilfered from their persons; in this way they have hoped eventually to accumulate a fund large enough to permit them to get away—to the South, by the sea, to sunlit beaches and open spaces.

One morning when there appears an obviously wealthy traveler, apparently without connections in the neighborhood, they are immediately fixed in their purpose to kill and to rob. In reality he is Jan, the prodigal son who left them years earlier to go out into the world to make his fortune. He has at last returned, to share his wealth and happiness with his mother and sister. Having arrived in the vicinity the previous night, he and his wife Maria are guests at a nearby hotel. And it appeals to his sense of the dramatic to present himself at his mother's inn first as a stranger, and then, after playing out his little charade of pretense and surprise, to disclose his identity—to say, "Here I am at last, I, Jan, come to take you away to a land of endless sunshine beside the sea." Maria insists that there's "something morbid" in this whole scheme and that he ought simply to identify himself at once, letting "one's heart speak for itself." But Jan cannot be dissuaded. So, on the fatal morning, he sets out, leaving his wife behind at their hotel. Before he can reveal who he is to his mother and his sister Martha, however, he is bludgeoned to death, and his body is tossed into a bordering river—but only after the pockets have been carefully picked. Then comes the denouement, when Jan is recognized by the women after Maria comes and tells them whom they have killed. And thus the drama culminates in the hideously awful irony of its conclusion: Maria's loss of her husband, Jan's of his life, and the loss by the women of the son and brother for whom they have long yearned.

What the play itself most wants to say is voiced at the end by Martha, who, before taking her own life, grimly says to Jan's griefstricken widow, " . . . it's now that we are in the normal order of things." Jan, of course, was a man tragically deluded; he imagined the world to be a place where things "work out." But the normal order of things is one in which nothing ever really works out, and this is why Camus placed at the center of this play what he called an "impossible situation." Such a circumstance he believed to be the most accurate image of what our life in this world most essentially resembles, controlled as it is by what is so frequently nothing more than blind chance. Indeed, Camus' was a sense of reality that conceived the world to which man is condemned to be one so indifferent to his happiness that (as the painter Gauguin once said) "one dreams of revenge."

It is clear, then, that in these works of the 1940's—the

novel *The Stranger* and the plays *Caligula* and *The Mis-understanding*—a distinct vision of human existence was taking form. Undoubtedly, as they have been represented in these brief summaries, they seem to be more didactic than they actually strike us as being. In fact, the novel is a piece of prose fiction, and the plays are extraordinarily gripping works of dramatic art which establish, all three, their meanings in the ways that are proper to the literary imagination—by nuance of implication and shape of plot, by the general pitch and tone of the authorial voice. But for all of what is fascinatingly indirect and roundabout, each in its own nervously tentative way proposes a kind of verdict, a kind of judgment about what, at bottom, is the chief source of man's basic distress—that distress which is the chief hallmark of our common humanity. The work of Camus' early period in which this verdict is most systematically set forth, however, is the little book which Gallimard published in 1943 and which remains a central expression of his genius, *The Myth of Sisyphus*.

The linchpin of Camus' argument in *The Myth of Sisyphus* is the notion of the world's absurdity, and the world is called absurd, because it so persistently frustrates our highest hopes. Camus conceives the great yearning of the human spirit to be for some evidence of the world's being governed by principles of coherence and intelligibility: it hopes to find some point of contact, some essential relationship, between the structure of the human mind and the structure of reality. Man wants to feel that he really *belongs* in the world, that it is his real home, that it is prepared to *answer* the questions he raises about the meaning and purpose of existence. To his dismay, however, what he actually confronts, over and over again, is "the unreasonable silence of the world." As he looks out upon the encompassing reality of the universe, everything seems simply to be *there*—but nothing is explained; things do not dovetail into one another in such a way as to give us any sense of their being established within a pattern of intelligibility and order. The ultimate discouragement derives, of course, from the certainty that we shall die, that our brief span on this earth is controlled by a most "cruel mathematics" which determines that our final destiny shall be the darkness of the grave. So, inevitably, in such a world "man feels [himself] an alien, a stranger. His exile is without remedy. . . ." And human existence appears to be a thing of utter absurdity.

Indeed, it might even seem that self-destruction is the one right response for a man to make to the world as given. And in fact the opening sentence of *The Myth of Sisyphus* says, "There is but one truly serious philosophical problem, and that is suicide." Yet the extreme despair which that sentence appears to be expressing turns out to be not a major emphasis of the book. What Camus most wants to declare is that no real solution to the problem of the Absurd is to be found in suicide, since the man who destroys himself is simply running away from the issue and is in effect accepting defeat. No, if we are not to consent to our humiliation, our choice must be *for* life, not *against* life: what we must learn is how to live *with* absurdity—not submissively but defiantly, without illusions, and with dignity and honor.

Then, having asserted the futility of trying to leap out of the human condition, Camus goes on to hold up for our attention certain styles of life which exemplify the kind of indifference with which we must learn to confront the indifference of the world. He speaks first of Don Juan, the Great Lover, who is a "hero of the absurd" because his intention in going from woman to woman is simply "to use up everything that is given," since nothing has any real significance. He is a "wise man" because, knowing that there is no escape from absurdity, he is simply bent on getting the greatest possible enjoyment out of this present life.

Camus also suggests that the actor offers still another example of "absurd" living. When the actor plays a part on the stage of a theater or before a movie camera, he is projecting a life that is not his own; and in pretending to be what he is not, he bodies forth the truth that the life of the fictitious person whom he is impersonating is no more uncertain than his own.

Camus' third example of *l'homme absurde* is the adventurer or conqueror who, in launching some large program of political or military action, behaves as if the "one useful action" could really be performed, "of remaking man and the earth."

Finally, *The Myth of Sisyphus* proposes that the fourth, and perhaps the greatest, example of man living "in" the Absurd is the artist or the "creator." "If the world were clear, art would not exist," and the artist's persistence in trying to give a kind of order and logic to the world is thus itself only a symptom of the world's absurdity.

These, then, Camus suggests, are the great models of man living amidst the Absurd—Don Juan, the actor, the conqueror, and the artist. They are all symbolized, for Camus, in the ancient figure of Sisyphus, that king of Corinth who, according to Greek mythology, as a punishment for having attempted to conquer death itself, was condemned eternally to roll to the top of a hill in the lower world a huge stone which incessantly rolls back again. It is such an "impossible situation" of which we have an image in the Great Lover who seduces many women but who can never quite reach infinity, or in the artist forever trying to fashion an order out of that which has no order. But Sisyphus is the symbol not only of the seducer and the actor and the conqueror and the artist, but of every man who refuses to consent to the world as it is. He knows that he shall never win his hill, yet he refuses to allow his rock to remain at the bottom of the slope. And, in his dogged perseverance, he embodies the kind of courage which Ernest Hemingway called "grace under pressure"—that grace by which man keeps a stubborn hold on his human dignity in the face of an absurd world. Sisyphus "teaches the higher fidelity that negates the gods and raises rocks. . . ."

As one looks back now on these early works—*The Stranger, The Myth of Sisyphus,* and the plays *Caligula* and *The Misunderstanding*—one feels that, in them, Camus was completing a phase of his thought. Here was a young man who had lived through much of the political and ideological debacle of the 1930's, who had experienced in the early 1940's the terrible havoc imposed upon Europe by the insanity of Nazism, who had lived through the awful humiliation of the French during the years of the Occupation, a young man whose experience of the world had very largely been an experience of violence and destruction and homelessness. And, not finding amidst all this disorder and calamity any confirmation of the great hypotheses of religious faith, he did, therefore, conclude that God is dead and that human life is unsupported by anything good or gracious in the fundamental constitution of reality: ours appeared to be a world in which nothing is at the center—nothing, that is, but Absurdity.

But *The Myth of Sisyphus,* in its tentative explorations of how the Absurd might be resisted, was already looking toward what was to become the second cycle of Camus' meditations. For, from the mid-1940's on, his most basic preoccupation came to be with precisely this issue— namely, with the question as to how, despite the world's absurdity, it might be so resisted as to make possible a decent life for mankind. This concern unified all his work during his last fifteen years and, in this second phase of his career, found its first important expression in his *Lettres à un ami allemand (Letters to a German Friend)*, which Gallimard published in 1945.

These letters to a young German whom Camus had known before the war were composed at various intervals between July of 1943 and July 1944. Here he is recalling that in the prewar period they were indeed at one in their shared conviction that there was nothing but emptiness and absurdity at the heart of the world. This being the case, for a time he found it impossible, as he also recalls, to summon any effective rebuttal when his friend, along with his fellow Germans, began to embrace the furiously anti-human politics of Nazism as a way of giving a meaning to human life. No, says Camus, "I . . . saw no valid argument to answer you"—none except "a fierce love of justice which, after all, seemed to me as unreasonable as the most sudden passion." His position was something like Cherea's in *Caligula*: the Roman nobleman had been unable to refute the Emperor's philosophy which seemed "logical from start to finish," and yet he could not bring himself to accept a doctrine whose only consequence was corpses. Which was precisely where Camus found himself in relation to the new religion of Nazism, as he candidly admits in the *Letters*. "For a long time," he says to his young German friend, "we both thought that this world had no ultimate meaning. . . ." And of this he is still convinced. Yet, he now declares, there is surely one affirmation that must be made: that "This world has at least the truth of man, and our task is to provide its justifications against fate itself."

Camus was here saying, in other words, that, though the Absurd must be resisted, our *method* of resistance must not be allowed to become something whose final effect is that of betraying man himself—which was the immense tragedy involved in the whole experiment of Nazism. Hitler's program may initially have been a kind of rebellion against the Absurd, against the sheer meaninglessness of life in the modern world. But because of its cynicism and unbridled violence, this rebellion against the Absurd became finally a revolt against man himself. "If nothing had any meaning," said Camus in the second of the *Letters*, "you would be right. But there is something that still has a meaning"—namely, the dignity of man. And this we must be *for*, not *against*; to adopt any other position is in effect to have decided to cooperate with the Absurd, and to accept man's defeat.

It is such ideas as these that are at the center of Camus' moving novel of 1947, *The Plague*. Its setting is the Algerian coast town of Oran, whose inhabitants are fearfully beset for almost an entire year by a murderous siege of bubonic plague. The epigraph which Camus chose for the novel is drawn from the English writer of the eighteenth century Daniel Defoe: "It is as reasonable to represent one kind of imprisonment by another, as it is to represent anything that really exists by that which exists not." These words immediately make clear Camus' intention that we should read the book as an allegory, and so indeed it proves itself to be. For the plague is an image of the irrational brutality of the Absurd itself, of everything that twists and badgers and crucifies the human spirit in a cruelly indifferent world.

Each character in the novel represents a distinct mode of response to the crisis. The leading physician in the town, Bernard Rieux— who, it finally appears, is the narrator of the story—throws all his energies into the organization of the "sanitary squads" that battle the epidemic: he simply knows that "there are sick people and they need curing." His one certitude is that "a fight must be put up . ¨ and there must be no bowing down. The essential thing was to save the greatest possible number of persons from dying and being doomed to unending separation." His closest associate in the struggle is Jean Tarrou, a veteran of revolutionary movements, who has grown disillusioned with the frequently unscrupulous tactics of the radical Left. He now sees that moral issues are never so simple and clear-cut as he had once assumed, that "each of us has the plague within him. . . ." So he has come to choose what he calls "the path of sympathy"— to follow which may be, he suspects, to learn "how to become a saint . . . without God." And, as the disastrous emergency wears on month after month, with an ever larger toll of victims, the various other characters illustrate one or another attitude of profiteering on the crisis, of cooperating with the scourge, or of resistance.

If there is anything at all that the novel wants to reject, it is the traditional Christian attitude—the acceptance of suffering as a divinely administered punishment for sin and as a fitting part of an eternal order in which all things somehow finally work together for good. This is the point of view represented by the priest, Father Paneloux, whom Rieux rails against for using his pulpit to advocate resignation to calamity. Yet, finally, Rieux, limited as his sympathy is for the faith of the priest, appears to feel the inappropriateness of heckling him, caught up as they all are by the fury of the plague. After they have shared the anguish of standing together at the deathbed of the police commissioner's little boy, the physician acknowledges that they are "allies"—"working side by side for something that unites us—beyond blasphemy and prayers." In such a common effort as that in which Rieux and Father Paneloux are engaged, the novel finds its moral center—the healing of what is broken in human life, the defense of men against the powers of darkness.

Rieux, however, remarks at a certain point to the jour-

nalist Rambert, "There's no question of heroism in all
this. It's a matter of common decency"—a matter, as he
says, of simply doing one's job. And it is such a renunciation
of all moral pretentiousness that is consistently conveyed
by the predominant tone of *The Plague*. Rieux tells Tarrou one night that heroism doesn't really appeal to him,
and they both take it for granted that fighting plagues
is "everybody's business." Indeed, the novel rather whim-
sically at one point designates its real "hero" as Joseph
Grand, a little clerk in Oran's municipal office whose job
during the crisis becomes that of keeping a careful statis-
tical record of the epidemic's progress; though only the
tiniest cog in the machinery that has been brought into
existence to fight the pestilence, in the conscientiousness
with which he performs his assigned role he is as involved
as anyone else in the great action of *résistance*.

This, the novel is proposing, is the central effort to
which all men are summoned. Camus is saying, in other
words, that we live in a strange and incomprehensible
world which is brutally indifferent to human life, a world
which in all likelihood we cannot alter very much. But at
least we can refuse to join forces with it, at least we can
choose to be *for* man and *against* whatever would bring
distress and humiliation to our brothers. And when this
is what we commit ourselves to, then we have, in effect,
chosen to *resist* the world's absurdity. It is not a question
of heroism, but simply a matter of common decency.

The Plague is today perhaps the most widely cherished
of all Camus' books, the one, no doubt, which we have
most immediately in mind when we begin to think of his
career. It is a book which occupies a very important
place in the total body of his work, for it was this novel,
when it appeared in 1947, that made clear, even more
emphatically than did the *Letters to a German Friend*,
that a profound change had occurred in the basic direc-

tion of his thought. The young author of *The Stranger* and *The Myth of Sisyphus*, of *Caligula* and *The Misunderstanding*, was a writer whose work had, at the center of its major impact, a vision of the world as absurd; and the essential emphasis represented a tragic pessimism of the most extreme sort. But with the appearance of *The Plague*, one could see that Camus was beginning to say that there is something more important, something more ultimate even, than the Absurd—namely, the human spirit itself. And he was also wanting to define man's principal obligation as being that of *resisting* whatever it may be in the world which imperils or threatens to assault our common humanity.

It is in this way, then, that *The Plague* may be seen now as anticipating his brilliant book of 1951, *L'Homme révolté (The Rebel)*, in which he undertook to trace out the history of the idea of "resistance" or "rebellion" in modern thought. Here Camus suggests that perhaps the purest example of rebellion is to be found in the "slave who has taken orders all his life [and who] suddenly decides that he cannot obey some new command." For when he stands up to say, " 'This you shall not do,' " he is saying "that there is something in him which 'is worth while . . .' and which must be taken into consideration": he is saying that for him *now* to bow down would be for him to commit blasphemy against that in himself which is the very essence of his manhood. So he acts "in the name of certain values . . . which he feels are common to himself and to all men. . . . It is for the sake of everyone in the world that the slave asserts himself when he comes to the conclusion that a command has infringed on something in him which does not belong to him alone, but which is common ground where all men—even the man who insults and oppresses him—have a natural community." In short, rebellion "goes far beyond [mere] resentment," for it reveals "the part of man which must always be defended," and thus it reveals how deeply the fate of mankind is at stake in the fate of the individual.

As Camus looked back, however, on the various ways in which the idea of rebellion has been conceived in the modern period, he was troubled by the frequency with which its interpreters have failed to perceive that it must itself be held under some principle of criticism if the rebel is to be kept from becoming simply intoxicated with rebellion in and for its own sake alone. Karl Marx, for example, and his various descendants in the tradition of Communist thought form one major line in the history of modern rebellion. And here one encounters a type of rebellion which is based on the assumption that God is dead, that history is therefore to be "written" in terms of the sheer manipulation of power, and that the revolutionary is entitled to do *anything* that promises to hasten the coming of a "classless society." But once the rebel gives himself the right to do *anything* for the sake of advancing his program, he surrenders any guarantee that a rebellion initiated *for* man shall in fact remain so dedicated. This is precisely the tragic irony that Camus considered the history of Russian socialism to exemplify, that what was initially a dream of absolute justice was turned, under Stalin, into a demonic fanaticism utterly destructive of all humane values—because a program of rebellion was not itself constantly held under criticism.

Now it is by the term *mesure* (meaning "limit" or "measure" or "moderation") that Camus designates that principle to which the rebel is to be held accountable. And his meaning was simply that any program of rebellion must always be "limited" by the understanding that the rebel's goal can never be *total* freedom, for the exercise of *my* freedom can never be valid if it destroys my neighbor's freedom: just here, in other words, is the "limit" beyond which rebellion must not trespass—"the limit being precisely . . . [my neighbor's] power to rebel. . . ." The freedom I claim for myself I must claim for all; the freedom I refuse, I forbid all other men to exercise. It is only in this way that I can manage to reject not only the condition of slavery for myself but the very structure of life in which master-slave relationships are possible. And it is only through the strict observance of such a *mesure*, of such a "limit," that rebellion or resistance stands any good chance of keeping faith with the human community and of redeeming it from the power of the Absurd.

Now the kind of concern to hold rebellion under the judgment of *mesure* which is so much at the heart of *The Rebel* is also the basic preoccupation being expressed in the plays which Camus was producing in the same period—*L'État de siège* (*State of Siege, 1948*) and *Les Justes (The Just, 1950)*: these are plays which dramatize the themes of his book of 1951, just as *Caligula* and *The Misunderstanding* had dramatized the central themes of *The Myth of Sisyphus*.

State of Siege, which was staged by Jean-Louis Barrault at the Théâtre Marigny in Paris in the autumn of 1948, never achieved the kind of large popular success that *Caligula* had enjoyed, perhaps because of its heavily allegorical character. Its setting is the Spanish city of Cadiz, which is beset by a deadly plague whose spirit Camus chose to put directly on his stage in the person of one bearing as his name "the Plague." This sinister personage appears shortly after the epidemic gets under way, accompanied by a young woman who is his secretary. Immediately he sets to work, directing his assistant to compile lists of the townspeople: no sooner does he order her to check off a name than the thud of the victim's falling body is heard. The Plague says:

> . . . from today you are going to learn to die in an orderly manner. Until now you died in the Spanish manner, haphazard—when you felt like it, so to say. . . . I shall impose

order on all that. There will be no more dying as the fancy
takes you. Lists will be kept . . . and we shall fix the order
of your going.

The Plague's great dream is of a total annihilation, since
Nothing "is the only thing that exists."

At last, however, the forces of revolt are rallied by the
young medical student Diego, who is filled with disgust
at the obscene wantonness with which human life is being
destroyed. He flings his anger into the face of the Plague's
secretary—and she, beginning herself to be repelled by the
endless assassinations, confides that the Plague's whole
system

 . . . has a weak point. . . . As far back as I can remember
 the machine has always shown a tendency to break down
 when a man conquers his fear. . . . I won't say it stops
 completely. But it creaks and sometimes it actually begins
 to fold up.

Once, in other words, a man has conquered his fear the
Plague can no longer get at him: then, even if his name is
scratched off the Plague's list, the thud of his falling body
will not be heard.

With new confidence now, Diego proceeds to organize
his fellow townsmen for revolt. In their scene of confrontation, the Plague offers Diego his fiancée in exchange
for the town: "I'll give you that girl's life and let you *both*
escape, provided you let me make my own terms with this
city. . . . No one can be happy without causing harm to
others. That is the world's justice." But it is a bargain that
Diego refuses: he will not purchase his private happiness
at the expense of the city's enslavement: he will make no
compromise with the "world's justice"—which is no
justice at all. He chooses to remain faithful to "the truth
of man": this is the supreme *mesure* which he will not
transgress by allowing his revolt to turn into a betrayal of
his fellowmen. And thus Camus appears to be offering

Diego as an example of the kind of integrity which he is pleading for in the closing pages of *The Rebel*.

Much the same kind of preoccupation with the ethics of revolt is also expressed in *The Just*, the stirring play which Camus based on that little group of Russian terrorists who assassinated the Grand Duke Sergei Alexandrovitch in Moscow in 1905. These socialist revolutionaries were people for whom Camus long kept a very great admiration. "The men of 1905," as he called them, were, as he said in *The Rebel, meurtriers délicats;* and he called them "fastidious assassins" because they so thoroughly despised bombs and revolvers, because they so profoundly regretted the methods they had to use in order to unsettle the foundations of Czarist Russia. It is a comparable fastidiousness which marks the acts of the conspirators in *The Just*—when they postpone by a day their assassination of the Grand Duke upon discovering that the carriage into which the bomb is to be tossed also has among its occupants the Grand Duke's little niece and nephew. Kaliayev, who is to perform the deed, says:

> Killing children is a crime against a man's honor. And if one day the revolution thinks fit to break with honor, well, I'm through with the revolution.

He refuses, in other words, to betray his sense of the sacredness of the human presence, merely for the sake of an uncertain and unknown future. "I can see the vileness in myself . . . I've got to kill—there are no two ways about it. But . . . I shall go beyond hatred." And thus, again, we are given what Camus intended to be an image of fidelity to the idea of *mesure*, to that "strange form of love" apart from which there can be no true rebellion.

That cycle of his work, then, which was formed by *The Plague* and *The Rebel*, and by the two plays *State of Siege* and *The Just*, clearly indicates that Camus was steadily moving beyond the chilling despair expressed in many of

his early writings. This is to be felt with especial force
in the lyrical essays he published in 1954 under the title
L'Été (*Summer*). In the essay called "Return to Tipasa"
there is a passage which epitomizes the spirit of the entire
book and what was increasingly the spirit of Camus'
general outlook in his last years. He says:

> At noon, on the half-sandy slopes, strewn with heliotropes
> like a foam that the furious waves of the last few days had
> left behind in their retreat, I gazed at the sea, gently rising
> and falling as if exhausted, and quenched two thirsts that
> cannot be long neglected if all one's being is not to dry up,
> the thirst to love and the thirst to admire. For there is only
> misfortune in not being loved: there is misery in not loving.
> All of us, today, are dying of this misery. This is because
> blood and hatred lay bare the heart itself; the long demand
> for justice exhausts even the love that gave it birth. In the
> clamor we live in, love is impossible and justice not enough.
> That is why Europe hates the daylight and can do nothing but
> confront one injustice with another. In order to prevent
> justice from shriveling up, from becoming nothing but a
> magnificent orange with a dry, bitter pulp, I discovered one
> must keep a freshness and a source of joy intact within,
> loving the daylight that injustice leaves unscathed, and re-
> turning to the fray with this light as a trophy. . . . In the
> depths of winter, I finally learned that within me there lay
> an invincible summer.

Apart from the political criticism he continued to publish
through the 1950's in the second and third volumes of
Actuelles (II, 1953; III, 1958), Camus' principal publications in his last years were the novel of 1956, *La Chute*
(*The Fall*), and the collection of short stories, *L'Exil et le
royaume* (*Exile and the Kingdom*), which appeared in
1957. There is a considerable variety of style and structure in the stories, and they recapitulate many of the
themes which are present in Camus' earlier work. But,
throughout, the quickness with which fictional narrative is
elevated to the level of parable tends to give these stories a

kind of thin, rarefied abstractness which keeps them from being very impressive pieces of work. *The Fall* is, however, despite its brevity, a major book—but one which may seem to suggest that Camus had somehow lost that "invincible summer" which he had earlier found in himself, and this has indeed been the verdict offered (somewhat mistakenly) by some of his critics.

The novel's protagonist, Jean-Baptiste Clamence, now living in Amsterdam, in earlier years had had a brilliant career as a lawyer in Paris, where he had spent much of his time defending the poor and the friendless. But, as he tells an unnamed acquaintance whom he meets in an Amsterdam bar, he was walking along the banks of the Seine one evening when, all of a sudden, he heard a drowning woman's cry for help coming from somewhere in the darkness. He ignored the appeal. And this act of cowardice destroyed him, for thereafter his life was broken by the sense that all along he had really been a fraud, that his charities had been calculated simply to give himself a sense of moral superiority, and his whole style of living had been something essentially vain and hollow and hypocritical. So he became what he calls a "judge-penitent," which is to say that the more he accuses himself, the more (he now believes) he has the right to convict other men of falseness and deceit and bad faith; the guilt he finds in his own heart he enjoys finding also in his fellowmen. Indeed, the novel—written in the form of Jean-Baptiste's "confession"—is very largely given over to a caustic, bitter indictment of man, of his capacity for truth and justice and decency and honor. So Camus' less careful readers, too quickly assuming Jean-Baptiste to be his direct spokesman, have sometimes quite failed to perceive the depth of his irony, and have concluded that he was himself moving toward a very bleak and pessimistic view of the human soul.

But among the many passages in the book which give Jean-Baptiste away there is one that ought most especially to be noted: he says:

> With me there is no giving of absolution or blessing. Everything is simply totted up, and then: "It comes to so much. You are an evildoer, a satyr, a congenital liar, a homosexual, an artist, etc." Just like that. Just as flatly. In philosophy as in politics, I am for any theory that refuses to grant man innocence and for any practice that treats him as guilty. You see in me, *très cher*, an enlightened advocate of slavery.

And this is precisely what Clamence is—an advocate of slavery. For he uses his doctrine of universal sin as a kind of club with which to bully people into a sense of their unworthiness. But, as he quite candidly says, "I navigate skillfully . . . in short, I adapt my words to my listener and lead him to go me one better." Which is his way of admitting that he is careful always to come out better than the other fellow: one must, he says, "permit oneself everything, even if, from time to time, one has to profess vociferously one's own infamy." But one cannot "permit oneself everything" and, at the same time, hold oneself accountable to any kind of *mesure*. And thus, as no one should ever have failed to perceive, Jean-Baptiste, far from being a direct spokesman for Camus himself, represents an attitude of mind that is absolutely opposed to what Camus conceived to be the disposition of the true rebel. In Clamence we have a memorable image of the absolute contradiction of everything Camus most wanted to speak out for in his last years; and thus *The Fall*, in a negative way, completes the circle of definition he was drawing in the 1950's about the idea of resistance.

Shortly before his death in January of 1960, Camus had remarked: "I have done nothing yet; my work is ahead of me." And it was said that he was then at work on a vast novel which was to be called *Le premier homme* (*The Foremost Man*) and on a long essay to be called *Le Mythe de Némésis* (*The Myth of Nemesis*). But though he was only in mid-career and though much of his work was doubtless still ahead of him, he had yet managed in the years that were allotted him to produce—in four volumes of fiction, in the plays, in his essays, and most especially in his great book *The Rebel*—a body of testimony that requires us to think of him today as one of the great spokesmen for the human spirit in this century. For here was a writer who did, indeed, use all his remarkable gifts to create for the men and women of his time an "image of our common joys and woes"—and who, as a consequence, is today thought of as one who helps us all to find an "invincible summer" amidst the doubts and uncertainties of our troubled age. A French critic once said of *The Stranger:* "If, a few centuries from now, only this short tale were left as witness to what man is today, it would be enough to give a fair image of what we are." But this is a remark that might be extended to cover Camus' work as a whole—and there is perhaps only a handful of twentieth-century writers of whom something like this could be said.

6

Jean-Paul Sartre—
Advocate of
"Responsibility in Solitude"

So SUDDENLY did Jean-Paul Sartre win an international reputation in the 1940's that one could almost name the very month and day in the winter of 1947 when the ideas and writings of this extraordinary Frenchman began all at once to dominate the pages of *The Nation* and *The New Republic* and the *Partisan Review* and the various other journals which young people of the time depended on for news of the latest developments in cultural life. In the big slicks and the Sunday supplements one constantly came across photographs of this thick-set little man, with his badly crossed but lively eyes squinting out at the reader through the clouds of smoke rising up from his pipe or cigarette. And wherever one was, it seemed, the people one talked to did, sooner or later, either venture or solicit an opinion about the playwright of *Huis clos* (*No Exit*) or the novelist of *L'Âge de raison* (*The Age of Reason*) or the philosopher of *L'Être et le néant* (*Being and Nothingness*). All across the country there was great exhilaration over the close of the war and, as the lines of communication with European intellectual life were being once again opened up, nothing quite caught the American imagination so much as this survivor of the French Resistance who, now that his people were liberated from the Nazi tyranny, besides editing the most exciting journal in Paris—*Les Temps Modernes (Modern Times)*— was producing plays and novels and philosophical treatises and political pamphlets and, in a spirit of absolute dedication and seriousness, throwing himself into the reconstruction of France.

In those years he was always thought and spoken of in connection with his friend Albert Camus (from whom he later became estranged) and the lady who was his constant companion, Simone de Beauvoir, herself also a novelist and philosopher and social critic. It was these three together—"bohemians" in their style of life, and leftists in their political allegiances—who appeared to be the very type and example of that new breed of French intellectual whose impassioned insistence on the absurdity of the human condition was summoning forth the revolutionary philosophic and literary movement called Existentialism. To be sure, the movement had other sources on the French scene—for example, the distinguished academic philosopher Jean Wahl; the Russian *émigrés* Leon Shestov and Nicolas Berdyaev; the Roman Catholic thinker Gabriel Marcel; the critic and man of letters Georges Bataille. But in the 1940's it was Camus and Mlle. de Beauvoir and most especially Sartre who seemed to be the principal exemplars of the new radicalism, and overnight they precipitated one of the major cultural episodes of the period. One heard of riots provoked in Paris by Sartre's public lectures, and it seemed that the pronouncements of this man on nausea and anxiety and despair as the fundamental elements of human experience were being felt by the French to be more important even than the uncertain actions of their politicians. So, as the

publishing firms of Alfred Knopf and James Laughlin
(New Directions) began to bring out English translations
of Sartre's books, each new volume was awaited impa-
tiently by young people in Cambridge and Chicago and
San Francisco and all across the nation.

Thirty years have now gone by, however, and, inevitably, new luminaries have appeared who compete for
our attention. Nevertheless, today it is clear how far off
the mark was a certain American critic whose first irri-
tated response to French Existentialism in the late 1940's
was the suggestion that it was something like an insult-
ing letter which arrives on a given morning and which, if
not answered the same day, need not be answered at all.
Certainly Sartre himself still demands to be reckoned
with, perhaps even more urgently now than three decades
ago. For now it is, with the subsidence of all the fierce
partisanship and hot commotion of that earlier time, that
we can truly see the author of *Nausea* and *Being and
Nothingness* and *No Exit* to be not only one of the great
intellectuals of France in this century, but one who has
added something permanent to the furniture of the modern imagination. He stands today, in other words, as a
great commanding presence on the contemporary scene:
not a "wise man" perhaps, for wisdom may not strike us
as his primary quality, but an audacious experimentalist
in ideas, a brilliant *provocateur*, who, like Nietzsche before him, dares to arraign the conscience of the age before the bar of his own vision—of the danger that is in our
streets and the terror that is in our hearts.

Sartre has produced one essay in autobiography, the
book of 1964 called *Les Mots (The Words)*, which presents a fascinating account of the early years of his life.
And in one sentence he quickly sums up what is undoubtedly one of the central facts of his existence, when he

says, "I began my life as I shall no doubt end it: amidst books."

He was born in Paris on the twenty-first of June, 1905, the first child of a young middle-class couple who had been married in the preceding year. His mother, Anne-Marie Schweitzer, was a member of an Alsatian Protestant family to one branch of which belonged the eminent musician-theologian and medical missionary to French Equatorial Africa, Albert Schweitzer. His father, Jean-Baptiste Sartre, after graduating from the famous École Polytechnique, chose the navy as a career. But only two years after little Jean-Paul's birth the young naval officer died prematurely of a fever he had contracted in Indo-China, whereupon Anne-Marie and her child took up residence with her parents, first in Meudon and subsequently in Paris. And her father, Charles Schweitzer, in order to support his daughter and grandchild, came out of retirement and resumed his teaching of foreign languages.

Grandfather Schweitzer, says Sartre, "so resembled God the Father that he was often taken for Him. . . . The fact is, he slightly overdid the sublime. He was a man of the nineteenth century who took himself for Victor Hugo" and who, in his florid theatricality, enjoyed striking heroic poses. Though he had dealt harshly with his own sons, he adored Anne-Marie's little boy and in all their relations together played the role of the benevolent and indulgent paterfamilias. "He would call me," Sartre relates, "his 'tiny little one' in a voice quavering with tenderness. . . . He would lift me from the ground, raise me to the skies, at arm's length, bring me down upon his heart, murmuring: 'My precious!'. . . . He would display the sublime, artless vanity that befits grandfathers, the blindness, the guilty weaknesses recommended by Hugo. If I had been put on bread and water, he would have brought me jam. . . ." But though Sartre speaks always of his grandfather with ironical condescension, he admits, nevertheless, as he looks back on those early years, that it was all "a riot of generosity. . . . It was Paradise. Every morning I woke up dazed with joy. . . . A kiss without a moustache, as was said at the time, is like an egg without salt; I add: and like Good without Evil, like my life from 1905 to 1914."

His early education was largely a hit-and-miss affair, partly self-administered amongst the vast hoard of books that spilled into every corner of his grandfather's house. Here it was that he read Corneille and Goethe, Chateaubriand and Hugo, de Maupassant and Flaubert: "I was a miniature adult and read books written for adults." "It was in books that I encountered the universe . . . and I confused the disorder of my bookish experiences with the random course of real events. From that came the idealism which it took me thirty years to shake off."

When the boy was eleven years of age his mother was remarried, again to one who was a graduate of the École Polytechnique, and who was then the superintendent of the naval yards in the seaport city of La Rochelle. Here, at the local *lycée* (a secondary school preparing students for the university—the French equivalent of the German *Gymnasium*), Jean-Paul, though frequently fractious and turbulent in his conduct, excelled in his studies and early distinguished himself as a brilliant pupil. But in the early 1920's Sartre's mother and stepfather, with misgivings about the wholesomeness of the ties which had developed between the boy and his youthful cronies in La Rochelle and wanting him to have a more stimulating school environment, returned him to Paris, where he began to prepare for the highly competitive examinations prerequisite to admission to the École Normale Supérieure. He was matriculated at this renowned academy in 1924, at the age of nineteen, and four years later sat for the competitive state examination, the *agrégation* (for him, in the field of philosophy), which is required for those wishing to teach in a *lycée*. Apparently his preparatory studies had not been sufficiently rigorous, for his papers were not adjudged satisfactory—which was not itself extraordinary, since the majority of the candidates normally fail this notoriously arduous examination. But when he sat again in the following year he came through with flying colors, with the rank of first *agrégé* in France for the year, in philosophy.

After a brief interlude of military service at Tours, where he served as a meteorological clerk, he was appointed a *professeur de lycée* and began his teaching at Le Havre, where—with the exception of the year '33-'34 which he spent at the Institut Français in Berlin—he remained until 1936. Here, the distaste for life in a French provincial town which he had first developed as a boy in La Rochelle was felt again and even more intensely because, set down as he was amidst the dreariness of this seaport town, he was now separated from Simone de Beauvoir, with whom he had fallen in love while they were students together at the École Normale in Paris and who had stood second only to him in the examination for the *agrégation* in philosophy in 1929. She had begun her own teaching in Rouen, a city which, as she tells us in her autobiography of 1960, *La Force de l'âge (The Prime of Life)*, she found to be quite as depressing as Sartre was finding Le Havre to be. But Rouen and Le Havre were barely more than fifty miles apart, and they could have weekends together and see each other with a fair amount of frequency. From this period in the early 1930's until the present time each has been the principal companion of the other's life; but, having early agreed that marriage was a "bourgeois" arrangement and having never

had children, they have chosen not to be formally united
as husband and wife. As Mlle. de Beauvoir has said (in
The Prime of Life) of their early years together,

> . . . we put our trust in the world, and in ourselves. Soci-
> ety as then constituted we opposed. But there was nothing
> sour about this enmity: it carried an implication of robust
> optimism. Man was to be remolded, and the process would
> be partly our doing. We did not envisage contributing to
> this change except by way of books: public affairs bored us.
> We counted on events turning out according to our wishes
> without any need for us to mix in them personally. . . .
> We had no external limitations, no overriding authority,
> no imposed pattern of existence. We created our own links
> with the world, and freedom was the very essence of our
> existence.

Yet, for all this early indifference toward the world of public
affairs, they were both to develop intense political commitments as Hitler's Germany began to loom ever more menac-
ingly on the European horizon in the late 1930's, and today
they are notable in France for the passionateness with
which they insist upon the obligation of intellectuals to enter the arena of politics.

But though these two were periodically enjoying the
careless rapture of lovers' holidays in these years, they
were all the while intensely hard at work, and most especially Sartre. In 1936 he published his first philosophical
work, *L'Imagination (The Imagination)*: and in 1939 his
book *Esquisse d'une théorie des émotions (Outline of a
Theory of the Emotions)* appeared. In 1938 Gallimard
brought out his first novel, *La Nausée (Nausea)*, which
was followed in the next year by a collection of his stories,
Le Mur (The Wall). And he was deeply engaged in the
studies that were to eventuate in 1943 in what is still the
magnum opus of his career as a philosopher, the great
book entitled *Being and Nothingness*.

After spending the year 1936-1937 as professor of philosophy in the Lycée at Laon, he accepted a similar appointment in 1937 at the Lycée Pasteur in Neuilly, a suburb of Paris, which enabled him at last to put the provinces behind him and to return to the beloved city of his birth where he has resided ever since.

The war years brought the same anguish and distraction from creative work to Sartre that they brought to other loyal Frenchmen. After the general call-up, he was drafted back into the meteorological service. In the summer of 1940 he was taken prisoner by the Nazis, but within a few months, by medically faking an extreme vertigo, he managed to hoodwink the Germans into releasing him for reasons of ill health. He thereupon returned to Paris and joined the underground Resistance movement, undertaking numerous writing assignments for its various clandestine publications. In 1941 he resumed his teaching, this time at the Lycée Condorcet in Paris, on whose faculty he remained until 1944.

Sartre has often spoken of how very nearly intolerable he finds any day to be in the course of which he has no opportunity to do a substantial amount of writing. And somehow, despite all the difficulties that were daily a part of life in France during the years of the Nazi Occupation, he appears to have continued, however intermittently, with his literary projects. Indeed, it was the production in 1943, a year before the Liberation, of a new play, *Les Mouches (The Flies)*, which first established his French reputation. The play presents a revised version of that ancient fable of Orestes on which Aeschylus based his famous trilogy, the *Oresteia*. As in the Aeschylean account, Clytemnestra, the Queen of Argos, has murdered the King, Agamemnon, and has married Aegisthus, who has usurped the throne and who now rules tyrannously over the people. At last, into this unhappy kingdom comes Orestes, Clytemnestra's son, who has been living in exile and whose mission is to avenge his father's murder. But, beyond this, Sartre's story entails a very radical transformation of the Aeschylean fable. The young prince finds the city of Argos to be overrun with swarms of flies which hold the people under the grip of a mysterious plague, an affliction which appears to be only an outward sign of the moral disintegration at the heart of the city's life. Orestes also finds the people to be obsessed with their past sins and with their own guilt, the careful cultivation of this obsession having been the tactic Aegisthus has used to bully them into submission to his tyranny. So Orestes undertakes to do something worse than any of the crimes the Argives believe themselves to have committed: as a protest against the injustice of the gods and in behalf of his dead father, he slays his mother and her evil consort. By these deeds he draws upon himself the avenging flies and thus liberates the people of Argos from the tribulation which has beset them. The entire design of the play would seem very clearly in part to have been intended to present, through its protagonist, an example of resistance and thus to offer a kind of encouragement to the Resistance movement in Vichy France. It is, therefore, astonishing that the Nazi censors permitted its production in Paris in the summer of 1943: perhaps the only explanation to be given of this remarkable oversight is that, normally, the censor is an imbecile. The Germans did, of course, finally discern the powerful subversiveness of the play, and thus after a series of initial performances it was banned. But by that time its impact had been felt: it had created a sensation, and Sartre was famous overnight.

In 1944 he withdrew from teaching altogether, in order to devote himself wholly to his writing, and he has never since resumed a professorial vocation. By that time he was, amongst young people, the most honored figure in French intellectual life. He lived in the Louisiana, a small hotel on the Rue de Seine, and he and Simone de Beauvoir did their writing each day in a little café (the Café de Flore) on the Boulevard Saint-Germain to which all sorts of people flocked in the afternoons—young writers wanting encouragement and evaluation of their manuscripts, students from the Sorbonne, bohemians of the Left Bank, visitors from abroad, journalists wanting an interview, and a host of others. The atmosphere was gay, intense, and filled with a great sense of importance, as the attendants listened to this ugly and charming little man talk in his captivating and brilliant way about his vision of the human voyager as one flung into an absurd world through which he must pick his perilous course—in anguish, and with unfaltering courage.

Once Paris was liberated, in the summer of 1944, with the glorious entry into the city of the Allied forces on the twenty-third of August, Sartre and his friends were deeply touched by the profound sense of relief and the great unshackling of hope that were felt throughout France. Now at last ideas could once again circulate without restraint in a climate of freedom; and, with the humiliation of 1940 behind them, men of vision and vigor could tackle the work of renovation, expectantly looking toward a new age of recovery and advance. Sartre's prestige was, of course, immense, and he became a central figure in the debates and controversies of postwar politics. His great hope was that France could find its internal stability in a genuine people's democracy whose foundation would be a leftist movement independent of the Communist Party, unaligned with either the East or the West, with either the Soviet Union or the United States. And it was toward this end that he helped to found the R.D.R. (*Rassemblement Démocratique Révolutionnaire* [the Democratic Revolutionary Rally]). The R.D.R. never managed to become a

decisive force in French politics, however, and it was Sartre's gradual disillusionment with the possibility of gal-
vanizing the non-Communist left into an effective party
that led him, increasingly in the late 1940's, to feel that it
was with the Communist Party itself that leftists must
make their peace if they were to remain identified with
the working classes. It was this reconcilement with Communism which his friend Albert Camus could not accept
and which finally brought their friendship to an abrupt
end in 1950, as it also ruptured many of Sartre's relations
with other old associates. But, despite the mistrust with
which he has always been regarded amongst theoreticians
of the Communist Party itself and despite his profound
disagreement with many aspects of Communist ideology,
his conviction has steadily deepened over these past decades that, in regarding the fundamental conditions of
work as one of the great primary realities of cultural life,
Marxism proves itself to have a profound grasp of the
nature of history. As he says in his last major philosophical treatise, the book of 1960 called *Critique de la raison
dialectique (Critique of Dialectical Reason)*, Marxism is
an "unsurpassable philosophy" that defines the climate
within which social and political thought must partly be
undertaken in our time. And his strictures against the
Soviet Union are prompted by his sense of how greatly
its own cynical amoralism often betrays what he conceives
to be the genuine humanism of classical Marxist theory.

Yet, for all the sharpness with which Sartre has occasionally denounced the Soviet Union since the Hungarian
tragedy of 1956, it would seem that, in facing the politics
of the Cold War and the bitter divisions between East
and West, his hostility toward the "reactionary" and
"bourgeois" values of the West has led him to reserve a
system of weights and measures for America and Western
Europe more exacting and severe than that he applies to

Russian Communism. And it is no doubt this partisanship that accounts for the heckling that has been directed at him in recent years by many of his American critics. But, whatever may be the extent of his prejudice and blindness, his political judgments and allegiances have never been governed by any kind of personal ambitiousness or opportunism. He is a man who has been deeply engaged by the great emergencies of modern politics and culture and who, whether right or wrong, has offered his own testimony with a passion and courage that will at least forever exempt him from that region of Hell which, in Dante's account, is reserved for the most contemptible—namely, the lukewarm. He is in fact, as the French would say, one of the great *directeurs de conscience* of our period, and one who occupies a focal place in the particular design of thought to which this book is devoted, for it is Sartre who is the most radical representative on the contemporary scene of that strain of existentialist thought which principally descends from Nietzsche. In Camus, the Nietzschean sense of the emptiness following upon the death of God is appropriated in such a way that it becomes a challenge to preserve man's dignity by achieving a decent *mesure*, and thus the result is a warmly affirmative kind of humanism. But, in Sartre, the sense of nothingness astir in the world, though felt to present a challenge to the moral imagination, remains an implacably blighting reality of human existence which nothing can finally assuage, and thus his is an Existentialism far more absolute than Camus'. He is, in short, a very hard taskmaster who refuses to be put off by anything bearing even the faintest resemblance to "positive thinking."

In the lively debate which Sartre's critics have carried on about the meaning of his work, one of the most frequently recurring issues concerns what his endeavor most

essentially has been. He is, of course, one of the most pro-
lific writers of this century; the body of work which he
has produced in drama, fiction, and philosophy is so vast
that his accomplishment in any of these fields alone might
be regarded as already the labor of a lifetime. So the
question is raised again and again as to whether he is a
philosopher who has used the media of fiction and the
theater to flesh out a speculative system, or an artist
whose explorations of concrete experience have driven
him into the thickets of theoretical thought. The answers
that are given tend to be so mutually contradictory, however, that no consensus yet appears to have emerged.
But, in the basic style of vision it expresses, Sartre's work
is so much all of a piece that it may well be that the question as to which he is, philosopher or literary artist, is of
no real importance. What perhaps deserves to be most remarked is simply that here is a writer who is immensely
compelling in the force and brilliance of his ideas, and so
prodigiously talented that, whether as novelist or playwright or philosopher, he can seize reality in ways that
permit him at once to render an arresting account of human experience and to remain perfectly consistent with
his own basic outlook.

However this issue may finally require to be adjudi-
cated, the book which gives us the most immediate access to the central themes of Sartre's thought is neither
one of his plays nor one of the formal philosophical treatises but a novel, the book of 1938 called *Nausea*. And it
is with this text that any brief review of his work properly begins.

Nausea, in its form, is something like the kind of novel
the French call a *récit*, for it is the recital, or even a kind
of diary, of one Antoine Roquentin, a bachelor of thirty
years of age who has an independent income and who,
after extensive travels in North Africa and the Far East

and Central Europe, retires in the year 1932 to the little town of Bouville-sur-Mer to complete a project of scholarship. He is apparently without family connections or ties of friendship, a man of virtually no affiliations except his commitment to the research in which he specializes as a professionally trained historian. So he is quite free to settle into a dingy little room in Bouville to write the biography of an obscure eighteenth-century nobleman, the Marquis de Rollebon. Day after day he works away at his book in the local public library, and he spends his leisure hours in the dismal streets and seedy cafés of the drab little coastal village. He sleeps occasionally with the woman who runs the particular café which he most frequents, but his tumbling with this lady is a joyless affair—in part because of his nostalgia for Anny, the girl he has left behind in Paris and whom he rejoins toward the end of the novel. But not only is he bored by his tavernkeeper: he seems bored by everything in Bouville, and nothing holds any interest for him except his work in the town's library, where he reads volumes upon volumes with an enormous voracity. Yet there comes a time when this begins to pall, and, admitting to his loss of interest in his research, Roquentin prepares to return to Paris.

These are the only substantial facts we are given about the protagonist, for Sartre's main purpose is not to weave about this man a realistic narrative, but rather to explore the inner drama of his nausea, of the absolute revulsion he experiences as he confronts the world's absurdity. We are told that, though he is a man who has widely roamed about over the world, Roquentin no longer believes in the possibility of what men call "adventures." It was while he was in Indo-China, some years earlier, that he first realized how delusive is the dream of "adventure," for there one day, while looking at a Khmer statuette, he had, all of a sudden, felt himself to be "full of lymph and lukewarm milk." And this sudden onset of nausea had borne in upon him how utterly formless and chaotic immediate experience is. That is to say, the actual process of living through an experience is quite without any sort of real meaning at all: it is only when we are able to view it retrospectively that we can proceed to make it a part of some kind of conceptual order. Roquentin now believes that immediate experience is utterly meaningless—and not only meaningless but unpleasant as well. And the novel is largely devoted to an analysis of the essentially disagreeable and nauseous sensation that is provoked in us by our encounter with the world.

Indeed, it is just here that we come upon what is the really primary fact about this desolate and lonely man, Antoine Roquentin. As he faces the world, he is overcome with nausea and disgust—simply because *things* do so stubbornly persist in being *there*; and the sheer *thereness* of *things* wounds him so deeply because it seems in no way to be related to his own existence, and seems therefore in fact positively to oppose his own human reality. So offended is he by the very shamelessness with which the things of this world seem to glory in their own actuality that he feels them to be contaminated by a kind of slimy obscenity. Standing on the seashore one day, he picks up a pebble, intending merely to throw it into the water. But no sooner does he glance at the pebble than he is overcome with a nauseous horror: so he drops it and walks away. Or, again, he is sitting in a café, and, as he looks at his glass of beer, he is suddenly overcome with "a sweetish sort of disgust." One morning, as he is about to shave, he looks into a mirror at his own face, and it suddenly strikes him as disgustingly slimy and fishlike. Indeed, in his experience, everything appears to be messy, slipshod, bedraggled; the world for this man has become simply a huge, bulging pile of scrap the obscenity of which makes him either twitch with fury or retch with disgust. Every object that he beholds, every person he meets, even his own flesh reflected in a mirror—all this nauseates him, and the images which the novel constantly employs for the projection of Roquentin's sense of reality are images of what is gummy and gluey: they are images of stickiness and sliminess, of thickness and viscosity. And things appear to be monstrously clotted with a soft, dank kind of glueyness because they exhibit no logic, no pattern, no definable reason for being just what they are rather than something else. Everywhere the scene of life appears to be nothing but a spectacle of absurdity, and it makes this man literally sick. The world to which he is condemned appears to be without stability or permanence; and, since he finds no evidence of things being governed by any real necessity, he has a sense of its being possible for them to be very nearly anything at all. So his concrete experience takes on at times a violently hallucinatory character. On one occasion, for example, he is on a streetcar, and he speaks of his seat in the following way:

> This enormous belly turned upward, bleeding, inflated—bloated with all its dead paws, this belly floating in this car, in this grey sky, is not a seat. It could just as well be a dead donkey tossed about in the water, floating with the current . . . and I could be sitting on the donkey's belly, my feet dangling in the clear water.

It is in such a moment as this that Roquentin is overborne by a sense of how loosely the names and the concepts that we apply to things sit upon them, and he feels that whatever order things may seem to be a part of is really an order that we have ourselves imposed. Inded, in such moments his sense of the world's derangement becomes so strong that he doubts even the possibility of conceiving experience as experience of "things." For, when he glances at a seat in a streetcar and suddenly feels that it might well be the bloated belly of a dead donkey, what is in fact being perceived is the inapplicability to the world of the very concept of "thing." This is a notion—the notion of the "thing"—which does already carry within itself the promise of concrete realities having a certain persisting stableness of identity: but, as Roquentin comes gradually to feel, what we actually confront is not even "things" but simply existence, which is utterly without reason or justification—and which is therefore absurd.

In short, there is nothing in the world that appears to have any preordained order or form: the world as a whole seems to be characterized by the complete absence of any kind of necessity. So this man's recoil is into disgust and nausea. And the nausea in turn becomes a profoundly unhinging horror and dread, as Roquentin discovers that the complete absence of necessity in the world means that things are, in every way, uncertain, indeterminate, and governed ultimately by a kind of primal lawlessness.

Amidst all the obscene sliminess in which he feels himself to be enmeshed, there is but one thing that lights up the dreariness of his world with a ray of hope: it is to hear, in his favorite café in Bouville, a phonograph record of a Negro songstress (Billie Holiday?) singing the jazz melody "Some of These Days." And, after giving up his researches on the Marquis de Rollebon and deciding to return to Paris, as his disquiet is reaching its climax, he sits one day in this dingy little barroom, listening for the last time to the song and its saxophone accompaniment. Then, in a sudden burst of realization, he knows what it is he has wanted all his life: it has been, as he says, "to chase existence out of me, [to] empty the moments of their fat, wring them out, dry them, purify myself, harden myself, so as to give out finally the clean, precise note of a saxophone." He wants to be disembodied into the purity of sound made by a blues saxophonist. He wants, in other

words, as he says, to be washed clean "of the sin of existing": he wants not to be a soft, bulging mass of flesh, not
a man, but a mere breath of music. And he begins to feel
that, if perhaps he can write a book that will be, like the
jazz tune, "beautiful and hard as steel," if he can create
a work of art utterly different from the gluey, indefinite
amorphousness of the world—why then, he feels, perhaps
in his own personal existence he may come to partake of
the beautiful necessity and hardness and steeliness that
are conveyed by "the clean, precise sound of a saxophone
note."

Now some of Sartre's critics have supposed that he wants
us to regard *Nausea* itself as the book that Roquentin did
eventually write. But the trouble with this line of interpretation is that Roquentin had intended to write a book
that would be so perfect a work of art that in its taut,
steely necessity it would stand in sharp contrast to the
formlessness of human experience, and thus make men
ashamed of the way they live. He had hoped, in other
words, that his book would offer a kind of refutation of the
world's absurdity. But *Nausea*, the book that we actually
have, far from being any sort of refutation of the world's
absurdity, is itself very largely devoted to an illustration
of that absurdity and does not appear to offer any alternative to absurdity.

Certainly no alternative to absurdity is to be found in
the man whom the novel refers to as the Self-Taught Man.
This infinitely pathetic figure is one who has devoted
seven years of his life to reading all the books in the public library of Bouville, proceeding in the alphabetical order of their authors. His whole life is lived amongst books,
and he is quite without any human contact. Indeed, he
does not give up his ramblings through the town library
until the librarian discovers him on a certain day in the
act of fondling an attractive schoolboy and turns him out:

only then does he leave, "to enter" as we are told, "into his apprenticeship of solitude." Which is perhaps Sartre's way of saying that there is no way out of absurdity through Great Books. And this, presumably, is what the Self-Taught Man represents: he is a man who tries to live off what Matthew Arnold called "the best that has been thought and said in the world": he is the traditional humanist. But Sartre seems to be saying that, given the incurable loneliness and frailty of man, no effective help for our condition is to be found even in humanism.

Nor does bourgeois morality offer any escape from absurdity. Indeed, the novel reserves much of its bitterest invective for the bourgeois populace of Bouville—the little clerks and merchants who, whether out of timidity or indolence, attempt to find a secure life in the formality and decorum of conventional propriety; who suppose that, if they quietly mind their own business, they can shut out of their lives the utter insanity of the world, with ceremonious greetings and Sunday visits and correct manners. But this, too, Roquentin declares to be an evasion; there is no refuge behind the rituals of bourgeois etiquette.

Nor does there seem to be any way out through love, through the communion of personal relationship. It is true that, as the days go by in Bouville, Antoine comes to be filled with longing for Anny, the woman back in Paris with whom he has had an affair; and finally he returns, to pay her a visit. But this meeting is a failure, and nothing comes of it. Since they were last together, Anny has had an experience very much like his, for, whereas she had always been searching for the absolute satisfaction of the "perfect moment," she has come to feel, as she says, that "there are no more perfect moments"—and this is a conclusion which has been prompted by her own experience of nausea. But she will not acknowledge that they have now any communion even in suffering and disillusionment.

When Antoine says, a little regretfully, "Then I must leave you after finding you again," she replies, "No . . . no. You haven't found me again." Whereupon she pulls away from his arms, opens the door leading out of her flat, and bids him farewell.

So, as the novel says in numerous ways, there is no way out: we are simply condemned, irrevocably and irremediably, to a world to which the appropriate response is one of nausea and disgust. And thus the texture of the novel is clotted with images of ugliness and nastiness—as, for example, the Bouville librarian's spitting into his handkerchiefs and then spreading them out to dry on the library stove, or the fish scales which Antoine beholds in the mirror image of his eyes, or the remark of the café proprietress as she is about to allow Roquentin to use her body—"I'll keep my stockings on if you don't mind." This kind of thing is constantly appearing throughout the book, and Sartre never loses an opportunity to describe some object or event as sickening, as abhorrent and disgusting and nasty: the image of nausea is, indeed, the dominating image of the book.

Now there are those who have argued that *Nausea* should not be regarded as a direct expression of Sartre's own basic point of view. They propose, in effect, that it be regarded instead as a satirical study of the kind of perverted and unhealthy spirit which is the consequence of a man's abdication from the life of action and social commitment. And we are urged by these critics not to draw a direct line from this novel to the fundamental perspective governing Sartre's comprehensive understanding of the world. But the internal evidence both within this book and his major philosophical writings, as well as that which is observable in his other fiction, would seem to suggest, on the contrary, that this early novel, written over forty years ago and the one segment of his fiction which is

indubitably a modern masterpiece, does in truth take us
very near to the center of his vision. For, again and again
in his philosophical writing, he is at pains to reiterate one
of the principal implications of his novel of 1938, that
ours is a world in which nothing is formally sanctioned,
in which nothing receives its shape and function from any
transcendent authority. In, for example, his book of 1940,
L'Imaginaire (*The Psychology of Imagination*), he speaks of
our fundamental "consciousness of reality" as being characterized by a "nauseating sickness." And in *Being and
Nothingness*, the central philosophical treatise of his
career, he speaks of the "dull . . . feeling of sickness"
which "perpetually" discloses our real situation in the
world to the human consciousness, and refers us to the
analysis in fictional form of this fundamental nausea
which he offered in the novel of 1938. Nor can one help
but be impressed by how much the language and phrase-
ology of the book of 1938 have, at certain crucial points,
entered into the warp and woof of *Being and Nothingness*,
where "nausea" becomes very nearly a technical term for
the immediate taste of existence.

So it would seem that, in Sartre's account of Antoine
Roquentin, we have a most powerful rendering of what he
does himself truly conceive the human situation to be. Indeed, the more formally philosophic phase of his writing
might well be regarded as, at bottom, an attempt at
comprehending what it is in the nature of the world that
gives rise to the fundamental nauseousness of experience.
As it will be recalled, the essential reason why existence
 has the taste of nausea for Antoine Roquentin is that he
is utterly appalled—and disgusted—by, as it were, the arrogant nonchalance with which the things of this world
(in their mode of existence) persist in being other than and
distinct from the human spirit itself. In one of the most
famous passages of the novel, Antoine is sitting one day on

a bench in a park, beside a chestnut tree. And, as it occurs to him to think of the roots of the tree buried in the earth beneath his seat, he is made breathless by the sudden realization of what it means "to exist." He thinks of the raw, black mass of the tree's roots lodged deep within the soil, and it is the very thought of their knotty inertness— utterly unrelated to his own being and, in its essential "thinginess," uncapturable by any theory or "explanation" he may contrive—which overwhelms him with a sense of the world's absurdity, and with nausea.

Now it is precisely what Sartre conceives to be the remoteness of all being, its massive indifference to the human spirit, which leads him to make the central distinction on which the whole of his philosophy rests. In the language of *Being and Nothingness*, it is the distinction between *L'Être-en-soi* (Being-in-itself) and *L'Être-pour-soi* (Being-for-itself). The *en-soi*, the In-itself, is simply the thing in the sheer irreducibility of its thinginess: it is the chestnut tree in its self-contained being *as a chestnut tree.* It is the term which Sartre uses to speak of the mute, voiceless impassivity with which the world stares at man. The *en-soi*, the in-itselfness of a thing, is that silent impermeability with which the world confronts the human individual and which makes him know that, in its midst, he is forever a stranger, an alien, an outsider. Opposed to the *en-soi*, the objective world of existing things, there stands the *pour-soi*, the For-itself—which is Sartre's term for man. He speaks of man as the creature who is "for" himself, because he thinks of man as the creature whose existence is forever in question. That is to say, man's nature is not something definitely established and immovably fixed, like the pebble which Roquentin disgustedly throws into the sea. He is, on the contrary, as Sartre says, "what he makes of himself." His existence precedes his essence: he encounters the world and projects all sorts of undertakings and, through his various endeavors and transactions, gives definition to himself—which is to say that, by means of his diverse plans and projects, he finds a way of choosing himself, a way of being "for" himself, of "making" himself. So he is the *pour-soi*.

In the analysis which he carries forward in *Being and Nothingness*, Sartre suggests, however, that it is a part of the immense irony of existence that the For-itself is ever and again being seduced by the dream of becoming the In-itself. The burdens of freedom prove to be vexatious and wearying: so we try to escape them, deciding perhaps that our lives have already been determined by God or by Fate or by History, and that we do not, therefore, carry the full weight of responsibility for our own existence, that we are simply those to whom things happen. Thus it is that we are often tempted to flee into the apparently impregnable solidity of the *en-soi*. But, as Sartre never tires of reiterating, man is, willy-nilly, "condemned" to freedom, for that is what he *is*: he has no fixed nature, and the human reality is, therefore, defined by nothing other than *possibility* and *freedom*.

Indeed, human freedom is something truly "dreadful," for it is absolute and unconditional. Man cannot choose to be free or to be unfree: it is freedom out of which he is constituted and in which his essence, if he can be said to have an essence, consists. He is not a creature of unconscious forces of the psyche, as in the psychology of Freud; nor is he a creature of social-economic forces, as in the Marxist theory of history. On the contrary, for Sartre, man *is* precisely what he *does*—which is to say that he *is* total freedom. Since God is dead, there is no freedom except that which man possesses. Even if I surrender my freedom to some authoritarian church or totalitarian state, it is my freedom I am exercising when I accept a condition of servitude. And suicide, for all its perversity and cowardice, is simply an ultimate expression of the sovereignty of the will. In short, as he said in a famous lecture entitled *L'existentialisme est un humanisme* (*Existentialism Is a Humanism*) which he delivered in Paris in October of 1945, "Man is condemned to be free. Condemned, because he did not create himself, yet is nevertheless at liberty, and from the moment that he is thrown into this world he is responsible for everything he does." Or, again, as he says toward the close of *Being and Nothingness*:

> . . . man being condemned to be free carries the weight of the whole world on his shoulders: he is responsible for the world and for himself as a way of being. . . . I am responsible for everything, in fact, except for my very responsibility, for I am not the foundation of my being. . . . I am *abandoned* in the world, not in the sense that I might remain abandoned and passive in a hostile universe like a board floating on the water, but rather in the sense that I find myself suddenly alone and without help, engaged in a world for which I bear the whole responsibility without being able, whatever I do, to tear myself away from this responsibility for an instant. For I am responsible for my very desire of fleeing responsibilities. To make myself passive in the world, to refuse to act upon things and upon Others is still to choose myself, and suicide is one mode among others of being-in-the-world. . . . I never encounter anything except my responsibility. That is why I can not ask, "*Why* was I born?" or curse the day of my birth or declare that I did not ask to be born, for these various attitudes toward my birth . . . are absolutely nothing else but ways of assuming this birth in full responsibility and of making it *mine*. Here again I encounter only myself and my projects, so that finally my abandonment . . . consists simply in the fact that I am condemned to be wholly responsible for myself.

But, despite the exhilaration which Sartre occasionally seems to feel at the thought of how radical man's freedom is, it remains to be remarked that freedom is itself also for him a tragic principle. For if man is what he makes of himself and is, therefore, to be defined in terms of possibility, then he is definable only in terms of what, in any given moment, he has not yet already become—which is to say that he is definable only in terms of what he is not. So there is nothingness at the very heart of his existence: his past is "what he is *not* now," his future is "what he is *not* yet," and, in the immediacy of any given instant, there is never any stable structure of being in which he can locate his identity. We are, in other words, creatures who can never catch up with ourselves. We must reckon with the unbridgeable chasm between the *en-soi* and the *pour-soi*. And there is no escaping the nothingness that is wrought into the very core of our humanity. But not only does man find himself estranged from himself by his freedom: he also finds estrangement to be the law most basically governing his relations with his human neighbors, for there, too, we face nothing but distance and alienation.

It is, indeed, the analysis of that whole dimension of experience embracing *L'Être-pour autrui* (*Being-for-others*) that constitutes a major phase of *Being and Nothingness,* and Sartre's exploration of the problem of "the Other" is one of his most brilliant performances. He conceives the relation between persons to be essentially an affair of disconnection and conflict, and he proposes that its central reality is what he calls the "look" or the "gaze." That is to say, I do not begin to exist for another man until he "looks" at me; nor does he come into my field of attention until I "look" at him. But to gaze at another person is immediately to make him "the Other": it is to reduce him to the status of an object, and thus to diminish his freedom; for, when he begins to exist only through another's gaze, he begins to be at the mercy of a freedom which is not his own. Thus no sooner is one looked at than one is by way of becoming a slave; for, when another man through his gaze reduces me to an object, my reality begins to depend not on my own freedom but on his. And, similarly, when

I gaze at him, his human reality becomes dependent on my freedom, and he begins to be my slave. This is what Sartre takes the interpersonal situation to be—a situation, that is, in which the chief components are threat and uneasiness and tension and struggle.

It is, indeed, such an analysis of the I-Thou relation that requires Sartre to deny, as he does, that love is ever any simple possibility for human beings. For if "the Other" is always encountered as one who threatens to make me "his" object and if my natural response is therefore that of trying to make him "my" object, if in fact the relation between persons is essentially an affair of conflict between competing egos, then love itself can be nothing other than the attempt of one human being to *make* another love him. The very possibility, in other words, of any kind of true charity, of any kind of genuinely selfless solicitude for another person, is extinguished from the outset by the "look" or "gaze." For I am either looking at another and threatening his freedom, or he is looking at me and threatening mine—and, as I move from the one condition to the other, I find myself forever "in a state of instability in relation to the Other." One of the characters in Sartre's play *No Exit* says at a certain point, *"L'enfer, c'est les autres"*—"Hell—is others." And it is such a vision of the threat and conflict that are inextricably a part of human togetherness that is being dramatized not only in this play but also in the novels—*L'Âge de raison* (*The Age of Reason, 1945*), *Le Sursis* (*The Reprieve*, 1945), and *La Mort dans l'âme* (*Troubled Sleep*, 1949)—which form his impressive trilogy, *Les Chemins de la liberté* (*Roads to Freedom*). Despite its sensationalistic profundity, it is, of course, a very narrow kind of vision—astonishing, indeed, in its narrowness. For so committed is Sartre to a view of the Other as enemy that whole ranges of experience are brushed aside: the affectionate tenderness in the relation

between parents and children, the bonds of love and
fidelity between husband and wife, the attachments of
fondness and devotion that make up the myriad phenom-
ena of friendship. But genius often tends toward some
sort of drastic one-sidedness of perspective: so, when the
imbalance is as obvious as it is in the case of Sartre, rather
than attempting to enumerate the "errors," it is more
profitable to try to see what it is which, despite all the
disproportionateness, is genuinely illuminating. And when
Sartre's thought is approached in this way, it must surely
be acknowledged that he is one of the great psychologists
of our time, for his *psychanalyse existentielle* ("existential
psychoanalysis") explores with an extraordinary freshness
and brilliance the dilemmas in our relations with one
another that are the result of the ultimate inaccessibility
of the Other.

It has often been urged, however—sometimes even by
his more friendly critics—that Sartre's analysis of the
human situation presents a picture so bleak and dispirit-
ing as to enervate the wellsprings of action. If man is
(as he says toward the close of *Being and Nothingness*)
"a useless passion" and if the world into which he has been
thrown is utterly absurd, can it then matter at all what he
does with his life? Are there, indeed, even any meaningful
alternatives for the conduct of life? Do they not all collapse
under the invading pressures of nothingness, and is not
Sartre's nihilism, therefore, incapable of yielding any kind
of robust ethic? Such questions as these have frequently
been raised about his whole testimony, and raised for the
sake of suggesting that there is in fact no significant
ethical guidance to be gleaned from the vast literature he
has produced over the past forty years.

Simone de Beauvoir, it is true, tells us in the third volume of her autobiography, *La Force des choses* (*The Force
of Circumstance*), that by the end of the 1940's Sartre had

abandoned any intention of producing an "ethics in the proper sense of the word"—by which she means that he had by then relinquished any intention to produce, in the terms of technical philosophy, a full-fledged system of ethics. But both he and she would want vigorously to deny that his thought is without any significant ethical dimension; and on this point they would be no doubt more nearly right than Sartre's detractors.

In the course of his book on the French dramatist Jean Genet (*Saint Genet: Comédien et martyr* [*Saint Genet: Actor and Martyr*], 1952), he does, to be sure, remark that " . . . morality *as such* is both impossible and necessary." Yet, when he speaks of the "impossibility" of morality, as in one way or another he often does, he means that no *system* of morality is possible because man himself is without any "essence," being simply whatever he happens to make of himself. But he is far from wanting to dodge the moral problem as such. Indeed, that is an issue with which Sartre is virtually drunk, and nothing could be more wrongheaded than to suppose that, at least in his own sense of things, his darkly tragic view of existence prompts any sort of unprincipled amoralism.

The real crux of Sartre's ethical vision is, undoubtedly, the notion of authenticity. And this is a conception which takes us back to that fundamental distinction in his thought between the *pour-soi* (namely, man himself) and the *en-soi* (i.e., the objective world of existing things). For by authentic existence he means nothing other than that courage whereby a man consents to bear the burdens of freedom. Man is the creature whose nature it is to be "for" himself: he must find ways of "making" himself, for he is radically free and is, therefore, his own great project. But the labyrinth of freedom is sometimes frightening, and thus the *pour-soi* finds itself envying the apparently unshakable solidity of the *en-soi:* that is to say, man is tempted to abdicate his freedom and to try to become a thing. The form which this abdication takes is that of what Sartre calls *l'esprit de sérieux* ("serious-mindedness'), or what he sometimes speaks of as *mauvaise foi* ("bad faith"); and, in his lexicon, "serious-mindedness" or "bad faith" is the very name of the *in*authentic life.

The man who has fallen under the grip of *l'esprit de sérieux* is the man who thinks of himself *as* a university professor, *as* the president of his bank, *as* an engineer, perhaps also *as* husband or *as* father. Indeed, the hallmark of *l'esprit de sérieux* or *mauvaise foi* is a man's identification of himself so completely with some particular function which he performs that he becomes little more than an automaton. There is, for example, in *Being and Nothingness* a remarkable passage in which Sartre gives a kind of anatomy of "serious-mindedness" by describing a certain waiter in a café: he says:

> Let us consider this waiter in the café. His movement is quick and forward, a little too precise, a little too rapid. He comes toward the patrons with a step a little too quick. He bends forward a little too eagerly; his voice, his eyes express an interest a little too solicitous for the order of the customer. Finally there he returns, trying to imitate in his walk the inflexible stiffness of some kind of automaton while carrying his tray with the recklessness of a tight-rope-walker by putting it in a perpetually unstable, perpetually broken equilibrium which he perpetually reestablishes by a light movement of the arm and hand. All his behavior seems to us a game. He applies himself to chaining his movements as if they were mechanisms, the one regulating the other; his gestures and even his voice seem to be mechanisms, he gives himself the quickness and pitiless rapidity of things. He is playing, he is amusing himself. But what is he playing? We need not watch long before we can explain it: he is playing at *being* a waiter in a café.

In short, what he is attempting to realize is the "being-

in-itself"—that is, the *en-soi*—of a café waiter, as if his entire
humanity coincided with this particular function which he
performs, as if he had no human reality *beyond* this particular role. In playing this game, what the waiter really
hopes to do is to escape the burdens of his freedom. He is
trying to be nothing other than a waiter, he is trying to
convert himself into a thing. But a man can never quite
manage to give to his existence this kind of simplicity.
There is no way in which he can get rid of his freedom,
for that is what he *is*. Which is why, as Sartre concludes,
there can be no universally valid *system* of morality:
because man is not a thing, because he has no fixed nature, no simple essence. The man who is possessed by
l'esprit de sérieux supposes, of course, that the whole
moral problem is a matter of finding universally valid
ethical rules by which to steer one's course; and he thinks
this to be the case, because he wants to be something
fixed and unchanging: he wants the security of the *en-soi*.
But this is the essence of *mauvaise foi*: whereas the truly
authentic man simply wants to be human and knows that
this means putting aside the sham security of "rules" and
assuming all the risks and responsibilities of freedom. As
Sartre says in a pamphlet of 1946 entitled *Réflexions sur
la question Juive (Reflections on the Jewish Question**),
"Authenticity . . . consists in having a lucid and truthful
awareness of the situation, in bearing the responsibilities
and risks which the situation demands, in taking it upon
oneself with pride or humility, sometimes [even] with
horror and hatred." And the largest purpose lying behind
much of his work for the theater—in such plays as *The
Flies; Les Mains sales (Dirty Hands); Kean;* and *Les
Séquestrés d'Altona (The Condemned of Altona)*—is that of
presenting, in the concrete terms of dramatic action, living

---

* The title of the published English translation is *Anti-Semite and Jew*
(New York: Schocken, 1948).

images of true authenticity and of its counterpart (in various forms of "bad faith").

The question may be raised, however, as to whether an "ethic of authenticity" entails anything more than the most nakedly formal kind of abstract principle. Does the notion of authenticity furnish any genuine illumination of the concrete dilemmas that men regularly face in the daily round of experience? Does it in fact provide a basis of ethical decision? Does it suggest any real directives for the moral life? These are, of course, questions to which more satisfactory answers could be given had Sartre ever produced a systematic statement of his ethical theory. But, however great a handicap the interpreter of his thought may feel the lack of such a work to be, it can nevertheless be maintained that the notion of authenticity is not altogether without content. As one looks at his plays and novels, at his philosophical writings, at his various discussions of politics and questions of public policy, it seems clear that, at least so far as Sartre himself is concerned, you cannot proceed to do *any*thing, and simply because it is done with *passion* claim that it represents "authenticity." You cannot, for example, act authentically while supporting anti-Semitic social policies and exclusivist sanctions against Negroes. You cannot claim to be acting authentically when you contribute in any way to the humiliation of other men. Always, the context in which the notion of authenticity is to be encountered in Sartre's writings makes it clear that, for him, a truly authentic mode of life entails a certain reverence for man and such a limitation in the exercise of one's own freedom as may be necessary for the preservation of one's neighbor's freedom. People who are free, in other words, want freedom generally to prevail in the human community. And Sartre's whole analysis of the "look" and of why "the Other" is threatening indicates that what is for him most intolerable in human relationships is any reduction of a man to the status of an object, any denial of his essential *person*hood. So, despite his great distaste for universal "rules" and ethical maxims, one of his recent critics is undoubtedly right in feeling that the doctrine of authenticity does in fact imply the traditional imperative: "So act as to treat humanity, whether in thine own person or in that of any other, in every case as an end, never as a means only."*

This same critic has also noticed a crucial passage in Simone de Beauvoir's brilliant novel of 1954, *Les Mandarins* (*The Mandarins*), which helps to enlarge our circle of definition about Sartre's ethical thought. One of the central personages in Mlle. de Beauvoir's narrative is Robert Dubreuilh, a distinguished Parisian editor and writer, who was intentionally modeled after Sartre. At a certain point late in the novel, Dubreuilh says to the gifted young writer Henri Perron (who was once his friend but from whom he is now estranged, and who is Mlle. de Beauvoir's rendering of Albert Camus), "You can't draw a straight line in a curved space. You can't lead a proper life in a society which isn't proper. . . . No [merely] personal salvation [is] possible." And so, indeed, Sartre has consistently maintained over many years, that in a curved space it is impossible to draw a straight line and that decent relationships amongst people can, therefore, flourish only in a society that is itself decently ordered. In short, the doctrine of authenticity in his thought entails not only a personal ethic but a social ethic as well. For, in his view, to suppose that I can simply contract out of an unjust and disordered society and live an authentic life in my own little private garden is to embrace the last illusion. So, increasingly, his movement as a thinker has been toward the issues of political theory; and, given his

* See Anthony Manser, *Sartre: A Philosophic Study* (London: The Athlone Press of the University of London, 1966), p. 158.

profound commitment to socialist ideology, his great concern appears now to be that of finding a way of recon-
ciling Existentialism and Marxism—the first step toward
which, he proposes, is his monumental book of 1960,
Critique de la raison dialectique (*Critique of Dialectical
Reason*).

These, then, are some of the principal "stages on Sartre's
way"—which, even when all its paths and byways are not
taken, is widely felt today to be one of the great feats of
moral and philosophical imagination in this century. Many
will no doubt want to reject this or that position which
the man has embraced: but the great thing is the *example*
he has provided of a thinker whose aim is nothing less
than that of wanting, as he suggests in one of his essays,
"to embrace from within the total human condition." And
it is this example, one suspects, which has helped to keep
alive amongst young people a sense of the dignity of the
philosophic vocation. The philosophers whom they encounter on university campuses today are, of course, many
of them, busy analyzing, as it were, the structure of sen-
tences: they are principally fascinated by the various ways
in which language behaves, and—whether their subject is
ethics or esthetics or politics or religion—they are generally
to be found studying what they call "language games."
This is, to be sure, a form of study that can be immensely
sophisticated and challenging. But when one looks back
on "the great tradition" in modern philosophy and recalls
the kind of audacity and seriousness with which the full
stretch of the human adventure was examined by Kant
and Hegel, by Bergson and Santayana, by Whitehead and
Dewey, one cannot then help but feel a most unfortunate
timidity and a great retreat being represented by a philosophy which specializes in nothing other than "linguistic
analysis." And it is a retreat which leaves so much of the

world behind that many of the most thoughtful and sensitive young people of our period might well have been prompted long since to despair of the philosophic enterprise altogether, had it not been for the career of such a thinker as Sartre, whose effect has in part been that of persuading us that it may still be possible for a man who (as the English would say) "does" philosophy to do it in ways that do not involve merely a sterile kind of logic chopping or a frivolous kind of tiddlywinks. Admittedly, Sartre—standing as he does so immediately in the line of Nietzsche—is (as it was earlier remarked), in his atheism and his consistently tragic perspective on the human situation, a very "absolute" kind of existentialist. But his great purpose over more than forty years has been that of helping us to discover how to live where Orestes in *The Flies* finally discovers himself to be—"on the far side of despair." And thus his *example* is felt to be among the most inspiriting on the intellectual landscape of our time.

7

Martin Buber—Guide to the World of *Thou*

THE DIFFERENCE between the two great ancestors of Existentialism in the nineteenth century—the difference between Kierkegaard's passionate advocacy of faith and Nietzsche's clamorous insistence on the death of God—is a divide that still cuts across the entire movement. For on the one side there are those who find the human universe to be invaded by intimations of the sacred and who believe man's pilgrimage to be one which looks toward eternity: whereas, on the other side, there are those who find the ultimate context of the human adventure to be one of emptiness and nothingness with a great abyss underfoot. And there are still others—like those two great German masters of philosophy Martin Heidegger and Karl Jaspers—who are to be found right on the divide itself, feeling apparently that human existence has a transcendent dimension but yet disinclined, finally, to name it God. The existentialist family, in other words, as one of its interpreters has remarked, is a "fractured family," a family broken by profound dissension on the issue than which (among all the great questions man wrestles with) there is none more ultimate. Some—like Job—say, "Behold, I go forward but He is not there; and backward, but I cannot perceive Him; On the left hand . . . I cannot behold Him; . . . on the right hand . . . I cannot see Him" (Job 23:8-9). But others find in the most intimate neighborhood of their experience a Presence which is radiant like the sun, and which soaks the heart as rain soaks a parched field. And the distance between the two types of witness seems to be very considerable indeed.

Yet existentialist atheism, even in its most stridently radical forms, seems always to be a religious atheism: in a curious way, the experience of the death of God appears to be itself a *religious* experience. Men like Sartre and Camus, it is true, conceive ours to be a godless universe, a world in which man can nowhere behold any sure sign of divinity. Yet in their way of talking about this fact they make us feel that, for them, it is a *theological* fact. God may be silent or absent or dead—but, whatever the case may be, secular existentialists appear to take this very silence or absence or death to be the most important reality which any man can confront. For all of its absurdity, the universe is still, in other words, conceived to be a religious universe—whose ultimate meaning is to be found in God (even if He be absent or dead).*

So there is a sense in which one ought not perhaps to distinguish between Existentialisms that are religious and non-religious but, rather, between those which support an atheistic and those which support a theistic world view. Yet, despite the religious cast of existentialist atheism, this remains a very fundamental difference indeed, and one which has prompted certain critics of the existentialist movement to conclude that what one confronts

---

* This whole theme—of the religious character of existentialist atheism —is suggestively explored in an essay by Susan Taubes entitled "The Absent God" in *The Journal of Religion*, Vol. XXXV, No. 1 (1955).

here, finally, is a type of thought so unstable at its very center as to be unworthy of serious consideration.

But, far from attesting to some essential fickleness or insolvency, the duality of emphasis arising out of the theistic and atheistic varieties of existentialist thought does in fact attest to the rough and invincible kind of integrity which has been at work throughout this whole enterprise. For if one thinks of Existentialism as having entailed, at bottom, an attempt—through passionate introspection and engagement with the concrete immediacies of experience—to clarify the nature of the road man travels, and if that road can be imagined to be something like "a road to Bethlehem, or better, to Calvary," then one must surely grant that at the end of it "one may as easily find only a manger of straw as . . . the Messiah. One may as easily find only two thieves as find the suffering savior."* Or at least this must be granted, if one is prepared to acknowledge—as one must surely be—that it is possible for an honest man to find no confirming evidence in his experience that supports any sort of traditional religious faith.

In Camus and in Sartre we have looked at two enormously compelling representatives of Existentialism in its secular and atheistic mode. But there have, of course, been many equally persuasive spokesmen on the contemporary scene for an Existentialism which is, in one way or another, positively allied with a religious perspective. The Protestant Reformation of the sixteenth century and the whole import of the thought of a man like Martin Luther are no doubt very greatly misconceived, if "the priesthood of all believers" is taken simply to mean that every man is on his own in the moment of the encounter with the naked

* Carl Michalson, "What is Existentialism?" in *Christianity and the Existentialists*, ed. by Carl Michalson (New York: Charles Scribner's Sons, 1956), p. 20.

glory of God. But there is no denying the strongly individualistic tendency which has traditionally been a part of
Protestant Christianity, and this may largely account for
the affinity that Protestant theology has felt between itself and the existentialist tradition. Indeed, it is a host of
distinguished Protestant thinkers who form the predomi-
nating majority of theistic existentialists. The work of the
Swiss theologian Karl Barth (1886-1968) looms now as
the most massive accomplishment not only in twentieth-
century Protestantism but in the whole of modern theology: nowhere else does one encounter a restatement of
the Christian faith so vast as that which this amazing
genius produced in the mountainous literature that came
from his pen during fifty years. In the late years of his career, as he moved more deeply into the exposition of his
thought in the great multivolume *Church Dogmatics*, his
profound commitment to biblical revelation led him drastically to rescind the enthusiasm he had felt for Kierkegaard
and existentialist thought in the early decades of his life,
when (in his Preface of 1921 to the second edition of his
Epistle to the Romans) he declared that, insofar as he had a
system at all, it derived from Kierkegaard. But, even in his
last years he suggested (in a little book entitled *The Humanity of God*, 1960) that Existentialism continued to offer
a valuable reminder to the Christian theologian, "that one
cannot speak of God without speaking of man." In the
famous opening passage of his *Confessions*, St. Augustine
said: "Great art Thou, O Lord, and greatly to be praised
. . . for Thou hast formed us for Thyself, and our hearts
are restless till they find rest in Thee." And Barth's whole
analysis of that inner restlessness of the human spirit which
gives rise to the leap of faith was heavily marked by the
accents of existentialist thought.

It is, however, the late Rudolf Bultmann (1884-1976)
and the late Paul Tillich (1886-1965) who best represent

the emphatically existentialist orientation of much recent Protestant theology. Tillich's overriding concern was to "correlate" the "questions" man's historical experience compels him to raise about the meaning of his existence with the great central affirmations of Christian theology. And Bultmann's principal concern was to "demythologize" the Christian faith, to strip it of that mythological overlay deriving from the world of the ancient Middle East in which it first took form, so that it might be freshly appropriated as what he took it in essence to be—namely, a type of "self-understanding." But though Tillich's fundamental project as a theologian was different from that of Bultmann, they may both be seen to be Christian thinkers for whom the basic theological task was one which entails, in part, a systematic analysis of the nature and structure of human existence; and, in this, their thought—along with that of the American theologian Reinhold Niebuhr (1892-1971)—manifests a very considerable indebtedness to existentialist tradition, most especially to the work of Martin Heidegger, but also to the legacy of Kierkegaard.

Roman Catholic thought has not itself been untouched by existentialist influence. Indeed, by 1950 the impact of Existentialism had been felt with sufficient force to arouse misgivings among the more conservative ranks of Roman Catholic churchmen, and it was, no doubt, partially this anxiety which prompted the publication in that year of a papal encyclical (*Humani Generis*) in which Pius XII anathematized "Existentialism, whether atheistic or simply the type that denies the validity of the reason in the field of metaphysics." Of course in the years that have followed the momentous Vatican Council convened by Pope John XXIII, all sorts of fresh winds have been blowing into every nook and cranny of the Roman Church, and today its intellectual life is far less restrictive than was the case even just a few years ago, so that many of its most

gifted thinkers are now to be found responding with enthusiasm to the various existentialist currents in recent philosophy and theology. But, among all these, it is the
French philosopher, the late Gabriel Marcel, who continues
to be the pre-eminent representative of Existentialism in
Roman Catholic circles. In a long series of brilliantly written philosophical works and dramas (for, like Sartre, he was
also a playwright) extending over nearly fifty years, Marcel took as his central theme the nature of personhood,
what it is that enables the human individual to become an
authentic person; and it is the categories of *fidelity* and
communion, of *presence* and *testimony*, of *hope* and *mystery* that govern his entire thought. His style is autobio-
graphical, intuitive, informal. He had a great fondness for
the term *disponibilité*—which means being available, being
at the disposal of another, being present: man, he believed,
is in fact definable as a creature who needs *disponibilité*,
who can survive in health and happiness only for as long as he
can find in his environment those who consent to be available to him, to be present. Indeed, as Marcel argued, any
doctrine or metaphysic of Being must, finally, be a metaphysic of Presence; and it is toward this kind of emphasis
that the whole body of his work is poised in a beautifully
delicate and moving way.

   In contrast to the traditionally individualistic tendency
of Protestant Christianity, Judaism has always found its
center in the communal realities belonging to the history
of the People of God; and it has conceived the integrity
of Jewish existence to consist in unremittingly faithful
observance of the Law. It is doubtless this dual emphasis
on Law and People which has to some extent restricted
the sympathy of the Jewish community for Existentialism, with its strongly individualist bias toward subjectivity and personal decision. Yet the greatest poet of Jewish
history is to be found crying out in the Psalms, "Save me,

O my God"; "Give ear to my words, O Lord"; "Hear me
when I call, O God." Certainly there is a sense in which it
can be said to be an existentialist voice which stutters forth
the Psalmist's anguish—"Out of the depths have I cried
unto thee. . . ." And the Job who declares that even after
"my skin worms destroy this body, yet in my flesh shall I
see God" is most assuredly a man who has a profound
awareness of what Nietzsche called "the eternal wound of
existence." So it should not be considered paradoxical
that Judaism, too, has had its representatives amongst
the ranking existentialists of our time.

That extraordinarily brilliant German Franz Rosenzweig (1886-1929), whose untimely death in 1929 at the
age of forty-three cut short a career of great promise, was
meditating primarily on the mystery of Israel in his masterpiece of 1921, *Der Stern der Erlösung (The Star of
Redemption)*; but at many points his thought shows a
striking resemblance to that of Kierkegaard—even, in certain respects, to Nietzsche's—and he is today considered
an important precursor of recent existentialist theology.
The distinguished Polish émigré scholar, the late Abraham Joshua Heschel (1907-1972), long a professor in the
Jewish Theological Seminary of America in New York
City, was also a theologian of enormous power who,
though steeped in the traditions of conservative Judaism,
yet gave an account of the life of faith which carries an
unmistakably existentialist stamp. Or, again, the American Jewish philosopher and social critic Will Herberg
(1909-1977), in his memorable book of 1951, *Judaism
and Modern Man*, and in various other writings disclosed
how his own pilgrimage in the 1940's from Marxism
back to a deeply biblical faith was guided in part by Reinhold Niebuhr and Paul Tillich and Kierkegaard and the
whole insurgency in those years of existentialist thought.
But, of course, the commanding figure who towers above
all others in the renascence of Jewish philosophy and

theology in this century is Martin Buber, and it is he more than anyone else who stands as the great exemplar of theological Existentialism in Jewish thought of the last several decades.

It will be recalled that, late in our discussion of Kierkegaard, reference was made to a relatively recent book which undertakes to distinguish Kierkegaard, Nietzsche, and Camus from the general family of existentialists by calling them "lyrical existentialists" because, as the author contends, they draw "us inward to become absorbed in the only existence we shall ever directly encounter: ourselves."° As it was suggested, however, the notion of "lyrical Existentialism" hardly designates any particular type of existentialist thought, since what is pervasively characteristic of existentialist literature is precisely this proclivity toward a subjectivistic outlook and this preoccupation with the interior drama of personal experience. But at least, in the case of Buber, it may be maintained that among those existentialists who claim a theistic faith he is the *most* lyrical, for, in those of his books which present the crucial expressions of his basic outlook, he—more consistently than any of the other "religious" existentialists—is to be found managing a kind of song, often stunningly beautiful in the haunting originality of its melody, about the infinite mystery which is embraced by the reality of the person. So it is to this eloquent sage of Israel that we turn for our chief example of twentieth-century Existentialism in its theological mode.

Martin Buber was born in Vienna on the eighth of February, 1878, but at the age of three, following his parents' divorce, he took up residence at Lemberg in Galicia,°°

° See page 53.

°° "Galicia" is the name formerly applied to that area of Poland lying on the northern slopes of the Carpathians, which constituted an Austrian crownland in the period between 1772 and 1918; its capital was the town of Lemberg.

where he was reared in his early years in the home of his grandfather, Salomon Buber. Salomon Buber was a wealthy banker and an astute businessman, but he was also a man of very considerable learning in the field of rabbinic scholarship. It was no doubt the atmosphere of his household, infused as it was at once with dedication to Jewish tradition and with the refinements of secular culture, that determined the direction of the boy's development. It was here, one imagines, as he began to master the Hebrew language and to study the Bible, that the lore and piety that formed his inheritance first began to enter deeply into his sense of reality and to establish what were to become his most basic perspectives on the world. And it was during these years, as the family took its summer holidays in the little Galician towns of Sadagora and Czortkov, that Buber had his first encounter with Hasidism, for there were still communities of Hasidim living in these towns. This was one of the decisive encounters of Buber's life, and some attention must shortly be given here to this remarkable East-European Jewish sect.

By the time Buber was fourteen his father had remarried and established another home in Lemberg; so the boy was transferred back to his father with whom he remained until he entered the University of Vienna in 1896. Vienna in the 1890's was a beautifully "romantic" city whose cultural life, particularly in the arts, was characterized by great exuberance and considerable brilliance. But, fascinating as he found the local scene to be, Buber was also drawn to other centers, in Leipzig and Berlin, and it was at the University of Berlin that he took his doctor's degree in 1904.

In Berlin, as he had earlier done in Vienna, Buber became very much a part of life in the Jewish community, most especially of the Zionist movement which was then just beginning to emerge. But, in a manner that was to remain characteristic of his position on the Zionist question throughout all the years to come, already in this early period Buber's Zionism began to take a "heretical" turn. For, though he believed it immensely important that world Jewry should have a state of its own where the Jewish people might find a refuge against the bitter penalties imposed by anti-Semitism, he could not conceive the establishing of such a state as the be-all and end-all of Jewish existence: it was instead for him and his circle in Berlin only one of many cultural tasks to which the Jewish community was summoned in the modern world. So at many points he found himself severely at odds with Theodor Herzl, the great leader of the Zionist movement of the time. But, even if Buber's Zionism did carry within itself a certain taint of heresy, it represented one of the most serious commitments of his life and, more than anything else, was the interest which shaped his early years. Before leaving Vienna he had edited the Zionist journal *Die Welt* (*The World*); and in 1902, together with a group of friends, he founded in Berlin a Jewish publishing firm, the Jüdischer Verlag, which was to be perhaps the most important single instrument in the development of the Zionist movement in Central Europe.

Buber's deepest intuitions, however, had always told him that the social and political dimensions of life do not circumscribe the full range of man's humanity; he had always believed that the human spirit reaches beyond the merely external mechanisms and arrangements of any social collective. Indeed, what he conceived to be religiously most profound in Judaism itself had convinced him that man is a creature too complex and too radically mysterious to be regarded as simply a "political animal," and he was therefore coming more and more to feel that the essential genius of Jewish tradition was bound to be betrayed in any simple equation of it with political Zionısm. So in 1904 he withdrew from the public sphere in which he had been active as an interpreter of Zionist thought, and for the next five years lived in semiretirement, devoting himself to an intense study of the Hasidic traditions which he had first encountered as a boy in Poland.

The Hebrew word *Hasid* means "a pious one," and the Hasidic movement has gathered its name as a result of the very exacting requirements of personal piety to which it has held its followers accountable. Hasidism was founded in the middle years of the eighteenth century by Israel ben Eliezer (1700-1760), who came to be spoken of as the Baal Shem Tov ("Master of the Good Name"). It was a kind of sectarian Judaism that seized Eastern European Jewry with enormous power, particularly the Jewish communities in Poland and the Ukraine, and represented in part a rebellion of the Jewish peasantry of these regions against the learned, sophisticated rabbinical religion of urban Judaism. The movement had its roots amongst rural Jews who found themselves ridiculed when they ventured into the synagogues of neighboring towns; but, for all their rude simplicity, they were a people intimately involved in an earthbound culture that was in direct contact with the elemental rhythms of nature, and thus they had a large vision of how a man might find his ultimate fulfillment not in some sort of monastic retreat from the world but in concrete communities situated in the midst of the ordinary affairs of life and dedicated to the "hallowing of the everyday." Indeed, as Buber says in his book *The Origin and Meaning of Hasidism,* these "unenlightened Polish and Ukrainian Jews produced," in their humble villages, an order of life whose scrupulousness is nowhere surpassed in religious history. They conceived the task of every man to be that of loving the world and of loving his neighbor and himself—for the sake of God. And in their fidelity to this vision they breasted all the changing currents of the modern period, being doggedly resolved, even as they moved into the twentieth century, to preserve intact a traditional pattern of life, however quaint it might seem to be in the larger world.

The Hasidic life which Buber had encountered as a boy in Galicia was not so vigorous as the communities that had been formed by earlier generations who had felt more immediately the impact of the Baal Shem Tov, but there still remained a sufficient grace, charm, and vitality to leave in him a deep and abiding impression of religious and moral greatness. So when, in 1904, he withdrew from public life to deepen his understanding of Jewish tradition, it was to the Hasidic movement that he felt impelled to turn; and his increasing mastery of its rich lore and literature over the next few years constituted what in retrospect appears to have been the crucial experience of his life. For the Hasidic vision of a world in which all human endeavor, no matter how mundane or humble, would be consecrated to God expressed a profound belief in the essential dignity of the common life that men have with one another in all their daily transactions: it expressed, at bottom, the conviction that the life of faith is to be lived not in any cloistered retreat from the world but in the very midst of all its urgencies and tensions. And it was just this belief which was to form the guiding principle of Buber's thought over all the decades of his life that were to come: indeed, the "hallowing of the everyday" is the deepest note being sounded in all the most characteristic writings of his long career.

By 1909, however, as Buber began to emerge from the five-year-long period of retirement that had been given over to meditation and study, he was also beginning to be touched by still another excitement—namely, the legacy of Søren Kierkegaard, whose writings were to have a profound impact on Buber's whole understanding of his task. In this case, what he was most quickened by was Kierkegaard's insistence on the subjective character of all vital philosophic truth, by his view of the philosophic task as one focused on the concrete actualities that make up the experience of ordinary men. As a university student, Buber had been stirred by the kind of critique of nineteenth-century rationalism which Nietzsche had rendered; but Nietzsche's program was one which was based on an atheistic humanism, whereas in the case of Kierkegaard the rejection of rationalist thought was prompted not only by concern for the concrete reality of the human person but also by a profound religious faith, and thus Buber was bound to be captivated by the thought of this bold and brilliant Danish thinker whose influence was just beginning to be felt in German intellectual life. There was to come a time when Buber in turn was to voice the gravest misgivings about the final adequacy of Kierkegaard's doctrine of man, for he did at last consider its extreme individualism to be irrelevant to what he took to be the essentially interpersonal character of human existence. Yet he never wholly lost his early esteem for Kierkegaard, nor did he ever shake off altogether the Kierkegaardian influence, for it can now be seen to have left its indelible stamp on his entire thought.

In the years that followed his return to public life in 1909, Buber's steadily deepening devotion to Hasidism did in no way deflect him from his early commitment to the Zionist movement. In 1916 he established the journal *Der Jude* as an organ for the dissemination of Zionist thought. Under his leadership it fast became German Jewry's most important journal of opinion, and he retained the chief editorial responsibility until 1924. From 1926 to 1930 he edited, jointly with the Catholic theologian Joseph Wittig and the Protestant physician and psychotherapist Viktor von Weizsäcker, the journal *Die Kreatur,* which was devoted to a variety of questions concerning the interrelationship between religion and culture. Then, in addition to his work as an editor, he constantly carried heavy burdens of writing and lecturing; and it was by such labors that his career was most fundamentally shaped.

In those years the most important relationship of his life was no doubt that which bound him to his friend Franz Rosenzweig, the brilliant principal of the Free Jewish Academy in Frankfurt, whose great book *The Star of Redemption* had a considerable influence on Buber after its appearance in 1921. It was with Rosenzweig that Buber undertook in the 1920's a new translation of the Bible into German which has been universally acclaimed "a miracle of fidelity and beauty," and it is the Buber-Rosenzweig translation (completed by Buber in the years following Rosenzweig's untimely death in 1929) which is largely responsible for the renascence of the study of the Bible among German-speaking Jews in the twentieth century. But their collaborative efforts extended far beyond this single project: each influenced the other on the deepest levels of his life and thought, and their impact on religious thought in the Jewish community of our time is very nearly without parallel.

In 1923 a new professorship in Jewish philosophy was created for Buber at the University of Frankfurt, and he held this post until he was ousted by the Nazis in 1933. Through the dark years of the Hitlerian insanity in the 1930's Buber was a pillar of strength for German Jewry, and through his writing and lecturing presented an example of resistance that the Jews who survived the Nazi scourge have declared to have been a source of profound inspiration for themselves and their beleaguered brethren. But there came a time when it was clear that he himself could not expect much longer to be allowed to remain at

large: so he fled to Palestine in 1938, where he became
Professor of Social Philosophy in the Hebrew University in
Jerusalem, a chair which he held until his retirement in
1951. But even then he was not allowed to rest, and for
the next two years he bore a commission from the state of
Israel to direct, through the Institute for Adult Education
(which he had founded in 1949), the training of teachers
for the settlements that had been established to receive the
great influx of immigrants into the newly established nation.

In the 1950's, now an old man, Buber paid several extended visits to the United States, in 1951-1952 and 1957
and 1958, where, in colleges and universities all over the
country, he was affectionately and reverently greeted as
the legendary figure he had become. For the modest and
lively old gentleman, with flowing white beard and haunt-
ingly beautiful and gentle eyes, whom American audiences
met in the 1950's was a man who—through such books as
I and Thou, Eclipse of God, Between Man and Man, and his
numerous studies in Biblical and Hasidic thought—had exerted an immense influence on several areas of modern
thought, on philosophy and theology (Protestant and Catholic as well as Jewish) and psychotherapy and theory of
education; and he had long since been acknowledged,
internationally, as one of the most truly seminal thinkers
of this century. Indeed, when he died on the thirteenth of
June, 1965, in his eighty-eighth year, it was felt throughout the world that one of the great saints of modern intellectual life had passed from the scene.

In the eighteenth century in England it was often remarked, and particularly by Samuel Johnson, that any man
worth paying attention to is the victim of an obsession,
what Dr. Johnson called a "ruling passion." And there is
more than a little truth in this old adage, for, as we dis-

cover again and again, any man who has something to say
to us that carries real weight is a man who is "centered,"
who has found his own angle of vision, his own perspective—from which he looks out at the immense panorama
of the world and in relation to which he then proceeds
to arrange and give order to the formlessness of the
spectacle that lies before him. This is especially true of
the man of genius whose work, as Camus once suggested
(in *The Myth of Sisyphus*), whether he be philosopher
or artist, will normally be found to be not simply "a series
of isolated testimonies" but an ordered whole, expressing
some particularly distinctive way of taking hold of the
world and making sense of experience. Martin Buber is
surely a case in point, for, as the Scots theologian, the
late Ronald Gregor Smith of the University of Glasgow,
once said, despite Buber's immense learning and the extraordinary breadth of his intellectual interests, he was,
nevertheless, "a man with a single insight." That is to say,
on every occasion of his undertaking some major project
of reflection on the fundamental realities of human existence, he appears to have found it necessary to start from a
certain assumption, a very simple assumption yet one
which for him carried an enormous freight of implication:
that the experiences which bring man the deepest joy and
the deepest fulfillment are not those in which he simply
explores his own inwardness, but are rather those in which
he encounters some presence which is separate from and
other than his own existence, and finds himself upborne—
reinforced, strengthened, invigorated—by this confrontation. The *essential*, the *normative* human situation is not
one in which a man stands over *against* the world: for
Buber any such picture promotes a greatly mistaken view
of what our human situation most essentially is. For, using
as he did the German language, to him the great reality is
that for which he reserved the term *Begegnung*—which

means "meeting": that, as he liked to say, is where *real* life is to be found, in "meeting." The English theologian J. H. Oldham once recalled the distinguished Roman Catholic historian Christopher Dawson remarking to him that he wasn't sure that he liked the notion that real life is meeting, for, said he, were the word "meeting" somehow to acquire a final "s," then it would be a most horrible thought indeed that would be conveyed. But, of course, Buber is not talking about committees or cocktail parties, for what he wants to lay down as a fundamental principle is not the importance of social gatherings but the notion that the portal which grants entrance to the profoundest things of human life is the portal of *relationship*—or, as he says, "In the beginning is relation." This is the conception on which his whole philosophy rests, and it was in this basic principle that he found the "ruling passion" of his life.

The *locus classicus* of this central theme in Buber's thought is, of course, that remarkable little book of 1923, *Ich und Du (I and Thou)*, which, as it has sung itself deep into the mind of our time, has become a modern classic. In Ronald Gregor Smith's elegantly rendered English translation of 1937 it runs to barely more than a hundred pages, and Gregor Smith has reported that Buber once said to him that no book should exceed 120 pages in length—a rule, however, to which Buber himself did not adhere in many of his other writings. Yet, in the intensity of the spell which it casts, this slender volume is unmatched in the philosophical literature of this century. But is it an essay in philosophy? Certainly, in its tone and idiom, it is not a conventional academic treatise. It is, to be sure, profoundly influenced by the kind of mystical piety that Buber had been deeply touched by through his studies in Hasidism; yet, in the consistency with which it adheres to the Hasidic emphasis on ultimate reality as hav-

ing its locus in the claim and responsibility brought by
each mortal hour of a man's involvement with his neighbor, it is not a "mystical" work, for it does not propose
that our true destiny is to be found in any realm which is
other than this present world. And though the beautifully
cadenced lyricism and intimacy of its language make us
want to call it a poem, it is written not in verse but in a
marvelously controlled and vibrant prose. So one doesn't
know quite to what class of literature it ought to be assigned, and on this level of analysis perhaps the best that
the interpreter can do is to speak of it, as Gregor Smith
does in his Introduction, as a "philosophical-religious
poem." But, however the genre of this extraordinary little book may be defined, it does most assuredly present
the crucial statement of Buber's vision and marks the
point at which any review of his thought must both begin
and end.

The whole substance of Buber's "philosophy of dialogue" is given in the opening passage of *I and Thou* which
says:

> To man the world is twofold, in accordance with his two-
> fold attitude.
> The attitude of man is twofold, in accordance with the
> two-fold nature of the primary words which he speaks.
> The primary words are not isolated words, but combined
> words.
> The one primary word is the combination *I-Thou.*
> The other primary word is the combination *I-It*; wherein,
> without a change in the primary word, one of the words
> *He* and *She* can replace *It.*
> Hence the *I* of man is also twofold.
> For the *I* of the primary word *I-Thou* is a different *I* from
> that of the primary word *I-It.*

Now there are two fundamental assertions being made
in this passage. Buber is, first of all, saying (by implication) that, though man may be an individual ego, he is not

an isolated ego, and the ultimate reality of human life is not an affair of the sovereign individuality of the single self but of man's relatedness to the world. When, in short, we say the word *I*, we are speaking not about any sort of self-contained atom but about a being whose nature and existence are interlocked with realities other than and beyond itself. And then, of course, Buber is also saying in this passage that man's involvement with the world is twofold: on the one hand, we deal with things, and thus the *I* finds itself related to the world of *It*; on the other hand, we are, as persons, involved with one another, so that the *I* dwells also in the world of *Thou*. So, says, Buber, there are two "primary words"—*I-Thou* and *I-It*.

Each of these "primary words" connotes a fundamentally different kind of orientation or attitude toward the world. When life is lived in the dimension of the I-It relation, man's tendency is to approach the world as something to be weighed and measured, to be manipulated and controlled. Here a man is bent simply on having experiences and on learning how to subject things to his own purposes. Here there is no spirit of give and take, of reciprocity, of mutuality—for the "It," whether it be a lifeless thing or a person, is faced simply as an object to be used, and is not permitted to have any real effect on the inwardness of one's own humanity. In the I-It dimension, our basic concern is to arrange and organize, to manage and to turn things to practical account. And Buber does not by any means suppose this orientation to represent something intrinsically evil, for he fully recognizes it to be the necessary basis of large spheres of human activity—in science and technology and commerce and government. The daily conduct of business in the human community cannot be accomplished without the mechanization of vast domains of life, and thus Buber is prepared to acknowledge that the human enterprise is inextricably involved in the world of "It."

Yet, as he faces this apparently inexhaustible world of things and processes which he is eager to explore and to taste and control, a man will suddenly find himself *addressed*, by the voice of another person. And here he is met by a kind of limit, by a reality which is not simply another object at his disposal, for now he is confronting another agent who is himself an independent center of consciousness, who has his own perspectives, his own purposes, and his own desires to explore and to subdue the objective world. And there is no controlling what he will say, there is no determining what word his voice shall utter. Now you are no longer in command of the situation, for your world has been invaded by another point of view, and you find yourself *engaged*, in a moment of *meeting*: you find yourself *addressed* and being invited to make a response. And if you accept that invitation, if you commit yourself to the presence which is before you, if you give up the attempt at manipulating and controlling and consent truly to be touched by the reality of him who confronts you, if indeed you make a candid response to the word which has been uttered by this other voice, then you are quitting the dimension of *I-It* and embarking on a new voyage, into the world of *I-and-Thou*, where the great discovery which is to be made is that I do not have the essence of what it means to be human in myself alone but that this resides in what there is "between man and man." For, as Buber says, "he who lives with It alone is not a man."

There is, of course, a sense in which Buber's analysis of the "two-foldness" of the world does not make for an absolute distinction between the realm of I-and-It and the realm of I-and-Thou. For he knew how frequently we undertake to deal with one another from an I-It standpoint: he knew how easily we tend to become so absorbed in our own plans and purposes that we fail to perform an act of true attention before our neighbors and thus retreat from the risks and responsibilities of genuine encounter with others. He knew indeed man's great besetting affliction to be his habit of wrapping himself up in his own ego and thus building walls between himself and his neighbor. Very often, instead of consenting really to encounter our neighbor, we choose simply to accumulate information about him, to reduce him to a kind of statistic, to stand *over against* him, insisting upon his separateness and upon our own. And human life is ever and again being corrupted and disfigured by the thousand different ways in which we ingeniously manage to refuse to pronounce the word "Thou," choosing instead—because of thoughtlessness or laziness or sheer insensitivity—to convert our relations with one another into what is essentially an affair of I-It.

But then, again, those regions of our experience which might be thought naturally to belong to the I-It dimension can and sometimes are stirred by the breath of the I-Thou relation. Buber's conviction seems to have been that, at every point in our dealings with the universe, we ought in fact to be striving to achieve the I-Thou relation. For he was prepared in effect to say that every non-human creature and every natural occurrence or object has the power of "speaking" to us, of breaking through the banalities in which we customarily live and of stirring the soul to new awareness and response. Indeed, for us to take up an attitude of "listening" in the presence of an object—whether it be a dog or a tree or some vast and awesome projection of the earth's terrain—is for us to permit that object to become a *thou*. And, just at this point, the immense difference in the quality of Buber's vision from that of Sartre is worth remarking. For it will be recalled what an immense disgust Sartre finds it natural for the protagonist of *Nausea* to feel, as he contemplates one day while sitting in a park a chestnut tree. But, with Buber, everything is

conceived in a startlingly different way. He remarks, for
example, at a certain point in *I and Thou*, that we may
think of a tree as simply a stiff column against a background of blue sky, or we may think of a given tree as an
example of this or that species, or as simply a certain sort
of natural phenomenon. But then, as he says, we *may*
consent to become so "bound up in relation to it" that the
tree before which we stand ceases to be merely an *It*, so
intensely have we begun to value it for its own sake, to
permit it to "speak" and to "listen" to the mysterious communication which it bodies forth. And in such a moment, through the reverent attentiveness with which we
face it, the tree does indeed attain to the status of a kind
of *thou*hood.

So the difference between the I-It and the I-Thou dimensions does not, in Buber's thought, make for an altogether
absolute distinction. But though he believes it to be a part
of man's dignity to be able to regard the non-human universe with a reverent piety, he is not, of course, ultimately
to be found trifling with any kind of romantic sentimen-
tality about nature. And thus it is most essentially our
life with other men that he conceives to be the realm of
the I-Thou relation, for here it is that life can be lived in
love—which is, he says, "the cradle of the Real Life":

> The man who does not know this . . . does not know
> love. . . . In the eyes of him who takes his stand in love,
> and gazes out of it, men are cut free from their entangle-
> ment in bustling activity. Good people and evil, wise and
> foolish, beautiful and ugly, become successively real to
> him; that is, set free they step forth in their singleness, and
> confront him as *Thou*. . . . Love is responsibility of an *I* for
> a *Thou*. In this lies the likeness . . . of all who love, from
> the smallest to the greatest and from the blessedly pro-
> tected man, whose life is rounded in that of a loved being,
> to him who is all his life nailed to the cross of the world,
> and who ventures to bring himself to the dreadful point—
> to love *all men*.

For Buber, then, "entering into relation" is, as he says, "the whole stuff of life," for it is only in those processes of exchange whereby we mutually confirm and recognize one another's presence that human personality comes into being. The child who, from the time of his earliest experience of the world, does not find himself surrounded by those who tenderly and affectionately acknowledge his *thou*hood becomes a stunted creature. And the man from whom such acknowledgment is consistently withheld will go literally insane. For we are so made that we can be truly human only *with* other men: here alone is authentic human existence to be found. So it was the genius of Buber to say—though the simplicity of the proposition (and all truly great ideas are ultimately simple) must not obscure the brilliant originality of the concept—that the life of humankind is a "life of dialogue," that we are so organized by the most basic laws governing the nature of human nature that, as W.H. Auden once declared (in the most famous line of all his poetry), "We must love one another or die." It is an ancient wisdom, which finds, in the English-speaking world, one of its most eloquent statements in the familiar lines of the seventeenth-century poet and priest John Donne:

> No man is an Iland, intire of it selfe; every man is a peece of the Continent, a part of the maine; if a Clod bee washed away by the Sea, Europe is the lesse, as well as if a Promontorie were, as well as if a Mannor of thy friends or of thine owne were; any mans death diminishes me, because I am involved in Mankinde; And therefore never send to know for whom the bell tolls; It tolls for thee.

It is, then, in the realm of what he called "the interhuman" that Buber located that form of existence which can alone be considered to represent for man a truly authentic mode of life. And he constantly likened the authentic life unto a form of "dialogue," taking a conversation between two speakers to present one of the purest instances of men's mutually recognizing and confirming one another's humanity. For the very idea of conversation presupposes a willingness on the part of the participants to reveal themselves to each other, to listen: two men cannot have a conversation unless each undertakes to bring himself to the other and to receive in turn the other's self-disclosure. One must try to convey himself (his attitudes and beliefs) with candor and clarity, with as little distortion as possible, holding back nothing that might advance mutual understanding—and one must also try to offer one's fellow interlocutor the very best attentiveness one can summon, for one wants really to grasp what he is attempting to say. You cannot have a genuine conversation, in other words, unless each participant makes an honest and serious effort to *see* the other, to enter into his perspective, to feel the rhythm that experience has for him, to understand how the world appears on his side of the fence. And Buber's whole point was that it is precisely in the interaction occurring in a true and serious dialogue that we have our clearest example of the kind of mutuality apart from which the relation between man and man can never become a means of grace and joy and fulfillment. So, in the way of a metaphor, he said—"real" life *is* "dialogue."

It is a metaphor, though, which may to some extent distort Buber's real meaning. For the image that is most immediately brought into our minds by the idea of dialogue or conversation is an image of two persons talking to each other. And thus Buber's readers are likely to conclude—as many unfortunately have concluded—that the world of I-Thou relations is a world of unattached and mutually exclusive personal duets, and that the chief relevance of the I-Thou ethic is to the relations of the private life. Buber himself was prepared to admit that it is in the more intimate contexts of one-to-one relationships that the life of dialogue is most fully realized, the purest case of the I-Thou relation being indeed the love between husband and wife. But, as his many writings on social and political questions consistently indicate, he never for a moment conceived the kind of human norm represented by the I-Thou relation to be relevant only to the intimacies of personal life. As he says in his book *Between Man and Man*,

> You put before me the man taken up with duty and business. Yes, precisely him I mean, him in the factory, in the shop, in the office, in the mine, on the tractor, at the printing-press; man. . . . I have him in mind. . . . Dialogue is not an affair of spiritual luxury. . . .
>
> No factory and no office is so abandoned by creation that a creative glance could not fly up from one working-place to another, from desk to desk. . . .

Which is to say that there is no realm of encounter that may not be stirred into greater supportiveness of the human spirit by the life of dialogue—and most especially did Buber conceive this to be the case in the larger structures of social and economic life, where men are all the more likely to become simply faceless statistics and where, if the office or the factory is to be a really human place, it is perhaps even more essential than in our simpler one-to-one relationships that the actual quality of life be constantly held under the judgment of the "dialogical" norm. For Buber would have agreed with the remark of Robert Dubreuilh in Simone de Beauvoir's *The Mandarins* (which was quoted in the previous chapter), that "You can't draw a straight line in a curved space. You can't lead a proper life in a society which isn't proper." And, as he is at pains to remind us in many of his books, if conceptions which derogate the dignity of the human person are allowed to find expression in systems of social and economic power, the inevitable result will be the emergence of an environment in which the life of dialogue must wither away and die.

But now it has also to be remarked that no account of Buber's "philosophy of dialogue" begins even to approach adequacy, if it leaves the impression that his thought bears only on the dimension of the "interhuman." This is, to be sure, the point at which he begins, but it does at last become apparent that his analysis of the "interhuman" is undertaken in part for the sake of disclosing that not only do we most truly encounter one another in the life of dialogue but that, in the moment of genuine "meeting" with the neighbor, we also "look out toward the fringe of the eternal Thou." God, in short, is the great silent partner of every human dialogue into which we enter: "in each [human Thou] we are aware of a breath from the eternal Thou: in each Thou [whom we encounter on this earth] we address the eternal Thou." It is toward this kind of affirmation that the whole movement of Buber's thought ultimately proceeds.

He knows, of course, how baffling the people of our time find the idea of God, for we in the West live now at the end of a long period in which for centuries the central traditions of philosophical and theological thought have conceived the relation between the world and God in "objective" terms, as though it could be understood by way of categories belonging to the sphere of I-and-It. God has been conceived to be *a* Being "out there" somewhere, far afield from the world—"the supreme Being, the grand Architect, who exists somewhere out beyond the world—like a rich aunt in Australia—who started it all going, periodically intervenes in its running, and generally gives evidence of his benevolent interest in it."* But, living as we

* John A. T. Robinson, *Honest to God* (Philadelphia: Westminster Press, 1963), p. 30.

do in a world of telephones and space travel and nuclear
fission, it is simply no longer possible for man to take
seriously the old picture—of *a* Being who "exists" *outside*
the world which science describes but who from time to
time enters into this world for the sake of altering in some
way its normal processes. The God who dwells "above"
nature but who yet comes "down from heaven" periodically
to intervene in human affairs and to redirect the course of
nature and history—this is a conception which has increasingly lost any real capacity to captivate the modern
imagination. So the very word "God" has become for many
so tarnished and so devoid of any specifiable content that
it cannot even be spoken without discomfort and embarrassment. The "objectivized" God who is "up there" or
"out there" is a notion which has simply lost its persuasive power. And thus, as Paul Tillich once suggested,
if human experience is any longer to be understood religiously it may be necessary for "you . . . [to] forget
everything traditional that you have learned about God,
perhaps even that word itself."* Yet, says Buber in effect, there is no accounting for the kind of unlimited and
unconditional demand that is exerted upon us in the I-Thou
relation except by way of the assumption that this relation
is itself the bearer of something that belongs to the fundamental structure of reality—and which must finally be
named God, even though (as he says in *Eclipse of God*)
this "is the most heavy-laden of all human words."

J. H. Oldham in a remarkable little book of 1953 called
Life Is Commitment puts the issue in a way of which Buber
would surely have approved. He says:

> Let us imagine a young man of brilliant promise standing on
> a pier, and beside him a wreck of humanity, a man advanced
> in years whose powers have been squandered and exhausted

* Paul Tillich, *The Shaking of the Foundations* (New York: Charles
Scribner's Sons, 1948), p. 57.

through dissipation. The latter stumbles and falls into the water. The younger man leaps in after him, risking, and perhaps actually losing, his own life. There is no rational justification for such an act. By every possible calculation, the younger life is the more valuable. The loss to the community by its sacrifice is incomparably greater. And yet we feel intuitively that humanity would somehow be a poorer, meaner affair if such things were not done. Such instances of sacrifice for the sake of others are not rare; they are the ordinary stuff of life. In wartime they abound. In peacetime we have only to pick up a newspaper and the chances are that we shall find some story of self-denying heroism, and the deeds that are recorded are only a fraction of those that are performed. We could never complete the tale of the sacrifices of parents for their children or of men and women for their friends, or even for strangers.*

Now here is a fine description of the inherent stuff of the I-Thou reality, for it is essentially an affair of being confronted by another who does in effect ask for a gift—for the gift of oneself. Self-giving is in fact the very meaning of love. As Dr. Oldham reminds us, "When you love another person you make a complete, unreserved commitment of yourself. You cannot help doing that, if you really love. In marriage you take the other 'for better or worse, for richer or poorer, in sickness and in health, to love and to cherish till death us do part.'" And, as we are also reminded by Dr. Oldham's hypothetical tale of the young man who plunges into the water to save an unknown derelict, we often find ourselves being summoned even to show unlimited devotion to a stranger. But how does it come to be that other human beings, with all their manifest faults and failings, can, nevertheless, make an absolute claim upon us, and one which our consciences goad us into acknowledging? It would seem that any absolute self-sacrifice could be exacted of us only by that which is itself

* J. H. Oldham, *Life is Commitment* (New York: Harper & Bros., 1953), pp. 54-55.

absolute and without imperfection. But how are we to account for one of the commonest realities of human experience—that in fact one person can and often does exert an *absolute* claim on another person, not in the way of any sort of tyrant but simply in the way of one who needs my help, my support, my love? How is this possible? Well, Buber's answer is beautifully summarized by J. H. Oldham, that "when we give ourselves in complete surrender to another person or persons, we are responding not merely to them in their finitude but to something greater of which they are the embodiment," that "when we really love to the point of giving our whole selves, we are . . . in some way reaching out to the infinite and relating ourselves to the ultimate meaning of the universe." Or, as Buber says: "Every particular *Thou* is a glimpse through to the eternal *Thou*. . . ." Which is to say that, in the I-Thou relations that give depth and substance to our lives, we discover that which seems somehow to be the ultimate Ground of reality—and we may call it *God*. God, in other words, is not an "object" above all other objects, in some spooky "superworld." But, rather, "God" is the name to be given to that radically mysterious depth of the I-Thou relation itself. And here, of course, is Buber's Hasidism again, for what he wants always to say is that God is to be encountered not by retreating from the world into some "religious" or "sacred" region but, rather, He is to be encountered as we move more deeply into the full reality of all the I-Thou encounters that are brought to us ever and again by the life of everyday. It is not the raptures of mystical ecstasy that are to be sought, but rather it is, as he says, "the central reality of the everyday hour"—which is a "simile of the relation with God," indeed the only simile of that relation which we shall ever have.

Here, then, is a drastically condensed version of the

testimony which is rendered about the human pilgrimage by one of the most challenging thinkers of the twentieth century. Yet one hesitates a little to speak of Buber as "thinker," for, as one looks at the immense body of work that came from his pen—at *I and Thou* and its more elaborate development in *Between Man and Man;* at such essays in social and political theory as *Israel and Palestine* and *Paths in Utopia;* at philosophical studies of religion like *Two Types of Faith* and *Eclipse of God;* at his numerous books on Hasidism and Judaism; and at various other writings—it is apparent that he was a man whose basic commitment was not to a "system" of thought. Indeed, he shared the existentialists' characteristic indifference toward "system," and Gregor Smith hits the nail on the head when he speaks of Buber as having been "a man with a single insight." The myriad ramifications which that insight underwent in his thought have, of course, in no substantial way been fully reviewed here; but perhaps the essential core of it has at least been set forth—and, in brief, it amounts to the proposal that Buber did himself contain within a single sentence of his inaugural lectures at the Hebrew University of Jerusalem in 1938, when he said, "The fundamental fact of human existence is man with man."[*]

Gabriel Marcel, it is true, in his own most important work—his Gifford Lectures at the University of Aberdeen in Scotland, published as *The Mystery of Being* (2 vols.) —declares ours to be a world in which "the preposition 'with' . . . seems more and more to be losing its meaning." And there is much which suggests that this is increasingly the case. Marcel's line was written in the late 1940's, in the light of all the dilapidation, particularly on the European scene, that followed in the wake of World War II;

[*] Martin Buber, *Between Man and Man*, trans. by Ronald Gregor Smith (New York: Macmillan Co., 1948), p. 203.

but now, as we approach the end of the 1970's, the outlook may be even bleaker, especially from an American perspective. Over a long period we in this country were providentially spared much of the social and political disorder that has been so regularly recurrent in modern Europe: but in recent years—through the terrible drama of racial crisis, through the increasing anarchy and decline that settle down upon our great urban centers, through our tragic involvement of the 1960's and early 70's in the tangled affairs of Southeast Asia—we, too, have been initiated into "the terrors of history." And, at whatever point to which one turns today on the Western scene, one finds the overwhelming need of the modern metropolis to be that of finding ways of preventing "personal existence from being submerged by impersonal forces and technical requirements, [ways of affirming] . . . the reality of love in face of the reality of power."* Indeed, it was doubtless some prevision of how much this would increasingly be the most difficult challenge facing modern society that led Buber in 1938, in his inaugural lectures at the Hebrew University in Jerusalem, to speak of his fundamental standpoint as a "narrow rocky ridge." And so perhaps it is, for, in our own late stage of modern history the world often seems to be ever more surely slouching toward a greater impersonality and a greater facelessness in the basic structures of human community, and nothing seems to be more doubtful than the future of the person. Yet, from his narrow ridge, Buber tells us that there is no "happy middle" to be found in any system of life that discounts the primacy of the I-Thou relation, for man, as he maintains, cannot dwell continuously in the world of *It* and remain, in any authentic sense of the word, truly human.

But, as we have noticed, the range of that dialogue to which Buber believes man to be called extends far be-

* J. H. Oldham, *op. cit.*, p. 91.

yond the realm of "the interhuman" and embraces, ultimately, that conversation between the human spirit and the
Lord of the world—which overflows the boundaries of all
speech and which carries the soul into the rich blessing of
companionship with the Eternal Thou. In an essay of 1929
called "Dialogue" (in *Between Man and Man*) Buber recalls how frequently through his lifetime a night's sleep
brought over and again the same dream. "I name it," he
says, "the dream of the double cry." He is at first wrestling
with an animal—like a small lion cub—which is tearing the
flesh from his arm and which only by a great effort is
forced to loose its hold. This first part of the dream "always unrolls at a furious pace" and is soon over. "Then
suddenly the pace abates," and it is as if he stood in some
vast cave "or on the fringe of a gigantic forest" in a
drear and desolate kind of "primitive" world. And he finds
himself uttering a cry—"sometimes joyous, sometimes fear-
ful, sometimes even filled both with pain and with triumph." At first it is only the merest wail or whisper, but
gradually it gathers strength until, through the strict
rhythms of its rising and falling, it swells to a fullness
which, as he says, "my throat could not endure were I
awake." And, at the climax, it seems that his very heart
must cease its beating, so powerfully is he overwhelmed
by the great billows of sound that come pouring up out
of his breast. Finally, this cry—which has become a kind
of tremendous song—completes itself and is finished. Then
he waits, and from somewhere, far away, across the vast
spaces of this primitive world, another cry begins slowly
to move toward him. At first he feels that this is somehow
the same cry that had come rushing up from the depths of
his own spirit, but as he listens more intently he realizes
that, no, *this* cry is no mere echo of his own but is "uttered or sung by another voice": it is a new voice and
another cry which is a true rejoinder to his own. At first it,

too, is something very muted and barely audible, but
gradually it grows deeper and larger, widening out until
finally, through the variousness of its rhythm and the
richness of its brilliant tonality, it seems to reproduce the
very music of the spheres, somehow gathering up the whole
mystery of Creation into a great symphony of glorious
sound: all this comes rushing back into his soul. It is a
moment of the most transcendent exaltation. Then, slowly,
all this jubilance dies away; and, at last, as a great silence
once more descends upon the empty plains of this primitive
region, Buber says that always in his dream there comes
to him the "certitude . . . that *now it has happened*"—
just so, nothing more, and in just this way: *now it has
happened.* So it has gone, he says, this "dream of the
double cry"—over and again, across the stretch of a lifetime.

It is a beautiful tale and makes a haunting figure of that
final dialogue into which the human spirit is called—
which is the dialogue with God. As one commentator on
Buber's parable has remarked, "It is only when out of the
wrestling and the agony and the tearing of our flesh and
blood, it is only when our own hearts actually suffer in the
travail of a new birth and we attempt to say what has
never been said before, that at last come all the rhythms
and glories of a song which transcends the emptiness and
space of this world. At the same time already prepared
and waiting from the foundation of the world comes the
answer, first a piping sound, and then the mounting
corroborations of history, until the symphony of it is completed and wedded with our own voice. We have entered
into a dialogue between ourselves and God and until we
have achieved that dialogue we will be unable to talk to
any living soul except in terms of pots and pans, profits,
advantages, position."* This is, indeed, the essential testimony constituting Martin Buber's legacy to the people of

our time: that there shall be no real communion and joy and peace among men until they rediscover God, and that our coming into our full human stature awaits each man's learning how, out of the depth of his soul, to speak forth the word that is more fundamental than any other—the word "Thou." For, as Buber reminds us, it is in the utterance of this word that man finds his true beginning and his true end.

° Samuel H. Miller, *The Life of the Church* (New York: Harper & Bros., 1953), pp. 131-132.

8

The Achievement
of Existentialism

OVER A LONG PERIOD, at least ever since the middle years
of the eighteenth century, a certain large, comprehensive
sense of reality has prevailed in the Western world and
has afforded the terms of reference whereby human experience has been most basically understood. It is an attitude of mind in accordance with which "the real world"
has been taken to be the things and events and processes
of Nature. And Nature has itself been conceived to be not
simply the world of inanimate matter and of subhuman
vegetal and animal species existing apart from man, but
the entire system of reality to which man also belongs.
Man himself has been thought of as a work of Nature,
no doubt its most important work; and Nature has been
supposed to be the scene and setting of his life—which has
itself been considered to be most essentially controlled by
the laws of Nature. This basic premise has guided the
main course of Western thought over the past two hundred
years and has very largely shaped its characteristic world
view.

To assume that man is integrally a part of the natural

order—not only his body, but his entire spiritual life as well—is inevitably to assume that the phenomenon of man requires to be understood by means of those methods of inquiry that have proved to be most illuminating of everything else in Nature: namely, the methods of empirical science. And this, too, is an assumption which has been deeply a part of that *sense of reality* whereby the world has been most basically interpreted in the modern period. Man has been thought of as situated squarely in the setting of Nature, as having a natural origin and a natural history, and as involved in a complex pattern of interactions with the forces making up his natural environment. But not only has he been conceived to be an animal species like any other, and thus amenable on all levels of his life to the kinds of understanding promoted by the natural and biological sciences: his whole mental and conscious life and his relations with his human neighbors have also been considered accessible to exact scientific description. For if his life is a truly natural life, then no aspect of his existence can be unamenable to scientific study and formulation.

Our modern habit of regarding man as a scientific object has entailed unquestionable advantages. "Fancies, Ghosts, and every empty shade" have been put to flight, along with the fears and superstitions of premodern experience. And surely it deserves to be thought of as a great advance, that men of the modern age have brushed aside those fantasies by which the people of earlier periods were often so grievously haunted—of human life as beset on every side by mysterious and supernatural agencies, angelic hosts and prankish devils. It is surely a good thing that we no longer regard our world as open to invasion from without by capricious spirits and strange potencies, that modern man conceives himself as solely responsible for his own feelings and thoughts and decisions.

The world in which we find ourselves often appears, it is true, to be a most inhospitable world. But the old terrors have been exorcised: at one or another critical juncture in experience we may find an abyss underfoot, but at least we know it to be a *human* abyss—and this is, undoubtedly, a great gain, in the increase of poise and equanimity which thereby becomes possible.

But, though it has brought substantial advantages, our modern habit of conceiving human experience as simply another sort of material for empirical observation and experiment has also entailed a certain loss of profundity in our sense of who we most basically are. Among all the great moral injunctions which our culture, in its most ancient expressions, lays down there is perhaps none so immemorially honored as that which was inscribed over the gateway leading into the Temple of Apollo at Delphi—"Know thyself." But it is more than a little doubtful as to whether or not any right and deeply true knowledge of man is achievable, if he is thought of simply as a certain kind of mammal occupying space in a certain way. This, of course, he undeniably is, but it is by no means so assured that such a definition of man affords any genuine illumination of distinctively *human* reality. He constitutes, it is true, one element or species of the animal kingdom, but it is exceedingly doubtful that the kinds of notations on his resemblance to other animals that are made by the sciences of anatomy and physiology and behavioristic psychology offer any real answer to the kind of question man himself is raising, when he begins to search for the driving principle of his life as one whose destiny it is to be a *human* being.

It is doubtless true that man is a "tool-making animal" and a "thinking animal," that in certain respects he is simply "an ingenious assembly of portable plumbing" or a kind of machine into which food is put and by which what we call thought is produced. And such a scientific culture as our own has been ingenious in devising dozens of similar definitions—all of which, however, are seen to be absurdly piecemeal, as soon as any man tests them against the immediacy of his own self-awareness. Yet it is precisely the reductionism of a piecemeal view of things which tends to be promoted by the notion that man is simply one of a multitude of scientific objects awaiting systematic description and classification. For the scientific enterprise always wants to strip things of human "distortion": it always wants to observe them in a spirit of utter detachment, to contain them within a quantitative formula, to place them squarely within the objective frame of Nature. But, of course, man is a creature a part of whose uniqueness consists in the impossibility of bottling him up in a mathematical theorem. You can say that he is definable as one the fat in whose body will yield seven cakes of soap, a creature containing enough iron to make a small nail, enough phosphorus for two thousand match heads, and enough sulphur to permit him to rid himself of his own fleas.* And such a description may in some sort be true, but it does not tell us anything that really helps us toward a deeper understanding of ourselves. In the critical moments of our lives, it is not some new method of chemically classifying ourselves that we want—not some formula that merely redefines our animality—but rather, it is a renewed understanding of our humanity and of the full depth of our personal existence.

The supposition that the scientific outlook affords a sufficiently comprehensive basis for the interpretation of man did, however, reign over a long period, without any effective challenge. For the spectacular successes of modern

* A statement which Abraham Joshua Heschel (in his book *Who Is Man?* [Stanford: Stanford University Press, 1965]) reports as having enjoyed wide currency in pre-Nazi Germany.

science in harnessing the energies of nature to human purpose
lent a seeming persuasiveness to the view that the inner
being of man himself must finally prove accessible to the
same modes of analysis which had been found to be so
useful in subduing the external world. But in our own late
stage of modern history this assumption has begun to lose
its old cogency, and we have begun to find ourselves overtaken by a renewed sense of what is profoundly mysterious in human existence and of how elusively that mystery
slips through the nets of purely scientific schemes of interpretation.

Martin Buber once proposed (in *Between Man and Man*)
that the history of the human spirit be thought of as an affair of alternation between "epochs of habitation and
epochs of homelessness." In epochs of habitation, man
does not experience his own humanity as anything prob-
lematic or particularly perplexing. He does not understand
the world with reference to himself, but, rather, under-
stands himself with reference to the world, and he dwells
in the world "as in a house, as in a home." Such a period,
for example, was the Middle Ages, when the Christian
cosmos offered man a world in which no region was uncharted and in which every human being knew himself to
be accommodated, to have his divinely ordained place.
In epochs of habitation there is no great anxiety about
the fundamental terms of existence, for the world is felt to
be so ordered as to guarantee everything its fixed place
in the hierarchy of being. But in epochs of homelessness
"man lives in the world as in an open field": the old secu-
rities are no longer effective, and, feeling himself to be
trapped in an icy kind of solitude, man becomes a great
question to himself: "the original contract between the
universe and man is dissolved and man finds himself a
stranger and solitary in the world." Such an age came into
being with the advent of the Renaissance, as the medieval

world system began to collapse and as man consequently began to inquire with a new earnestness into the ultimate issues of human destiny.

It is most especially, though, our own age that Buber wants to speak of as an epoch of homelessness, for now, again, men are confusedly searching for the basic ground-plan of the universe and are driven ever more deeply back in upon themselves. And one could say that ours is an age of homelessness, in part because the sheer terror which is a part of the world we have made is itself incomprehensible within the terms of the classic modern outlook, which sees man as simply one among countless scientific objects. The creature who has produced a scientific establishment capable of ushering in the nuclear age, and who has produced a political establishment generating the unnerving tension with which we live today in the world community is, we now feel, very much like Mary Shelley's Frankenstein, who created a "second nature" threatening to surpass man's capacity to control. But though Victor Frankenstein's monster may be conceivable as a "scientific object," surely the creative capacity that could invent such a prodigy deserves something like the Psalmist's exclamation, that man is a being "fearfully and wonderfully made!" And not only does the fearsomeness of what we make of nature itself inspire in us a strange kind of marveling at ourselves, but so too does what we do to one another, in the demonic ingeniousness with which it manages to liquidate the human presence—through the dehumanized impersonality of our great cities, through our brutal indifference to the suffering of the poor, through the sluggishness of moral imagination with which we respond to the humiliation of oppressed racial and ethnic minorities. So that, finally, we begin to wonder what are the limits beyond which human beings cannot go, in the acquisition and use of power, if they are to remain human.

What, indeed, does it mean for a human being to be human? What is the distinctively *human* component in humankind? How does a man properly go about discovering and reverencing and preserving his humanity? What *is* "the human"?

It is such questions as these that constitute the great burden for reflection in our time. And what is innovative in Existentialism, as a tradition of modern thought, is precisely the immediacy and straightforwardness with which it addresses this kind of issue. For here we have a family of thinkers whose chief interest has been not at all in the objective classification and quantification of human experience in accordance with any "scientific" model; instead, they have wanted, as it were, to bracket off the dimension which is designated by the attribute "human" in the term "human being," and then to make the distinctively *human* reality the essential datum for philosophical thought and literary meditation.

If I am asked who I am, I can, of course, give my name and date and place of birth, followed by other vital statistics and a résumé of my professional career. But any man looking at such a catalogue of information about himself knows that it does not even remotely manage to touch anything truly central to the reality of his existence: it may, of course, do some sort of rough justice to what he is in so far as he is an item of the fact world, of the world *out there*. But viewed merely as a scientific object, as an item of the fact world, a man is simply a certain sort of biological creature struggling to adjust to his environment, and is in no great way different from a cat or a monkey. His full reality cannot begin to be broached merely by the ticking off of certain vital statistics, for what is decisive is the total life-situation of the individual and his own sense of that situation, the whole horizon within which he apprehends the meaning of his name and family origins and personal involvements. And one does not begin to penetrate the *human* dimension until *this* order of questions becomes the ruling focus of one's inquiry.

Now it is precisely in its recovery of philosophical prestige for the human world that the great achievement of Existentialism may be said to consist. In this, of course, it has been very greatly assisted by the psychologies descending from Freud and Jung and by numerous developments in modern art and literature. But here, we feel now, is the tradition—whether in its more purely philosophical or theological or literary aspects—which, perhaps more than any other, has reinstated as a datum for reflection the specifically *human* life-world, what the Germans call *Lebenswelt*.

Those philosophers who suppose that the true vocation of philosophy is only to be that of a sort of handmaiden to empirical science offer, to be sure, a very determined resistance to the whole existentialist movement. For, as they say, it is too *literary* a form of philosophy to deserve being thought of as genuinely philosophical: the themes of memory and time, of anxiety and death, of suffering and love, of alienation and despair, of homelessness and nostalgia, belong, we are told, in the cinema perhaps and in poetry and drama and fiction, but they are not the material of which philosophical treatises are properly made. To which one can only answer that, if this is so, then so much the worse for philosophy. For men do lose their moorings and find themselves suddenly homeless; men are stung by the knowledge of their frailty and finitude, and they do worry anxiously about what the morrow will bring forth; they are baffled by "the cruel mathematics that command our condition," and they do contemplate in a spirit of profound unease the certainty that they shall ultimately die. All of this belongs most deeply to the essential character of specifically *human* existence: man moves "on the edge of chaos within and without"[*]: he is a creature often insecure and filled with alarm. A large part of his uniqueness consists in his capacity and compulsion to ask questions about himself: not only can I look at myself and interrogate myself, but I can also in turn ask questions about the interrogator—and thus the self's transcendence of itself can proceed almost infinitely. Which means that man is a creature who "exists," who can stand out from or apart from himself, disclosing himself to himself or concealing himself from himself, and thus finding himself to be one for whom life is an affair either of authenticity or inauthenticity. So he is a creature whose nature requires him to ask himself *who* he is and *what* he is; and the moment of self-confrontation is a moment of suspense and shock and mystery.

Now this can, of course, all be taken for granted, in a spirit of indifference, if it is assumed—as it tends to be today by academic philosophy on the Anglo-American scene —that the locus of the real lies not so much within the human person as in that outer world with which he carries on various sorts of transactions. And the absolute tangibility of this outer world is surely undeniable: if a man requires reassurance that there is indeed a world outside his own brainpan, all he need do is to knock his head vigorously against a tree. But the specifically *human* world —and this, in a way, is the whole claim of Existentialism —is discoverable only when one descends into the interior of the person and begins to study the self's experience of itself and of its relatedness to the environing reality of nature and human society. Here it is, the existentialists declare, that the real "bite of existence" is to be felt, in the deep things of personal experience which make us know— through love and sorrow, through nostalgia and joy,

[*] Ralph Harper, *Existentialism: A Theory of Man* (Cambridge: Harvard University Press, 1948), p. 13.

through death and loss—that a man's life is not any sort of intellectual puzzle to be ferreted out but a gift to be received and a task to be fulfilled. And it is in the definitiveness with which it has broken the silence of modern philosophy about the distinctively human world that the great achievement of Existentialism may be seen to consist.

It may be the case that this movement has sometimes tended to overestimate the inclemency of the human weather: its propensity for sounding a hue and cry may sometimes have made for an excessively melodramatic account of man's experience, with too great a sense of panic, too great an emphasis on the narrowness of the ledge on which we live, on the cracking of the earth beneath. It may sometimes have tended too much to represent human life (in Kierkegaard's figure) as an affair of shipwreck on an empty sea, with 70,000 fathoms of water our sole support. But, though their attentiveness to man's inner distress may occasionally have prompted the existentialists to render an exaggeratedly alarmist kind of testimony, it is precisely this attentiveness which has helped them to keep a very lively sense of man as a highly unique kind of reality which is irreducible to anything other than itself.

The exact measurements of empirical science have, quite obviously, an absolute indispensability on many levels of life, and no one in his right mind would deny this to be so. But when, for the sake of exactitude, man is so objectified and rationalized as to be made simply one item among many in the realm of "scientific objects," then, as the existentialists maintain, it is a bogus exactitude which is being honored. What Buber calls the world of *It* is open to human manipulation and control, and is therefore fully accessible to scientific method. But the world of *I*-and-*Thou*, unlike the world of *It*, is not a world which man holds but is, rather, a world by which he is held—and thus what is precision in the one dimension may be the wildest kind of imprecision in the other, in the *human* world, where systematic reason must, to be sure, be at work but where it needs also to be informed (as in existentialist procedure) by the sorts of insights that go into the making of memoirs and autobiographies and poetry and prayer. And it is the important achievement of Existentialism to have reinstated in our age a sense of the irreducibility of the *I-Thou* dimension to the world of *It*, to have reinstated a sense of how highly specialized is the kind of reality represented by the *human* being.

"Existentialism is a humanism," says Jean-Paul Sartre. And if he is taken to mean, as he does, that it is inevitably committed to his own special sort of atheistic humanism, then one will regard his proposition as simply descriptive of Sartre's own philosophic program. But, if one interprets "humanism" more spaciously and more traditionally, as that type of philosophic and poetic vision which insists on the radical dignity and uniqueness of the human presence, then the movement in modern literature and philosophy and theology which is called Existentialism may well be considered to be the most robust and influential humanism of our period, and the one which, perhaps more than any other, represents the characteristic contribution of the twentieth century to the humanistic tradition.

Selected Bibliography

The brief checklist below has been prepared only for non-specialist readers who wish to broaden their view of modern Existentialism. And thus neither the citations of critical literature on Existentialism nor those of works by the particular writers discussed in this book are in any way comprehensive. Only materials in the English language are included in the bibliography.

GENERAL STUDIES OF EXISTENTIALISM

William Barrett, *Irrational Man: A Study in Existential Philosophy*. Garden City. N.Y.: Doubleday Anchor Books, 1958.
_____, *What Is Existentialism?*. New York: Grove Press, 1964.
H. J. Blackham, *Six Existentialist Thinkers*. London: Routledge & Kegan Paul Ltd., 1951; New York: Macmillan Co., 1952.
James D. Collins, *The Existentialists*. Chicago: Henry Regnery Co., 1952.
Marjorie Grene, *Dreadful Freedom: A Critique of Existentialism*. Chicago: University of Chicago Press, 1948.
Ralph Harper, *Existentialism: A Theory of Man*. Cambridge: Harvard University Press, 1948.

F. H. Heinemann, *Existentialism and the Modern Predicament.*
New York: Harper and Bros., 1958.

Helmut Kuhn, *Encounter with Nothingness: An Essay on Existentialism.* Chicago: Henry Regnery Co., 1949.

Carl Michalson, ed., *Christianity and the Existentialists.* New York: Charles Scribner's Sons, 1956.

Kurt F. Reinhardt, *The Existentialist Revolt.* New York: Frederick Ungar Publishing Co., 1960.

David E. Roberts, *Existentialism and Religious Belief.* New York: Oxford University Press, 1959.

Roger L. Shinn, ed., *Restless Adventure: Essays on Contemporary Expressions of Existentialism.* New York: Charles Scribner's Sons, 1968.

Søren Kierkegaard

Søren Kierkegaard, *Fear and Trembling,* trans. by Walter Lowrie. Princeton: Princeton University Press, 1941.

————, *Repetition: An Essay in Experimental Psychology,* trans. by Walter Lowrie. Princeton: Princeton University Press, 1941.

————, *Stages on Life's Way,* trans. by Walter Lowrie. Princeton: Princeton University Press, 1940.

————, *The Sickness Unto Death,* trans. by Walter Lowrie. Princeton: Princeton University Press, 1941.

————, *Concluding Unscientific Postscript,* trans. and ed. by David F. Swenson and Walter Lowrie. Princeton: Princeton University Press, 1941.

————, *The Concept of Dread,* trans. by Walter Lowrie. Princeton: Princeton University Press, 1944.

————, *Either/Or: A Fragment of Life,* trans. by David F. Swenson and Lillian M. Swenson. Princeton: Princeton University Press, 1944.

————, *Training in Christianity,* trans. by Walter Lowrie. Princeton: Princeton University Press, 1944.

————, *Works of Love,* trans. by David F. Swenson and Lillian M. Swenson. Princeton: Princeton University Press, 1946.

————, *Attack upon "Christendom,"* trans. by Walter Lowrie. Princeton: Princeton University Press, 1944.

————, *Philosophical Fragments,* trans. by David F. Swenson and rev. by Howard V. Hong. Princeton: Princeton University Press, 1962.

_____, *The Present Age*, trans. by Alexander Dru. New York: Harper and Row, Inc., 1962.

_____, *The Point of View for My Work as An Author*, trans. by Walter Lowrie. New York: Harper and Row, Inc., 1962.

_____, *The Last Years: Journals, 1853-1855*, trans. and ed. by Ronald Gregor Smith. New York: Harper and Row, Inc., 1965.

_____, *The Concept of Irony*, trans. by Lee M. Capel. New York: Harper and Row, Inc., 1966.

_____, *Journals and Papers*, ed. and trans. by Howard V. Hong and Edna H. Hong. 4 vols. Bloomington: Indiana University Press, 1967-1976.

_____, *Armed Neutrality*, ed. and trans. by Howard V. Hong and Edna H. Hong. Bloomington: Indiana University Press, 1968.

Robert Bretall, ed., *A Kierkegaard Anthology*. New York: Modern Library, 1959.

James D. Collins, *The Mind of Kierkegaard*. Chicago: Henry Regnery Co., 1953.

Louis K. Dupré, *Kierkegaard as Theologian*. London: Sheed and Ward, 1963.

Vernard Eller, *Kierkegaard and Radical Discipleship*. Princeton: Princeton University Press, 1968.

Eduard Geismar, *Lectures on the Religious Thought of Søren Kierkegaard*. Minneapolis: Augsburg Publishing House, 1937.

Theodor Haecker, *Kierkegaard the Cripple*, trans. by C. Van O. Bruyn. New York: Philosophical Library, 1950.

Howard A. Johnson and Niels Thulstrup, eds., *A Kierkegaard Critique*. New York: Harper and Bros., 1962.

Regis Jolivet, *Introduction to Kierkegaard*, trans. by W. H. Barber. New York: E. P. Dutton and Co., 1951.

Walter Lowrie, *Kierkegaard*. New York: Oxford University Press, 1938.

_____, *A Short Life of Kierkegaard*. Princeton: Princeton University Press, 1942.

Louis Mackey, *Kierkegaard: A Kind of Poet*. Philadelphia: University of Pennsylvania Press, 1971.

Gregor Malantschuk, *Kierkegaard's Thought*, ed. and trans. by Howard V. Hong and Edna H. Hong. Princeton: Princeton University Press, 1971.

George Henry Price, *The Narrow Pass: A Study of Kierkegaard's Concept of Man.* New York: McGraw-Hill and Co., 1963.

Adi Shmuëli, *Kierkegaard and Consciousness,* trans. by Naomi Handelman. Princeton: Princeton University Press, 1971.

Paul R. Sponheim, *Kierkegaard on Christ and Christian Coherence.* New York: Harper and Row, Inc., 1967.

Mark C. Taylor, *Kierkegaard's Pseudonymous Authorship: A Study of Time and the Self.* Princeton: Princeton University Press, 1975.

Josiah Thompson, *The Lonely Labyrinth.* Carbondale: Southern Illinois University Press, 1967.

————, *Kierkegaard: A Biographical Essay.* New York: Alfred A. Knopf, Inc., 1973.

FRIEDRICH NIETZSCHE

Note: The only complete English edition of Nietzsche's writings is that which Oscar Levy edited many years ago (*The Complete Works of Friedrich Nietzsche,* 18 vols.; New York: Macmillan, 1909-1911) and which was reissued in 1964 (New York: Russell and Russell). The general unsatisfactoriness of the translations in the Levy edition has been long recognized, however, and currently the most reliable Englsh versions of Nietzsche's texts will be found in the collection edited by Walter Kaufmann for Random House's Modern Library "Giant" series, *Basic Writings of Nietzsche* (1968), which contains Mr. Kaufmann's superb translations of *The Birth of Tragedy, Beyond Good and Evil, On the Genealogy of Morals, The Case of Wagner,* and *Ecce Homo.* This volume supplements *The Portable Nietzsche* (New York: Viking Press, 1959), which is edited by Mr. Kaufmann and which contains his translations of *Thus Spake Zarathustra, Twilight of the Idols, The Antichrist, Nietzsche contra* Wagner, and his translations of selections from Nietzsche's various other writings. Mr. Kaufmann's translation of *The Will to Power* is published separately (New York: Vintage Books, 1968); and his English version of *The Gay Science* appeared in 1974 (New York: Random House).

David B. Allison, ed., *The New Nietzsche: Contemporary Styles of Interpretation.* New York: Delta Books, 1977.

Conrad Bonifazi, *Christendom Attacked: A Comparison of Kierkegaard and Nietzsche.* London: Rockliff, 1953.

Erich Heller, *The Artist's Journey into the Interior and Other Essays*. New York: Random House, 1965. See the sixth essay, "The Importance of Nietzsche."

R. J. Hollingdale, *Nietzsche: The Man and His Philosophy*. Baton Rouge: Louisiana State University Press, 1965.

Walter Kaufmann, *Nietzsche: Philosopher, Psychologist, Antichrist*. 3rd ed. New York: Vintage Books, 1968.

F. A. Lea, *The Tragic Philosopher: A Study of Friedrich Nietzsche*. New York: Philosophical Library, 1957.

George A. Morgan, Jr., *What Nietzsche Means*. New York: Harper Torchbooks, 1965.

H. A. Reyburn, *Nietzsche: The Story of a Human Philosopher*. London and New York: Macmillan Co., 1948.

MARTIN HEIDEGGER

Martin Heidegger, *Existence and Being*, trans. by Douglas Scott *et al*, with an Introduction by Werner Brock. Chicago: Henry Regnery Co., 1949.

_____, *What Is Philosophy?*, trans. by William Kluback and Jean T. Wilde. New York: Twayne, 1958.

_____, *The Question of Being*, trans. by William Kluback and Jean T. Wilde. New York: Twayne, 1958.

_____, *An Introduction to Metaphysics*, trans. by Ralph Manheim. New Haven: Yale University Press, 1959.

_____, *Being and Time*, trans. by John Macquarrie and Edward Robinson. New York: Harper and Row, Inc., 1962.

_____, *Kant and the Problem of Metaphysics*, trans. by James S. Churchill. Bloomington: Indiana University Press, 1962.

_____, *Discourse on Thinking*, trans. by John M. Anderson and E. Hans Freund. New York: Harper and Row, Inc., 1966.

_____, *What Is a Thing?*, trans. by W. B. Barton, Jr., and Vera Deutsch. Chicago: Henry Regnery Co., 1967.

_____, *What Is Called Thinking?*, trans. by Fred D. Wieck and J. Glenn Gray. New York: Harper and Row, Inc., 1968.

_____, *The Essence of Reasons*, trans. by Terence Malick. Evanston, Ill.: Northwestern University Press, 1969.

_____, *Identity and Difference*, trans. by Joan Stambaugh. New York: Harper and Row, Inc., 1969.

_____, *On the Way to Language*, trans. by Peter D. Hertz and Joan Stambaugh. New York: Harper and Row, Inc., 1971.

————, *Poetry, Language, Thought*, trans. by Albert Hofstadter. New York: Harper and Row, Inc., 1971.

————, *On Time and Being*, trans. by Joan Stambaugh. New York: Harper and Row, Inc., 1972.

————, *The End of Philosophy*, trans. by Joan Stambaugh. New York: Harper and Row, Inc., 1973.

————, *Early Greek Thinking*, trans. by David Farrell Krell and Frank A. Capuzzi. New York: Harper and Row, Inc., 1975.

————, *Basic Writings*, ed. by David Farrell Krell. New York: Harper and Row, Inc., 1976.

Walter Biemel, *Martin Heidegger*, trans. by J. L. Mehta. New York and London: Harcourt Brace Jovanovich (A Harvest Book), 1976.

Manfred Frings, ed., *Heidegger and the Quest for Truth*. Chicago: Quadrangle Books, 1968.

Michael Gelven, *A Commentary on Heidegger's "Being and Time."* New York: Harper and Row, Inc., 1970.

Marjorie Grene, *Martin Heidegger*. New York: Hillary House, 1957.

Magda King, *Heidegger's Philosophy: A Guide to His Basic Thought*. New York: Macmillan Co., 1969.

Joseph J. Kockelmans, *Martin Heidegger: A First Introduction to His Philosophy*. Pittsburgh: Duquesne University Press, 1965.

————, ed., *On Heidegger and Language*. Evanston, Ill.: Northwestern University Press, 1972.

Thomas Langan, *The Meaning of Heidegger*. New York: Columbia University Press, 1959.

John Macquarrie, *Martin Heidegger*. Richmond, Va.: John Knox Press, 1968.

Werner Marx, *Heidegger and the Tradition*, trans. by Theodore Kisiel and Murray Greene. Evanston, Ill.: Northwestern University Press, 1971.

J. L. Mehta, *Martin Heidegger: The Way and the Vision*. Honolulu: The University Press of Hawaii, 1976.

James L. Perotti, *Heidegger on the Divine*. Athens: Ohio University Press, 1974.

William J. Richardson, S.J., *Heidegger: Through Phenomenology to Thought*. The Hague: Martinus Nijhoff, 1974 (3rd ed.).

John Sallis, ed., *Heidegger and the Path of Thinking*. Pittsburgh: Duquesne University Press, 1970.

Nathan A. Scott, Jr., *Negative Capability: Studies in the New Literature and the Religious Situation*. New Haven: Yale University Press, 1969. See the third chapter.

——, *The Wild Prayer of Longing: Poetry and the Sacred*. New Haven: Yale University Press, 1971. See the second chapter.

Laszlo Versényi, *Heidegger, Being, and Truth*. New Haven: Yale University Press, 1965.

Michael Wyschogrod, *Kierkegaard and Heidegger*. London: Allen and Unwin, 1954.

ALBERT CAMUS

Fiction

Albert Camus, *The Stranger*, trans. by Stuart Gilbert. New York: Alfred A. Knopf, 1946.

——, *The Plague*, trans. by Stuart Gilbert. New York: Alfred A. Knopf, 1948.

——, *The Fall*, trans. by Justin O'Brien. New York: Alfred A. Knopf, 1957.

——, *Exile and the Kingdom*, trans. by Justin O'Brien. New York: Alfred A. Knopf, 1958.

——, *A Happy Death*, trans. by Richard Howard, with Afterword and Notes by Jean Sarocchi. New York: Alfred A. Knopf, 1972. (The stories making up this novel represent Camus' apprentice-work in fiction [of the period 1936-1938] rescued for publication from his literary remains by Mme. Camus.)

Drama

Albert Camus, *Caligula and Three Other Plays*, trans. by Stuart Gilbert. New York: Alfred A. Knopf, 1958. (Contains, in addition to *Caligula*, *The Misunderstanding*, *State of Siege*, and *The Just Assassins*.)

——, *The Just and The Possessed*, trans. by Henry Jones and Justin O'Brien. Harmondsworth: Penguin Books, 1970.

Essays

Albert Camus, *The Rebel*, trans. by Anthony Bower. New York: Alfred A. Knopf, 1954.

——, *The Myth of Sisyphus*, trans. by Justin O'Brien. New York: Alfred A. Knopf, 1955.

————, *Resistance, Rebellion, and Death*, trans. by Justin O'Brien. New York: Alfred A. Knopf, 1961.

————, *Carnets: 1935-1942*, trans. by Philip Thody. London: Hamish Hamilton, 1963. (Selections from Camus' *Notebooks*)

————, *Notebooks: 1942-1951*, trans. by Justin O'Brien. New York: Alfred A. Knopf, 1965.

————, *Lyrical and Critical Essays*, trans. by Philip Thody and Ellen Conroy Kennedy. New York: Alfred A. Knopf, 1968. (This volume presents translations of three small books of Camus—*L'Envers et L'Endroit, Noces*, and *L'Été*.)

————, *Youthful Writings*, trans. by Ellen Conroy Kennedy, with an Introductory Essay by Paul Viallaneix. New York: Alfred A. Knopf, 1976. (In addition to the collection it presents of Camus' early essays, this volume also contains some fragments that appear to be sketches of projected stories.)

Germaine Brée, *Camus*. New Brunswick, N.J.: Rutgers University Press, 1961.

Robert J. Champigny, *A Pagan Hero: An Interpretation of Meursault in Camus' "The Stranger,"* trans. by Rowe Portis. Philadelphia: University of Pennsylvania Press, 1969.

John Cruickshank, *Albert Camus and the Literature of Revolt*. New York: Oxford University Press (A Galaxy Book), 1960.

E. Freeman, *The Theatre of Albert Camus: A Critical Study*. London: Methuen and Co. Ltd., 1971.

Emmett Parker, *Albert Camus: The Artist in the Arena*. Madison: University of Wisconsin Press, 1965.

Leo Pollman, *Sartre and Camus: Literature of Existence*, trans. by Helen and Gregor Sebba. New York: Frederick Ungar Publishing Co., 1970.

Roger Quilliot, *The Sea and Prisons: A Commentary on the Life and Thought of Albert Camus*, trans. by Emmett Parker. University, Ala.: University of Alabama Press, 1970.

Nathan A. Scott, Jr., *Albert Camus*. London: Bowes and Bowes Ltd., 1962; New York: Hillary House, 1963.

Philip Thody, *Albert Camus: A Study of His Work*. London: Hamish Hamilton, 1957.

Fred H. Willhoite, *Beyond Nihilism: Albert Camus' Contribution to Political Thought*. Baton Rouge: Louisiana State University Press, 1968.

JEAN-PAUL SARTRE

Fiction

Jean-Paul Sartre, *The Chips Are Down*, trans. by Louise Varèse. New York: Lear, 1948.

————, *Intimacy and Other Stories*, trans. by Lloyd Alexander. New York: New Directions, 1952.

————, *Nausea*, trans. by Lloyd Alexander. New York: New Directions, 1949.

————, *The Age of Reason*, trans. by Eric Sutton. New York: Alfred A. Knopf, 1947.

————, *The Reprieve*, trans. by Eric Sutton. New York: Alfred A. Knopf, 1947.

————, *Troubled Sleep*, trans. by Gerard Hopkins. New York: Alfred A. Knopf, 1951.

Drama

Jean-Paul Sartre, *No Exit and The Flies*, trans. by Stuart Gilbert. New York: Alfred A. Knopf, 1947.

————, *Three Plays*, trans. by Lionel Abel. New York: Alfred A. Knopf, 1949. (Contains *Dirty Hands, The Respectful Prostitute,* and *The Victors.*)

————, *The Devil and the Good Lord and Two Other Plays*, trans. by Kitty Black, and Sylvia and George Leeson. New York: Vintage Books, 1962. (The second and third plays in this collection are *Kean* and *Nekrassov.*)

————, *The Condemned of Altona*, trans. by Sylvia and George Leeson. New York: Alfred A. Knopf, 1961.

Autobiography

Jean-Paul Sartre, *The Words*, trans. by Bernard Frechtman. New York: George Braziller, 1964.

Philosophical and Critical Writings

Jean-Paul Sartre, *Imagination: A Psychological Critique*, trans. by Forrest Williams. Ann Arbor: University of Michigan Press, 1962.

————, *The Emotions: Outline of a Theory*, trans. by Bernard Frechtman. New York: Philosophical Library, 1948.

————, *The Psychology of the Imagination*, trans. by Bernard Frechtman. London: Rider, 1949.

_____, *Being and Nothingness*, trans. by Hazel Barnes. New York: Philosophical Library, 1956.

_____, *Existentialism and Humanism*, trans. by Philip Mairet. London: Methuen, 1948.

_____, *Anti-Semite and Jew*, trans. by J. Becker. New York: Shocken Books, 1948.

_____, *Baudelaire*, trans. by Martin Turnell. New York: New Directions, 1950.

_____, *What Is Literature?* trans. by Bernard Frechtman. New York: Philosophical Library, 1949.

_____, *Literary and Philosophical Essays*, trans. by Annette Michelson. London: Rider, 1955.

_____, *Saint Genet: Actor and Martyr*, trans. by Bernard Frechtman. New York: George Braziller, 1963.

_____, *Situations*, trans. by Benita Eisler. Greenwich, Conn.: Fawcett, 1966.

_____, *Search for a Method*, trans. by Hazel Barnes. New York: Vintage Books, 1968.

_____, *Critique of Dialectical Reason: Theory of Practical Ensembles*, trans. by Jonathan Ree. Atlantic Highlands, N.J.: Humanities Press, 1976.

Robert Denoon Cumming, ed., *The Philosophy of Jean-Paul Sartre*. New York: Vintage Books, 1972.

Hazel E. Barnes, *Existentialist Ethics*. New York: Alfred A. Knopf, 1967.

Robert Champigny, *Stages on Sartre's Way, 1938-1952*. Bloomington: Indiana University Press, 1959.

Maurice Cranston, *Sartre*. New York: Grove Press, 1962.

Wilfred Desan, *The Tragic Finale: An Essay on the Philosophy of Jean-Paul Sartre*. Cambridge: Harvard University Press, 1954.

Norman N. Greene, *Jean-Paul Sartre: The Existentialist Ethic*. Ann Arbor: University of Michigan Press, 1960.

Thomas M. King, *Sartre and the Sacred*. Chicago: University of Chicago Press, 1974.

Anthony Manser, *Sartre: A Philosophic Study*. London: The Athlone Press of the University of London, 1966.

Iris Murdoch, *Sartre: Romantic Rationalist*. New Haven: Yale University Press, 1953.

Leo Pollmann, *Sartre and Camus: Literature of Existence*, trans.

by Helen and Gregor Sebba. New York: Frederick Ungar Publishing Co., 1970.

Philip Thody, *Jean-Paul Sartre: A Literary and Political Study*. London: Macmillan Co., 1960.

Mary Warnock, *The Philosophy of Sartre*. London: Hutchinson, 1965.

MARTIN BUBER

Martin Buber, *I and Thou*, trans. by Ronald Gregor Smith. New York: Charles Scribner's Sons, 1958. 2nd ed., with Postscript added.

———, *I and Thou*, trans. by Walter Kaufmann. New York: Charles Scribner's Sons, 1970.

———, *For the Sake of Heaven*, trans. by Ludwig Lewisohn. New York: Meridian Books, 1958. 2nd ed., with new Foreword.

———, *The Revelation and the Covenant*. New York: Harper and Bros., 1958.

———, *Between Man and Man*, trans. by Ronald Gregor Smith. New York: Macmillan Co., 1965. 2nd ed.

———, *Daniel: Dialogues on Realization*, trans. by Maurice Friedman. New York: Holt, Rinehart and Winston, Inc., 1964.

———, *Israel and the World: Essays in a Time of Crisis*. New York: Schocken Books, 1963. 2nd ed.

———, *Paths in Utopia*, trans, by R. F. C. Hull. Boston: Beacon Press, 1958.

———, *The Prophetic Faith*, trans. by Carlyle Witton-Davies. New York: Harper Torchbooks, 1960.

———, *Two Types of Faith*, trans. by Norman P. Goldhawk. New York: Harper Torchbooks, 1961.

———, *At the Turning: Three Addresses on Judaism*. New York: Farrar, Straus and Young, 1952.

———, *Eclipse of God: Studies in the Relation between Religion and Philosophy*, trans. by Maurice Friedman *et al.* New York: Harper Torchbooks, 1957.

———, *Israel and Palestine: The History of an Idea*, trans. by Stanley Goodman. New York: Farrar, Straus and Young, 1952.

———, *Hasidism and Modern Man*, ed. and trans. by Maurice Friedman. New York: Harper Torchbooks, 1966.

————, *The Origin and Meaning of Hasidism*, ed. and trans. by Maurice Friedman. New York: Harper Torchbooks, 1966.

————, *The Knowledge of Man*, ed. by Maurice Friedman; trans. by Maurice Friedman and Ronald Gregor Smith. New York: Harper Torchbooks, 1966.

Arthur A. Cohen, *Martin Buber*. New York: Hillary House, 1958.

Malcolm L. Diamond, *Martin Buber: Jewish Existentialist*. New York: Oxford University Press, 1960.

Maurice Friedman, *Martin Buber: The Life of Dialogue*. New York: Harper Torchbooks, 1960.

Paul Schilpp and Maurice Friedman, eds., *The Philosophy of Martin Buber*. LaSalle, Ill.: Open Court Publishing Co., 1967.

Ronald Gregor Smith, *Martin Buber*. London: Carey Kingsgate Press Ltd., 1966.

Acknowledgments

T. & T. CLARK, Edinburgh; and Charles Scribner's Sons, New York: *I and Thou*, by Martin Buber (trans. by Ronald Gregor Smith), 1937.

HARPER & Row, INC., New York: *Life Is Commitment*, by J. H. Oldham, 1953; and *The Life of the Church*, by Samuel H. Miller, 1953.

ALFRED A. KNOPF, INC., New York: *The Stranger* (trans. by Stuart Gilbert, 1946), *Caligula and Three Other Plays* (trans. by Stuart Gilbert, 1960), *Lyrical and Critical Essays* (ed. by Philip Thody and trans. by Ellen Conroy Kennedy, 1968), *The Fall* (trans. by Justin O'Brien, 1957), and the Nobel Prize Speech (trans. by Justin O'Brien, 1958)—by Albert Camus.

NEW DIRECTIONS, INC., New York: *Nausea*, by Jean-Paul Sartre (trans. by Lloyd Alexander), n.d.

OXFORD UNIVERSITY PRESS. New York: *The Journals*, by Søren Kierkegaard (trans. by Alexander Dru), 1938; and *Preludes*, by Conrad Aiken, 1966.

PHILOSOPHICAL LIBRARY, New York: *Being and Nothingness*, by Jean-Paul Sartre (trans. by Hazel Barnes), 1956.

PRINCETON UNIVERSITY PRESS, Princeton: *Repetition*, by Søren Kierkegaard (trans. by Walter Lowrie), 1941; and *Concluding Unscientific Postscript*, by Søren Kierkegaard (trans. and ed. by David Swenson and Walter Lowrie), 1941.

VIKING PRESS, INC., New York: *The Portable Nietzsche*, by Friedrich Nietzsche (trans. and ed. by Walter Kaufmann), 1954.

WORLD PUBLISHING COMPANY, Cleveland-New York: *The Prime of Life*, by Simone de Beauvoir (trans. by Peter Green), 1962.

INDEX OF NAMES AND TITLES

About the Author

Nathan A. Scott, Jr., formerly Shailer Mathews Professor of Theology and Literature at the University of Chicago (where he taught for more than twenty years), is now Commonwealth Professor of Religious Studies and Professor of English at the University of Virginia, where he is a member of the University's Center for Advanced Studies. He has also held appointments as a visiting professor at John Carroll University, the University of Michigan, and Indiana University (as Fellow of the School of Letters).

He is a graduate of the University of Michigan (B.A., 1944), Union Theological Seminary in New York City (B.D., 1946), and Columbia University (Ph. D., 1949); and he holds honorary degrees from Ripon College, General Theological Seminary, Denison University, and numerous other institutions.

He is married to the former Charlotte Hanley, who is University Professor of Business Administration and Commerce at the University of Virginia. They have two children.